Contesting the Boundaries
of Liberal and Professional Education

Contesting the Boundaries of Liberal and Professional Education

The Syracuse Experiment

Edited by
PETER T. MARSH

Syracuse University Press

The paper used in this publication meets the minimum requirements of American National Standard for Information Sciences—Permanence of Paper for Printed Library Materials, ANSI Z39.48-1984. ∞™

Library of Congress Cataloging-in-Publication Data

Contesting the boundaries of liberal and professional
    education.

    Bibliography: p.
    Includes index.
    1. Syracuse University—Curricula. 2. Education,
Humanistic—New York (State)—Syracuse. 3. Professional
education—New York (State)—Syracuse. 4. Curriculum
change—New York (State)—Syracuse. 5. Inter-
disciplinary approach in education—New York (State)—
Syracuse. I. Marsh, Peter T.
LD5231.C66 1988 378'.199'0974766   87-33635
ISBN 0-8156-2428-X (alk. paper)
ISBN 0-8156-2429-8 (pbk. : alk. paper)

Manufactured in the United States of America

Contents

Foreword

Syracuse University, with a dozen professional schools and colleges in addition to its College of Arts and Sciences, is an ideal laboratory for the exploration of relationships between liberal and professional undergraduate education.

In my inaugural statement as dean of the College of Arts and Sciences in 1979, I spoke of "the interface between Arts and Sciences colleges and undergraduate professional schools as one of the relatively unexplored frontiers in higher education, one which we at Syracuse, with our tradition of flexibility, may be particularly well qualified to explore." I voiced the belief that such exploration "might be of great significance for the future vitality of Syracuse University—leading . . . to a greatly enriched and nationally distinctive undergraduate program, which is characterized in part by a strengthened liberal arts education for all, and in part by strengthened professional training for many."

In the years that followed, a number of such bridges were indeed constructed in the Syracuse curriculum. The "Liberal Arts Core" curriculum that had been adopted by the College of Arts and Sciences was extended to a number of our professional schools, among them the S. I. Newhouse School of Public Communications. Professional studies minors for Arts and Sciences students were created in the School of Management and in the School of Architecture. A new dual degree program, combining Arts and Sciences with Computer and Information Sciences, was initiated to supplement our existing array of dual and combined programs, in which nearly 10 percent of our student body now matriculate. An interdisciplinary six-course minor developing analytical and communications skills (writing, speech communications, critical thinking, computing, statistics, and data bases) was implemented cooperatively by Arts and Sciences and three professional schools.

The success of this series of curricular innovations, which brought together existing courses and programs of study, suggested that we might go further to explore the potential for integration of liberal and professional education through the creation of a new type of course in our All-University Honors Program. We sought courses that would provide approaches to such questions as: What are the liberal and conceptual foundations of specific professional disciplines? Can the teaching of the liberal disciplines be enriched by exploring their application to problems associated with the professions? In view of the fact that the preponderance of our Honors students are narrowly focused either in professional schools or with a pre-professional orientation within the College of Arts and Sciences, how can we awaken them to the interrelationships among the various liberal arts and professional subjects in their prescribed programs of study?

The Andrew W. Mellon Foundation recognized the creative nature of this project and offered generous support. Miss Claire List of the foundation was most helpful in clarifying the nature of the project, and I acknowledge her contributions and guidance with gratitude. As frequently happens with pioneering efforts, the completed project has gone well beyond the boundaries of the initial foundation proposal in curricular results, in intellectual impact on faculty and students, and in the refinement of concepts concerning the essential nature of liberal and professional disciplines. This book, through which we share the experience at Syracuse, is another unexpected result. For the University, I extend deep thanks to the project director, Professor Peter Marsh, for his vision, intellectual leadership, and tenacity, and to the faculty group who have become the true "owners" of the project.

The efforts begun when I became dean of Arts and Sciences are entering a new and most interesting phase. The faculty of the Mellon Foundation project have charged the University with extending their conceptions beyond the Honors Program to all the undergraduate curricula. They propose that we develop new courses throughout the University which acknowledge the essential "embeddedness" of all the disciplines and professions. Through these courses, students will perceive the larger fields of knowledge, action, and responsibility in which their special subjects are "embedded." The dual questions of "relation" and "self-reflection" will be transformed from a marginal position at the boundaries into the very center of each academic department. It is my hope that the Syracuse faculty will accept this challenge enthusiastically.

January 1987

Gershon Vincow
Vice Chancellor for Academic
Affairs, Syracuse University

Contributors

GERARDINE CLARK has her Ph.D. from Indiana University in theater with a specialization in dramatic criticism. She is an associate professor of drama in the College of Visual and Performing Arts, and literary manager for Syracuse Stage, a professional regional theater associated with Syracuse University. Her curricular assignments include courses in acting, theater history, and dramatic theory and criticism. She has recently begun research into the relationship of "Method" acting to certain recent discoveries in cognitive science. In addition to her academic work, she is a professional actress, director, and playwright. Her play, *Garcia Lorca's Bicycle Ride*, was featured at the opening of the Salvador Dali Museum in St. Petersburg, Florida. She is currently finishing a musical adaptation of Molière's *The Doctor in Spite of Himself*.

SAMUEL P. CLEMENCE has his Ph.D. in civil engineering from the Georgia Institute of Technology, and chairs the Department of Civil Engineering at Syracuse. He served six years in the Civil Engineering Corps as a naval officer in the Seabees (construction battalion), supervising construction of airfields, roads, and dams in the South Pacific, Thailand, Vietnam, and Spain. He was a consulting engineer for several years before entering academia, and is a registered professional engineer in New York and Missouri. An active researcher in the field of geotechnical engineering, he has done work on the morphology of the Mississippi River, strip mining reclamation, collapsible soils, and—now that he's moved north—frost heave in stabilized soils. He received the Outstanding Teacher Award for two years at the University of Missouri at Rolla where he taught before coming to Syracuse. He is the author of more than twenty technical papers, editor of two recent books on geotechnical engineering, and is currently director of several research projects in the disposal of hazardous wastes.

DENNIS GILLEN, assistant professor of organization and management in Syracuse's School of Management, teaches corporate strategy and policy on both the graduate and undergraduate level. He has several publications in the areas of management development and organizational effectiveness. He has consulted or conducted research for Allied Chemical Corporation, Georgia-Pacific Corporation, American Can Corporation, International Paper Co., Fairchild Space and Electronics Co., Pitney Bowes Inc., Oneida Limited, IBM, and Eastman Kodak Co. He has also developed a large computer-based diagnostic program for individual development of managers, and is currently conducting a study for IBM on university communication networks.

ERICH HARTH received his training in experimental physics at Syracuse University, completing his Ph.D. with a dissertation on cosmic rays. The experiments were carried out at the High Altitude Laboratory on top of Mt. Evans in Colorado. After a few years' work in nuclear physics at the Naval Research Laboratory in Washington, D.C., he returned to his original interest in elementary particle research. While in the physics department of Duke University, he was instrumental in building the first liquid helium bubble chamber, and carried out research at the cosmotron at Brookhaven National Laboratory and the bevatron of the University of California at Berkeley. He joined the Syracuse faculty in 1957, where he founded an experimental high energy team and continued collaboration with groups at Duke, Northwestern, Johns Hopkins, and Cornell. In the 1960s Harth abandoned high energy physics to concentrate entirely on a study of brain function, using both theory and experiment, and approaching the subject from a physicist's perspective. This work has resulted in a large number of publications in scientific journals and *Windows on the Mind*, a popular book on the subject.

MARGARET HIMLEY, with a Ph.D. in composition and rhetoric, is an assistant professor in the English department, and teaches undergraduate writing courses as well as graduate courses in composition theory and research. She works in the new Syracuse University Writing Program on curriculum development and program evaluation. She is interested in working out a post-phenomenological approach for studying written language development, and is currently writing a book-length study of how and why one child became a writer.

SHARON HOLLENBACK earned her degrees from the University of Texas at Austin, first in history and then in American Studies, culminating in a Ph.D. in communications. Further study at the University of Michigan and the Slade School of Art in London fueled an interest in cross-cultural and international television and film. The holdings of the Humanities Research Center in Austin led to her study of screenwriting and its role in the collaborative creation of feature films. An associate professor in the S. I. Newhouse School of Public Communications, she oversees the undergraduate writing program in television, radio, and film, and teaches courses in media criticism and dramatic writing. Long active in the University Honors Program at Syracuse, she was one of the original designers of the Mellon Foundation project and team teaches the course developed through it on social and cultural issues in mass communications. Having written, produced, and hosted television productions for fifteen years, she is currently researching the effects of new technologies on public broadcasting.

JOHN PHILIP JONES, a Welshman, read economics at Cambridge. He spent twenty-five years with J. Walter Thompson, the advertising agency, managing the advertising for major brands of consumer goods. Many of his responsibilities were multi-national, and he was based at various times in London, Amsterdam, and Copenhagen. He joined the faculty of the S. I. Newhouse School of Public Communications in 1981, published *What's in a Name: Advertising and the Concept of Brands* in 1986, and is currently at work on a book of marketing and advertising cases.

SALLY GREGORY KOHLSTEDT, who received a Ph.D. from the University of Illinois, teaches in American history and American studies. Her account of *The Formation of the American Scientific Community* is a study of emerging scientific professionalism in the nineteenth century. Her current attention is focussed on science in public culture, as represented in *Historical Writing on American Science* which she co-edited. She has chaired the Women's Studies Program at Syracuse and regularly teaches courses on women in American history, as well as topical courses on other aspects of American life. During the final months of this book's preparation, she intermittently rejoined the group, taking leave from research on natural history museums being conducted at the Woodrow Wilson Center in Washington, D.C.

H. RICHARD LEVY was born in Leipzig, Germany, received his secondary education in England, and then moved to the United States where he received his Ph.D. in biochemistry at the University of Chicago. A professor of biochemistry, he is an active research scientist in the field of enzymology, specializing in the mechanisms of action and regulation of dehydrogenases. This research includes collaborative projects with scientists in Canada and England. He has been an active participant in numerous university-wide endeavors including the Honors Program, the editorial boards of the *Syracuse Scholar* and the Syracuse University Press, and the University Senate Committee on Academic Affairs. He has a deep love of music which he satisfies by singing with the Syracuse University Oratorio Society and as general manager of a professional chamber orchestra, Syracuse Camerata.

PETER T. MARSH, born in Canada and educated in Toronto and Cambridge, is a professor of history and has directed the University Honors Program at Syracuse. It was on the basis of that experience that he drew up the proposal for the Mellon Foundation project which he has since led. The recipient of fellowships from the Canada Council, the Guggenheim Foundation, All Souls College, Oxford, and Emmanuel College, Cambridge, his books and articles deal with various aspects of nineteenth-century English political culture. His interest in the connections among differing occupational fields has been quickened by the biography that he is writing of Joseph Chamberlain, the English radical, municipal reformer, and imperialist whose first career was as a manufacturer of screws.

CLEVE MATHEWS is a professor of journalism in the S. I. Newhouse School of Public Communications at Syracuse University. After earning a master's degree at the University of Michigan, he served on the staff of the *St. Louis Post-Dispatch* for nine years and on the *New York Times* for twelve years. His positions there included that of assistant foreign news editor in New York and associate editor of the *Times* bureau in Washington, D.C. He joined National Public Radio as its first director of news and public affairs in 1971, and was the first executive producer of "All Things Considered." He was chairman of the journalism department at Wichita State University before coming to Syracuse. In 1960/61 he was the first occupant of the Robert and Evangeline Atwood Chair of Journalism at the University of Alaska, Anchorage. He is co-author with William L. Rivers of a book on ethics and the media scheduled for publication in 1988.

STEPHEN MELVILLE earned his B.A. and Ph.D. through a variety of interdisciplinary programs at the University of Chicago. He is currently an assistant professor in the English department, specializing in critical theory with a strong interest in contemporary visual art. Areas of special interest to his teaching and publication include modern European philosophy and psychoanalytic theory. The Mellon Foundation project continues a longstanding commitment to interdisciplinary work and theory that is reflected in his involvement with the Humanities Doctoral Program and the structure of the English department at Syracuse University.

GARY M. RADKE did his undergraduate work at Syracuse University and received his Ph.D. in art history from the Institute of Fine Arts at New York University. He has spent extensive periods of time in Florence and Rome. Attracted by the opportunity of teaching at Syracuse's center in Italy, he returned to his alma mater in 1980, where he is now associate professor and chair of the Department of Fine Arts. The holder of grants from the Fulbright Commission, the National Gallery of Art, and the American Academy in Rome, he is engaged in research and publication on the history of late medieval and early Renaissance art.

MARSHALL H. SEGALL, trained mostly at Northwestern University, with input from Yale and l'Université de Genève, is an internationalist social scientist. Best known for his work in cross-cultural psychology, including a study of visual perception done with Donald Campbell and Melville Herskovits and a widely used text, he has spent more than twenty years at Syracuse in the Maxwell School, where an interdisciplinary version of social psychology is embedded. His innovations in the undergraduate curriculum prior to his involvement in the Mellon Foundation project included a course that applies psychological findings to the analysis of public policy, and another that challenges the universality of psychological findings generated mainly by research performed on American undergraduates. He is now Associate Dean of the College of Arts and Sciences.

JAMES STEWART is a civil engineer and assistant professor of engineering who received his bachelor's degree from Syracuse University, and M.S. and Ph.D. from Cornell. Before beginning an academic career, he worked several years as a consulting soils engineer on such projects as high-rise office buildings, dams, offshore platforms, subway tunnels, waste containment facilities, and petroleum refineries. Since joining the faculty at Syracuse, he has taught courses in geotechnical and geological engineering. His research interests are in the fields of waste containment and foundation engineering.

DELIA C. TEMES has her Ph.D. in modern American literature from Syracuse University. An instructor in the Writing Program, she teaches lower and upper division writing courses. She serves as a consultant to local industry on writing, and has written and edited technical manuals and designed informational brochures for physicians. Before settling into a teaching career, she was the documentation specialist and senior technical editor for an engineering consulting firm in Washington, D.C.

STEPHEN ZAIMA, an artist born and educated in California, is now associate professor in the School of Art of the College of Visual and Performing Arts. In addition to a one-person exhibition at the Everson Museum of Art, he has shown in numerous exhibitions across the country. His works are in many public and private collections, and he has received awards from the Ford Foundation, the Edward Albee Foundation, the California Arts Council, and the National Endowment for the Arts. The co-author of Chapter 11, Professor Zaima also carried out image research for this book.

Contesting the Boundaries
of Liberal and Professional Education

1

Introduction

Preface

PETER T. MARSH

The boundaries between liberal and professional education are the most perplexing lines of demarcation in American higher education today. A large majority of American undergraduates now qualify for their bachelor's degrees by taking mixtures of courses categorized as either liberal or professional, a distinction emphasized by the administrative separation within universities between liberal arts and professional colleges. Various curricular arrangements —some of long standing, some more recent—have been made to package courses of the two sorts together. Yet all these arrangements have accentuated the dichotomy. The challenge to understand and to help students appreciate the depth of the interrelationship remains to be met.

An experiment to meet this challenge is being conducted at Syracuse, a university long distinguished by its provision of both forms of undergraduate education. The Syracuse experiment has a good way to go before it can claim full success. But the approach that it has developed already has proved singularly fruitful. We present this study of the experiment as a call and encouragement for further exploration across the boundaries between liberal and professional education.

Among the practical components of the experiment, two are crucial and inseparable. One is the creation of courses that take the relationship between liberal and professional coursework from the margins of the curriculum to its center. The other is collaborative learning among the faculty who teach these courses. This twofold approach is not simply useful pedagogical practice. It implies and fosters the belief that no discipline or profession can be rightly grasped without appreciating its embeddedness in the larger world. The approach has potentially radical curricular and administrative implications for American universities. It will require a reconfiguration of liberal and professional education.

The experiment at Syracuse has drawn moral reinforcement

3

from a succession of national reports on American higher education that have come out with striking frequency from the inception of the project to the present: in 1984 from the National Institute of Education and from the chairman of the National Endowment for the Humanities, William Bennett (now Secretary of Education); in 1985 from the Association of American Colleges; and in 1986 from the Carnegie Foundation for the Advancement of Teaching. Though written from varying standpoints, all make essentially the same point: American undergraduate education has lost its coherence and integrity, and hence much of its value. The blame tends to be placed on the rapid expansion of career-minded professional studies and the parallel abandonment of "one of the principle aims of liberal education, . . . to integrate what one has learned in different disciplines."[1]

Instead of further documenting the situation described by these national educators and agencies, the project at Syracuse has attempted to meet the challenge that they present. To do so we assembled faculty, not across the country, but across colleges within this one university. From the arts and sciences, we drew an English political historian who was to lead the project, an American social historian, a historian of art, an enzymologist, a physicist in neuroscience, a philosopher of science, a social psychologist, two literary theorists, and a professor of composition. From the professional schools, we recruited two civil engineers, management specialists in organization and in transportation/distribution, a nurse specializing in family practice, an analyst of advertising, a television and film writer-producer, a news journalist, an actor-director, and an artist.[2]

The cardinal weakness in undergraduate education as analyzed by the national commissions and experienced among our own faculty and students has much to do with failure to grasp and to convey understanding of the bearing of the many fields of liberal and professional learning upon each other. The cardinal need, so it seemed, was to find new, effective ways to integrate liberal and professional education. That was our initial objective. In order to meet it we had to dig beneath the surface of and also between each other's fields of study. Learning, reading, writing, and discussion in this collaborative context placed us collectively outside our individual specialities and thus moved us toward our goal. At the same time the goal changed. Integration, it became clear, is a bland term. It lacks the incisiveness needed to reflect the concepts and concerns that cut through all fields of learning, and it does not do justice to the distinctive contributions that each field has to make in the world of learning. What is needed in liberal and professional education is not integration but a reconfiguration, the shape of which we have only begun to discover.

This book is intended as an invitation to colleagues in our own and other American universities to join in this process of discovery. As befits that process, all of the following chapters, though signed by the contributers particularly responsible for them, have benefitted from close collaborative discussion and revision. Far from muting individual voices, this collaboration has encouraged each to make a distinctive contribution to the common enterprise.

The project has involved a mixture of components: (1) collaborative enquiry among faculty from a variety of departments and colleges; (2) various forms of communication—visual as well as spoken and written; (3) the identification of some concepts or themes of interest that run through all fields of learning; and (4) the creation of undergraduate courses. But none of these components stood by itself. They developed in fertile interaction with each other. To present each by itself—for example separating the faculty seminar from the concepts it identified and the courses it created—would be to misrepresent the essential process. The entire process, therefore, is deliberately reflected in each of the five sections into which this book is divided. Every section begins with an editorial preface to explain its place and draw out its implications.

The introductory section contains an interpretive account (chapter 1) by the editor of the Syracuse experiment as a whole. That is followed by an analysis (chapter 2) of the faculty seminar—the forum through which the enterprise was conducted—by Margaret Himley from her standpoint as a professor of composition, alert to the barriers that impede communication and to ways of dealing with them. The development that gave rise to the project is the vast expansion of professional education over recent years in response to the earlier and continuing growth of the professions. Sally Gregory Kohlstedt, quickened by her familiarity with the institutional history of American sciences, deals in chapter 3 with this set of phenomena by describing the seminar's discussion of the issues involved. In no field of professional education is the consequent debate more acute than in engineering, where demands for greater technological sophistication and for more humane social sensitivity compete for space in the undergraduate curriculum. In the final chapter of this section James Stewart, a civil engineer, dissects and responds to this dilemma, which epitomizes the difficulty in bringing liberal and professional education to bear upon each other.

The next two sections are unified around conceptual themes that emerged throughout the enterprise, that focused its enquiry, and that figure in all the courses we created. The first chapter in each of these sections sets the theme upon which the subsequent chapters play in a variety of analytical essays and course descriptions. The fourth section describes a constellation of the methods we have used and discoveries we have made in approaching the central task of learning and teaching. The final section presents the great remaining challenges. Pictures and captions are interspersed throughout the book by the artist in the project, Stephen Zaima, not to illustrate points made in the text, but rather to offer their own pertinent observation.

Those who wish to fathom the relationship between liberal and professional education must leave their home ports at least for a while. The treasure to be discovered far outweighs the risks the explorer must accept. Even the home ports can then be seen with new eyes. The following pages describe our ports of call, the winds that have filled our sails, the crosscurrents that continue to complicate our journey, and our sense of the barriers that we have yet to pass. We are still travelling, by land now as well as by sea. We hope to encourage those in other universities to join in. For what we have discovered is that the relationship between liberal and professional education is not so much a subject as a process that transforms teaching and learning.

Notes

1. *Involvement in Learning: Realizing the Potential of American Higher Education:* Final report of the study group on the conditions of excellence in American higher education, sponsored by the National Institute of Education (1984), 44.

2. See "Contributors."

Garry Winogrand, *Apollo II Moonshot, Cape Kennedy, Florida. 1969,* Photograph. © 1984 by the estate of Garry Winogrand, courtesy Fraenkel Gallery, San Francisco, and the estate of Garry Winogrand.

The Syracuse Experiment

PETER T. MARSH

The Problem

The most remarkable development in American higher education over the past decade has been the massive escalation of undergraduate enrollment in professional programs of study and the corresponding fall of enrollment in arts and sciences degree programs. High school seniors have been flocking in unprecedented numbers into professional colleges and departments, looking upon them as gateways to promising careers. By now, substantially more than half of all American undergraduates are enrolled in professional programs of study: management or engineering; public communications or the visual and performing arts; social work, education, or a host of fields under the heading of human development, nursing, dental, pharmaceutical, veterinary, computer, or library science. Since the mid-1970s, the number of bachelor's degrees conferred by institutions of higher education across the United States in engineering and management has increased by more than 75 percent; in public communications it has more than doubled; in computer science it has multiplied more than fivefold.[1] Meanwhile, the number of bachelor's degrees earned in the humanities and social sciences has fallen by roughly 40 percent. Though the natural sciences have fared better, their enrollment has been sustained to some extent by students seeking qualifications for entry to medical, veterinary, and other professional schools. This general pattern may change and there are, in fact, signs that it is already doing so; but no one believes that it will disappear.

The temptation to analyze the phenomenon in antagonistic terms as a struggle between liberal and professional education is strong. It is reinforced by the administrative division of universities into colleges of arts and sciences on the one side, and professional colleges on the other. But in reality, the phenomenon is immensely complex and is daily becoming more so. The relationship between liberal and professional education is not a straightforward dichotomy. It is more like the facets of a diamond or the bits of color in a kaleidoscope—one that is shaken and transformed by every advance in pure and applied learning.

Our enquiry was precipitated initially by realization that the conventional distinction between liberal and professional education is anachronistic and dysfunctional. It does not fairly reflect what most undergraduates in either the arts and sciences or the professional colleges expect from their education. Nor does it rightly reflect either the pedagogical aims or the scholarly objectives of most members of the faculty, again whether in liberal arts or professional colleges. To talk of the education of the chemical engineering student as professional and of the pre-medical student as liberal is to draw a distinction that makes little sense, at least to the students. Engineering and pre-medical students typically approach their undergraduate education in the same light and hope that it will serve essentially similar purposes. While pre-professional students in the liberal arts may be classed as a special group, the rest of the students in the arts and sciences quite correctly refuse to believe that their undergraduate education will not prepare them for work as well as for life. At the same time, to change the perspective from student to faculty, biology professors treat their majors as potential professionals, while faculty in some of the visual and performing arts—recognizing that, however fervent the hopes of their students, few of them will secure professional careers in their undergraduate field of study—regard the education that they provide as essentially liberal.

In terms of scholarly commitments, the faculty in the arts and sciences think of themselves as thoroughly professional, while the most eloquent statements that we hear these days about the importance of liberal learning come from faculty in professional colleges. Echoing complaints from executive officers of American corporations, professors of management insist that it is not enough to be a skilled technician. They demand breadth of mind, depth of culture, and an understanding of human nature. Professors of public communications pride themselves on the predominantly liberal character of their curricular requirements. Professors of engineering insist that education for their profession must involve more than the acquisition of technological skills.[2] The very rapidity of technological advance makes it more important for their students to grasp the underlying theories and principles than to master current practice. Rising concern with environmental issues makes it vital for the students to be able to assess the social and ecological impact that their work as engineers may have. They need also to prepare for the managerial responsibilities to which they may be promoted.

More generally, the preoccupation of professional colleges with the sphere of work overlaps the concern of liberal education with personal life. As one educator has observed, "For many in our complex, mobile, and frequently impersonal society, the work setting has replaced more traditional personal anchors—the church, the family, the local community. Thus, professional identity both parallels and supplements the liberal education goal of developing a feeling of personal identity."[3] The participants in our project have been impressed in this and many other regards by the capacity of the concerns of the professional schools to stimulate broad-ranging reflection. And, as the president of Cornell University writes, "It is the spirit of inquiry, as much as the subject of the inquiry, that is the benefit of a liberal education."[4]

Once when I was describing the composition of the faculty seminar at the center of our project, I was stopped when I mentioned the professor of transportation management. "Why transportation?" asked the skeptical inquirer; and I thought of Harold Innes. The greatest Canadian scholar of his generation, Innes is remembered for his study of two transportation networks—those that underlay the North American fur trade and fisheries in the eighteenth century. In doing so, Innes laid the foundation for two social science disciplines on this continent—economic history and historical geography—and also, as Marshall McLuhan later attested, for study of the flow of information and hence of the media. From the fur-trading or fishing entrepreneur to the social scientist to the public communicator: Could there be a better illustration of the capacity of what are now professional activities to provide food for liberal thought, thought that in turn stimulates the professions?

Another interplay between the professional and liberal dimensions of higher education ties the two inextricably together. The credentials of the faculty for their positions, as much in the arts and sciences as in professional colleges, are derived from their professional qualifications in their special fields. At the same time they are all professional educators, though rarely with formal credentials for this aspect of their work. As such, whether they are teaching skills or technology or theoretical subject matter, they work in a consciously critical and reflective frame of mind—one of the traditional hallmarks of liberal education. Hence, as the social psychologist in our project put it, "Liberal education is a redundant phrase. If we educate (not merely train) we do so 'liberally.'"

There is, however, no denying the thickness of the administrative walls that divide liberal arts and professional colleges or the depth of the material interests that they entrench. Universities are supposed to bring lively minds together, yet contrive to keep them apart. Though when our seminar first met the majority of its members had been teaching at Syracuse University for many years and were recognized in their colleges as outstanding scholar-teachers, most of them were complete strangers to each other. Those not yet promoted to full professor with tenure were also anxious about the impact that their participation in a demanding cross-campus seminar would have on their future.

In all other regards it became clear that the conventional distinction between liberal and professional education has disintegrated. Their assimilation has been going on as long as the two forms of education have existed. The explosive expansion of specialized knowledge over the past century has not only professionalized the disciplines of the arts and sciences, but has also reduced the historic rationale for purely liberal education to a faint memory. While the arts and sciences now stand to a large extent on professional foundations, there are liberal components at the base of professional education. The statements of principle and codes of conduct that have marked the birth of every profession are, among other things, expressions of public accountability. While the lawyer serves his client he is also an officer of the court, and the statements of a fully accredited accountant provide certification to the public as well as to the company that has hired her. The professions have gone on to encourage the formation of colleges to serve their needs because they want something more from their practitioners than skills.

In practice, the distinction between liberal and professional education is by now little more than a tautology denoting the different subject matter that liberal arts and professional colleges teach. That reality is obscured by lingering evaluative connotations that associate liberal education grandly with thought and professional education crudely with skills. It is time to discard those connotations. Where they are not misleading, they are harmful. They weaken the natural penchant of the liberal arts for self-reflection, and they have a self-fulfilling impact in professional schools. We have reached the point at which the liberal and the professional need to be appreciated as dimensions present in every field of higher education.

That is easier said than done. Both sides are still encumbered by invalid conventions and expectations. Requests from faculty in professional colleges for help from the arts and sciences in analyzing the historical roots and clarifying the central concepts of the professions are too often ignored as unwelcome distractions from pursuit of the pure learning that the disciplines prefer to reward. At the same time, while many of the faculty in professional colleges would like to see a higher value placed on conceptual than on technical competence, their attempts to bring the curriculum into line with these priorities are impeded by acceptance of the old stereotypes within their schools and professions, commonly reinforced by the desire of students for the obviously useful. As the professor of drama in our project commented about the curriculum in her school, "Liberal education has to be slipped in. It's basic, but it's not what the students come for."

Professional accrediting associations and the demands involved in credentialing exert ambivalent pressures in this regard. Many accrediting authorities, not least in engineering, attempt to increase the proportion of liberal arts courses in the undergraduate curriculum. Yet it is not easy to do so and still meet the expectations of undergraduates, parents, and the public if not of seasoned practitioners, that the student will have acquired enough technical competence by graduation to qualify as a professional. Professions such as nursing, whose status as such are not yet recognized to full satisfaction, feel obliged to devote a good deal of attention in the undergraduate curriculum to the substantiation of their claims.

The existing patterns for reconciling the need for liberal and professional education often serve to accentuate the division between them. Apart from engineering—which is an outstanding exception in many regards—the high-status professions, preeminently law and medicine, have equated liberal with undergraduate and professional with graduate education. That arrangement continues to be praised for ensuring that students receive the best of both worlds. Yet, at least in the case of medicine, the result has too often been the reverse. This demarcation has not alleviated the single-mindedly utilitarian approach characteristic of pre-medical students toward their undergraduate education, and has had dehumanizing implications for the graduate curriculum in medical schools.[5]

Liberal arts and professional colleges engaged in undergraduate education have negotiated curricular treaties to enable their students to take advantage of both. Colleges of arts and sciences are gaining access for their students to courses in, for example, management. Every professional college requires its undergraduates to take a certain proportion of their course work in the liberal arts. But once again these arrangements can accentuate the tension. Curricular treaties rarely include provisions to help students appreciate the intellectual bearing of their arts and sciences and professional fields of enquiry upon each other. Failure to explain the underlying rationale for liberal arts requirements to professional college students leave them often sullenly resentful. They are left to ponder the relationship among their various courses as they hurry from class to class, from a lecture in art history to one in accounting.

Alternatively, the curricular treaties may be sharply structured to point students in professional colleges toward liberal arts courses directly pertinent to their professional interests. Where the courses in the college of arts and sciences fail to conform to this pressure, professional colleges have created for themselves liberal arts courses that focus on their immediate concerns. The reason for doing so is persuasive. As one eminent engineer has put it, "Unless the liberal arts can be approached *through engineering* they seem lifeless and frivolous to those of us who are professional engineers."[6] But the loss of food for understanding in examining one field only as it pertains to another can be substantial. As the physicist in our project sought to explain with regard to his course on the natural sciences, "It would be a disservice to the students to omit mention of black holes (to pick an example) just because future physicians or engineers are not soon likely to run into one."[7] Though undergraduates cannot be introduced to the entire world of learning, they should be able to glimpse something of the rich fullness of a range of fields in which unexpected associations may prove more revealing than the predictable ones.

So long as we think of the liberal and the professional as different categories of higher education rather than as dimensions present in every field of learning, the old dichotomy will reassert itself and continue to blind us. Before the faculty seminar reached this conclusion, we debated the rival merits of two proposals to bridge the seeming chasm. One member suggested redesigning some lower division liberal arts courses to make them serve as gateways to upper division study in the professional colleges. Another argued that the arts and sciences courses should be treated instead as reflective pauses before professional coursework. But both proposals reinforced the conflict. It is implicit even in the common metaphor of

the bridge, for that draws attention to the intervening chasm. A similar sense is conveyed by the general education or liberal arts core
requirements in many American universities, including Syracuse.
Perverting the good intentions of their designers, as James M. Powell pointed out a few years ago, such requirements "have tended to
reinforce in students' minds the non-professional significance of the
liberal arts."[8]

While all these existing curricular arrangements have their merits, they have in one way or other reinforced a dichotomy between
liberal and professional education. The need to understand and appreciate the interpenetration of the two is urgent.

The Response

We addressed this challenge through an experiment at Syracuse
University funded by the Andrew W. Mellon Foundation. Syracuse
provided an unusually congenial site for the experiment, for it has
offered various forms of professional as well as liberal education for
undergraduates virtually since it was founded just over a century
ago. By the early twentieth century, the Syracuse catalogue was
proudly pointing out that "while the University presents exception-
ally strong courses in the liberal arts, it offers peculiar advantages
to students in these courses by the proximity of its professional
schools."[9] Rapidly expanded and consolidated since the 1950s, the
combination of liberal and professional education at Syracuse has
become the most distinguishing feature of the university's undergraduate curriculum.

In addition to its College of Arts and Sciences, Syracuse University contains professional colleges for architecture, computer science,
education, engineering, human development (including community,
family, and child studies, consumer studies and retailing, interior
design and textiles, and nutrition), information studies, law, management, nursing, public administration, and social work. Two other
broad areas of study that some universities house within their colleges of arts and sciences, namely public communications and the
visual and performing arts, have their own professional schools at
Syracuse. The S. I. Newhouse School of Public Communications
embraces advertizing, photography, and public relations in addition
to broadcast journalism, newspaper, magazine, television, radio, and

film. The College of Visual and Performing Arts deals with art, music, drama, and speech communications. All these colleges except for the College of Law are engaged in undergraduate teaching. It is the prominence of the professional colleges in undergraduate education that makes Syracuse University distinctive. The physical layout of the university conveys the message unmistakably to even the casual visitor. While the buildings of the College of Arts and Sciences ring the top of the hill on which the university stands, they are surrounded by the imposing structures of the professional colleges. The Hall of Languages, the original building of the university, still dominates the prospect, but from a distance the most salient feature on the skyline is the Victorian gothic tower of the College of Visual and Performing Arts.

Syracuse University possesses another component that was critically important for purposes of the experiment. With 12,000 undergraduate and another 5,000 graduate students, Syracuse is one of the largest private universities in the United States, much too big as a whole for a pilot project. But the University Honors Program constituted a manageable microcosm of the university. Though born like most American honors programs within the arts and sciences, it is no longer restricted to the college of its birth, nor is it a federation of essentially autonomous programs in the individual disciplines and colleges. It is a closely coordinated, genuinely all-university program with 250 students. Academically able and ambitious, they take thematic honors seminars and disciplinary honors courses and eventually write theses in their majors while pursuing regular courses of study in their home colleges. Over the past dozen years, an increasing proportion of the ablest freshmen coming to Syracuse have enrolled in its professional colleges. When our experiment began, two thirds of the students in the Honors Program were matriculated in professional colleges, and a further 15 percent were dually enrolled in a professional college and the College of Arts and Sciences.

Yet, like virtually all other university-wide honors programs, the courses that ours offered were drawn exclusively from the arts and sciences, apart from an occasional section in one of the large introductory professional schools courses reserved for honors students but not otherwise different in character from the standard sections. Aside from honors seminars offered by faculty from professional colleges on issues of current interest—such as artificial intelligence or the concept of comparable worth in employment—our Honors Program did not provide its students with any guidance on the bearing between the professional college courses in which they were en-rolled and their arts and sciences requirements. As the enrollment in honors from the professional colleges soared, this failure provoked increasing discontent among the students. Far from being merely trendy, questions of the relevance of the liberal arts and professional concerns to each other are in all probability the most pertinent to distinction in work, advances in thought, and the enhancement of personal life that students can raise. Yet no courses were devoted to these questions. If they were dealt with at all in existing courses, the treatment was fleeting and patently inadequate. Apparently we did not know how to subject these questions to sustained examination. While the demand we faced was pedagogical, the root of our failure to deal with it was intellectual. Here was the challenge.

It seemed clear that the best way to begin to meet the challenge was to bring faculty from the arts and sciences and the professional colleges together to explore the bearing of their fields upon each other and to give their discoveries curricular expression. In order to secure such a commitment of intellectual and pedagogical energy from the faculty, we had to find means to release them from part of their teaching load, which was particularly heavy in professional colleges with high enrollment, or from some of the institutional ex-pectations for research, especially exacting in the arts and sciences. Someone would have to be freed up still more to provide the leader-ship that the enterprise required. The Andrew W. Mellon Founda-tion responded generously to an application for funding of the project that we envisioned.

The project generated among the participating faculty a stance transcending individual fields of study, a stance for which we could not find a word until we coined the term "Mellonized." We all recall the afternoon in May 1985 when that experience began to take hold. The faculty seminar had met for the first time that January. Sepa-rately during the spring semester we read books in each other's fields of expertise. After the graduation ceremonies at the beginning of May, we convened daily for three weeks to discuss the reading. For some time these sessions were characterized by an exchange of monologues as each of us sought to explain his or her stance on the book, paper, or topic under discussion. It took an unlikely book, on a socially disengaged, minimalist painter from California—Robert Irwin—called *Seeing is Forgetting the Name of the Thing One Sees*,[10] to force us out of monologue toward dialogue.[11]

As organizer of the seminar, I was very apprehensive as to how the members would respond to the study of an artist who had spent three years putting a few short lines on a canvas. In a flight of fancy, Irwin had turned from lines to dots, and eventually reached the ultimate minimalism by removing every distinctive feature from the surface on which he worked. A civil engineer volunteered to kick off our discussion of the book, and we expected a dismissive attack. He proceeded, indeed, to say that his first reaction was that spending three years putting a few lines on a canvas was absurd. But when he recalled the research on which he had spent his past six months, his disdain turned to empathy. "I have occasionally gone to extremes myself," he confessed, "obsessed with perfection of some sort to the point where even minor details became a central focus."

That remark sparked impassioned responses from the group. Most of us discovered reflections of ourselves on Irwin's seemingly plain surfaces or in his utterly uncompromising pursuit of nonrepresentational visuality. A professor of management saw entrepreneurship, the professor of composition saw discourse, a literary theorist saw disciplinarity, the news journalist saw objective communication, the enzymologist saw relentless research, and the art historian saw art.

Four others felt their sensitivities touched to the quick. The artist who had proposed the book for reading by the seminar insisted that we were missing the point emphasized by the title, that a literal reading of what the artist puts on the canvas is precisely what Irwin was telling us to avoid. "The intent," the artist insisted, "is for us to go beyond what is familiar and to leave the comfortable but simplistic process of identification." That sentence could have served as the text for the next two years.

The actor-director, while admiring Irwin's total dedication to his art, deplored his rejection of the artististic heritage of the past. But the more others attacked Irwin, the more she bristled at their criticism of his art. The artist in her responded, "This is none of our business!" Undaunted, the physicist sustained the attack, not, however, from his disciplinary base, but from his life experience. As a young man, he had fled from Austria hoping to participate in the Spanish civil war—and he was infuriated by Irwin's complete disengagement not only from the heritage of art but also from the social and political concerns of the society that surrounded him. "If Weschler's book, which portrays Irwin's life as one grandiose repudiation, is a valid account of the man," he remarked angrily, "then neither his art nor his life merit our attention."

However much we differed, suddenly we all cared enough and had enough in common to want to persuade each other of the validity of our individual perspectives. At that point we set sail on a voyage to explore the relationship between liberal and professional education.

The plans were blessed with serendipity, though they also had their limitations—both of which became apparent as we proceeded. Half of the seminar of scholar-teachers that was to function as the central motor for the enterprise were recruited from the arts and sciences, half from professional colleges. Though most of those who were invited to join accepted the invitation with enthusiasm, not all did so, and two who joined eventually withdrew. Competing demands on people of talent accounted for the initial rejections; an unwillingness to move beyond treasured disciplinary commitments characterized the dropouts. The great majority who accepted the invitation and stayed have found the enterprise to be an addictive adventure.

The particular composition of the seminar shaped and also limited its vision. The professional college faculty in the seminar came from the major schools at Syracuse with a currently substantial enrollment in the Honors Program—Public Communications, Management, Engineering, and Visual and Performing Arts—plus Nursing where the experiment had begun. Hence it did not include either the smaller professional colleges like Architecture, or larger colleges such as Human Development and Education with a low enrollment in the Honors Program, nor did it include the College of Law, which was not involved in undergraduate teaching. The two-person contingent from the Department of History—and still more the three from the Department of English, all of whom had a theoretical bent—lent an unusual weight to the balance of representation from the College of Arts and Sciences. The presence of six women in the project pressed an expanding appreciation of gender as a determinant in intellectual and professional life on its deliberations.[12] Five members of the seminar were foreign-born, a fact that reinforced the efforts of the social psychologist to keep it alert to cross-cultural perspectives. On the other hand, the fact that all but one of its members were white imposed a corresponding limitation on its vision.

Our pedagogical assignment was to create or redevelop nine Honors courses, which we eventually expanded to twelve (Table 1). Four are in the arts and sciences; three deal with the broad divisions

Table 1

Courses Developed through the Project

a.   in the arts and sciences

    i. The Humanities and Human Understanding
    first offered in spring 1984; redeveloped (see chapter 14) in 1985/6

    ii. Individual, Social, and Professional Identity (social sciences)
    first offered under a different title and in different form in spring
    1985; redeveloped in its present form (see chapter 6) in 1986; of-
    fered in new form spring 1987

    iii. The Advancement of Learning in the Natural Sciences
    first offered in spring 1983; redeveloped in 1985

    iv. Reading and Interpretation
    first offered in fall 1985 (see pages 26–27).

b.   in professional colleges

    v. Technology and Its Practitioners (engineering)
    first offered in fall 1985 (see below pages 161, 163–67)

    vi. The Conceptual Foundations of Management
    first offered in fall 1985

    vii. Images of Healing (nursing)
    first offered in spring 1984

    viii. The Creating Mind
    first offered in fall 1985 (see chapter 5)

    ix. Social and Cultural Issues in Public Communications
    first offered in fall 1985

c.   with wider affiliations

    x. The Impact of Science on Medicine (in the College of Arts and
    Sciences with a view to medical school)
    first offered in spring 1986 (see chapter 9)

    xi. Gender and the Professions (housed currently in the College of Arts
    and Sciences)
    first offered in spring 1986 (see chapter 10)

    xii. Seeing, Reading and Interpretation (between the Department of
    English and School of Art)
    first offered in spring 1987 (see chapter 11)

of the liberal arts into natural and social sciences and humanities,
and a fourth examines the fundamental activities of reading and interpretation. These subjects were to be dealt with in a manner alert
to the concerns of students from professional colleges. Five courses

were to be created to examine the historical roots and formative concepts of the professions of engineering, management, the visual and performing arts, public communications, and nursing. Of the three further courses that we developed, one deals with a concern that cuts through every field: gender and the professions. Another tackles the phenomenon of pre-professional education in the College of Arts and Sciences by examining the impact of science on medicine. The third investigates a notable intermingling of literal and visual imagery in the current worlds of literature and art associated with poststructuralism and postmodernism.

Rather than plunge into the designing of courses, we sought first to educate ourselves. And rather than conduct the seminar amid the distractions of the teaching year, we agreed to meet for concentrated stretches of time, occasionally over weekends but mainly during three weeks each May. After an initial weekend in January 1985—in order to escape from the cloud of unknowing that often besets interdisciplinary discussion—the members of the seminar were asked to designate books that provided some acute appreciation of their particular fields of study or dealt with potentially integrating concepts, in either case written in a manner accessible to educated laymen. From the accumulated list we selected seven to be read before we reconvened in May. Three addressed themes or bodies of ideas of overarching importance: Burton Bledstein's *Culture of Professionalism*, Thomas Kuhn's *Structure of Scientific Revolutions*, and Terry Eagleton's *Literary Theory*. Four explored central issues in painting, art history, management and medicine. Subsequently we read *Windows on the Mind*—the introduction that one of our own members, Erich Harth, has written to his field of neuroscience —and also a pile of chapters and articles in the professional and disciplinary fields represented in, but not yet discussed by the seminar.[13]

This order of proceeding proved to be even more fruitful than we anticipated. Not only did it bring about greater mutual understanding and open up promising lines of intellectual advance, it also generated an ongoing discussion which turned the seminar into a model that the undergraduate courses we were creating began unwittingly to emulate.

Whenever we turned our attention from the common reading to proposed course syllabi—or "syllabustering" to use the delightfully dismissive word that the physicist coined[14]—discussion flagged. We discussed the syllabi systematically when they were first drawn up in May 1985, and thereafter the new courses were continually on our minds. Most of them were offered for the first time in the 1985/86 academic year; and we reexamined and revised them in the light of that experience. Yet nothing bores university faculty more than direct discussion of pedagogy. Pedagogical concerns in higher education are better approached inadvertently through discussion of the intellectual matter that the pedagogy is meant to convey. Even so, the seminar was composed of faculty recruited for their talent in teaching as well as scholarship, and the courses they were creating involved subject matter, perspectives, and writing with which they needed each other's help. In providing it—again inadvertently but with all the more compelling force—they learned much from each other's technique, style, and approach to teaching.

The discussion of reading in each other's fields was not without its problems. Yet these problems pushed our understanding forward pedagogically as well as intellectually. The debate provoked by the biography of Robert Irwin encouraged hope for still closer engagement over the next assignment, Kuhn's *Structure of Scientific Revolutions*, since its central idea of paradigm shifts in the evolution of scientific thought could illuminate many fields. But that discussion fell flat, for it was immediately dominated by one member with expert knowledge in Kuhn's field. Still the discussion—or rather failure of discussion—forced us to recognize that so long as we stayed where we were all most comfortable, in our individual fields of expertise, we could not move forward collectively. We also experienced first-hand the deadening impact that the assumption of an expert/novice relationship could have in teaching and learning, with students as well as among faculty. Though we placed a high value on expertise and were anxious to gather all we could from each other, to make an effective contribution, each expert had to accept the risk of involvement in collective learning. Repeated attempts to draw upon outside experts rarely, if ever, proved successful.

Windows on the Mind helped put us on track. It provided metaphors—and more—to fathom the way the mind works in many fields of intellectual enquiry and professional application. In particular, the loop-backs that the author describes in the functioning of the mind seized the seminar's attention. Were they related to what the professor of advertising said was the key to creativity in his field —the ability to see interconnections between seemingly unrelated things? Along the same line, one of the authors we read on management pointed out that, "Developing most strategies requires numerous loops back to earlier stages as unexpected issues or new data dictate."[15]

Well before the first year (1985) of the project was complete, it was generating a momentum of its own. A number of the new courses were offered for the first time that autumn and elicited a good response from the students. But it was the faculty seminar that set the pace. Its collective force proved far stronger than had been anticipated. It moved us generally forward—though in frequently surprising directions—and transformed the original conception of the enterprise.

Toward the end of 1985 we identified four foci or conduits for enquiry that run through each discipline and profession. One naturally is the compound phenomenon of professions, professionalism, and professional education.[16] Another has to do with the notion of objectivity as pursued by, or discounted in, each discipline and profession.[17]

A third, obvious and seemingly promising, vein had to do with the skills, craft, art, or technology that distinguish the various disciplines and professions. The familiar identification of professional education with skills, particularly of engineering with technology; the relationship between the acquisition of skills and professional credentialing; the mastery of skills required in the visual, performing, and industrial arts; the refinement of techniques for analysis in the humanities and the pure and applied social sciences; and the methods of the natural sciences surely provided plenty of common ground for exploration. But here we came upon intractable differences. The disciplinary and professional skills that each professor has painstakingly refined not only enhance ability to learn and act, they have become part of us. The professor of drama put it even more strongly: "We are in a very fundamental way our knowledge, practices, and terms of discourse." The atypical resistance that we displayed to debate the subject of skills, craft, and technology suggested that it was fraught with implications that threatened to drive us back into separate enclaves. The theme also bore upon an acute pedagogical problem in colleges such as engineering and nursing. The undergraduate curriculum there has to meet so many technical demands for purposes of professional credentialing that reflection on the historical and conceptual roots and sociocultural embeddedness of these professions may all too readily be bypassed as an impractical luxury. Yet this "luxury" is essential to liberal education, and is indispensable to sound understanding and performance in the professions. For whatever reason, in spite of repeated attempts, so far we have not managed to grapple satisfactorily with this whole vein of concern.

On the other hand, the fourth—and least familiar—vein that we came to recognize as formative in each discipline and profession proved to be the most illuminating. It revolves around the idea of embeddedness,[18] and can be defined negatively as the distorting tension caused by the extraction of each profession and discipline from immersion in the totality of things. But the concept is perhaps best explained by describing the way it came up in the seminar. A literary theorist was first prompted to speak of embeddedness by the enzymologist's exploration of the impact of science on medicine. The central concern in that pre-medical course is with the paradoxical impact of the advances in medical science over the past generation, enabling doctors to offer cures to a previously unimaginable extent, yet dehumanizing the practice of medicine, as the escalation of suits for medical malpractice attests. Generalizing from this paradox, the literary theorist argued that "no discipline or profession exists except by virtue of an extraordinary effort of interpretive abstraction that lifts an object from the world and poses it as autonomous. But this act of abstraction is at odds with the real embeddedness of its objects in the world, giving rise to a seam of contradictions and problems within the discipline and profession, like the seam that we have found between science and medicine—at once crucially constitutive of the medical profession and profoundly problematic for it."

To lay the basis for the next intensive stretch of discussions scheduled for May 1986, we identified and read articles and chapters from each field of study that bore upon these four lines of common interest. That approach helped to move discussion beyond individual fields. Every discipline and profession wrestles with the tension between objectivity and subjectivity. No field of learning, however pure, can rightly claim complete objectivity. Even in physics, the conceptions of time and space, the theory of relativity, and the development of quantum mechanics depend upon allowance for the perspective of the observer or for the intervention of the investigator. Many academics nevertheless assumed that pursuit of objectivity, however impossible a goal, still fosters the right frame of mind for disciplinary learning and professional effectiveness—many but not all. Does the assumption apply to the visual and performing arts? Commentators on the field of management are increasingly skeptical of reliance on objective statistical analyses and prescriptions for managerial action, insisting that the human dynamics within each business, as well as in the marketplace, are of overriding importance. A literary theorist also pointed out that disciplines and professions have used their own definitions of objectivity for purposes of self-protection. "We have the habit of taking a certain disciplinary or professional objectivity as a substitute for, or insurance against, social or personal kinds of responsibility," he contended. "The advertiser does not make the culture to which he or she sells; the engineer makes only the machine and not our relation to it." The professor of advertising hotly disputed this line of argument. Nonetheless, exploration of such veins of common concern strengthened the sense of the need to recast the initial conception of our charge.

Instead of pressing toward conclusions, the enquiry became more adventurous. As that occurred, some worried that absorption in intellectual enquiry would distract attention from the practical needs of the new courses. Another pleaded for devotion of much more thought to plans for extending the pilot project beyond the Honors Program in order to permeate the undergraduate curriculum of the University as a whole.[19] We must begin to do so now.

Yet the dynamic of the faculty seminar was indispensable to the success that the new courses were already enjoying. In addition to the techniques and examples of teaching that the faculty were imbibing through the seminar, its ferment was spilling into the classroom, Initially, students had approached the new courses with uncertainty, but once they began to explore through these courses relationships among their other liberal and professional subjects of study, we heard again and again the exclamation that the new courses "made me think for the first time!"—a sobering observation for those who had been teaching for a long time.

Team teaching contributed to this success.[20] A historian shared responsibility with an engineer for the course in the College of Engineering. Two professors from different departments in management taught the course there jointly. The professor of nursing recruited a string of special lecturers for her course on "Images of Healing." And writing specialists worked with the subject faculty in many of the courses. Yet the courses taught by single members of the seminar proved no less stimulating. This experience suggests that, for courses that seek to address both the liberal and professional dimensions of undergraduate fields of study, while collaborative teaching arrangements are desirable, collaborative *learning* among the teaching faculty is the key to success. That conviction is reflected in the frequency with which the pages of course description later in this book take the proceedings of the faculty seminar as a point of reference. Far from indicating self-absorption, this habit reflects the reliance each of us came to place on that indispensable opportunity to examine the subject matter of the new courses from a range of standpoints other than his or her own.

The Way Forward

Quickened by the veins of common interest that the seminar has identified, it moved forward along several interrelated avenues of advance.

One is drawn from the contemporary wave of theoretical enquiry in literature and the parallel development of thought and practice in the teaching of composition. Interestingly, both of these movements are to some extent assertions of professional credentials in fields hitherto deemed fully accessible to the educated layman. Discouragingly, these theorists have elaborated a language for themselves, fulfilling their own diagnosis of autonomous "discourse communities." This language can be impenetrable to outsiders. As such, it exacerbates the difficulty that the various disciplines and professions have in communicating with each other. Literary theory thus heightens the walls of division as often as it penetrates them; yet it has given rise to potentially incisive lines of analysis applicable to fields far beyond the customary sphere of literature.

From the outset, we recognized that reading and writing must be central components of the project and we came to appreciate that both needs apply as much to faculty as to students. Among the first courses to be embraced within the project was "Reading and Interpretation." At a basic level, as the professor of drama put it, "students need to be constantly reminded that truth is not one—that there are many valid lenses through which to view the world in a meaningful way." That is one of the cardinal messages of liberal education, voiced in this instance, as so often, by someone from a professional college. Still, most of us, faculty as well as students, tend to forget that every text—in management as much as in literature—is the product of interpretation and is inevitably read interpretively. "Reading and Interpretation" is designed to convey that message, and hence to inculcate one of the most important intellectual skills that liberal education has to impart. The ability to recognize the interpretive nature of any text and of the act of reading it is a boundlessly enlightening skill. It alerts students to the interpretive assumptions or canons that characterize each particular discipline or profession that they study.

The "Reading and Interpretation" course is not the only benefit that we have reaped from the rise of literary theory. Some members of the seminar welcomed Terry Eagleton's book on the subject as the seminar's single most valuable reading assignment. The professor of nursing responded to its resonances with nursing theory. The social psychologist was gratified by the attention that Eagleton—like his own course on individual, social, and professional identity—drew to "the non-obvious impact of our multiple identities on our thinking." He also agreed with Eagleton that, as he put it, "the most mysterious thing about human beings is that they use language." *Windows on the Mind* makes a cognate point: "it is language which, like a good interpreter, mediates between the different factions . . . consciousness emerges in this picture as a unitary thing, tied closely to the verbal system."[21]

In an allied way, we tend to think of reading as the intellectual counterpart of breathing. Professors, who never cease to be astounded by the ignorance of undergraduates, are therefore prone to assume that they need to ingest a great deal of knowledge before they are ready to write. But reading is just half of breathing—it is inhaling. Writing, like exhaling, is the other half. Given the tiny amount of writing that undergraduates do in most courses, it is little wonder that their intellectual capacities remain stunted.

Though, to begin with, we were only dimly aware of the significance that the arrangement would have, a professor of composition formed part of the seminar, and she was authorized to recruit and supervise writing instructors to help with the new courses. Most of the participants welcomed that help, daunted by the prospect of adding the cultivation of student writing to responsibility for course content, especially if it involved unfamiliar subject matter. The professor of composition and her colleagues furnished us with a flexible array of devices for encouraging students to write,[22] and also with direct help. In doing so they gave rise to the most successful form of collaborative instruction that we have found.

The professor of composition also fostered awareness of the intellectual and professional dividends of the enterprise into which she led us. If students indeed need to be taken beneath the practical expertise of the professions in order to grasp the principles that explain and clarify their aims and claims, what better way of doing so is there than the "slower, more mediated process of analyzing and synthesizing" that writing entails? The professional dividends of writing far exceed the ability, say, to deal with business correspondence or submit a report on an engineering project, however useful that may be. Professions and disciplines are also, she stressed, "communities in which people talk or write to each other, guided by some agreement about what counts as a relevant contribution, what counts as a question, what counts as having a good answer to that question —and how to challenge those ways. In this sense, knowing how to talk or write constitutes active membership in that community."

What's good for the student goose is good also for the faculty gander. At the outset, the seminar faculty had no thought of writing down their unpolished thoughts for each other's consumption. Some were diffident of their ability to express themselves in prose, particularly in comparison to colleagues from more literary disciplines who in turn disliked issuing anything that they had not finely polished. But once we broke into effective oral dialogue over the biography of Robert Irwin, the professor of composition prompted us to pursue the discussion through an exchange of short position papers. They launched us into more free ventures in writing. As with teaching, so with writing, we learned by inadvertence, concentrating on what we wanted to communicate rather than on how to do so. Working ideas out on paper, then clarifying and developing the line of thought in response to each other's questions, fostered confidence and propelled the seminar forward more boldly than fleeting discussion could have done.

This process deepened the engagement of the faculty from the arts and sciences in the combined enterprise. Previously, the flow of information and energy in the enquiry had come predominantly from the professional schools' faculty, eager for cooperation from their colleagues in the liberal arts, who did not know quite how to respond. Once we settled into writing, words and ideas flowed both ways, generating the opposite danger that the liberal arts faculty, having found their voice, would not listen to and learn as much as before from their professional-school colleagues.

The process of writing also accelerated the demand for a more radical reconfiguration of the world of learning than had been envisioned at first. In one draft paper, a literary theorist argued that the various fields of pure and applied learning have so much in common that it is not helpful to divide them into two spheres—the liberal and the professional—as essentially different though perhaps complementary.[23] He cited a passage by a literary scholar, Suzanne Gearhart, on the relationship between history and fiction in eighteenth-century France, as suggestive in this regard. "The problem with the boundary separating history and fiction," Gearhart has written, "is that it . . . is much more open than closed, . . . as much within each field as at the limits of each. . . . It is not just open, then, in the sense that it permits passage over it—all boundaries do this. It is open in a more radical sense, for the very domains it is supposed to separate and delimit continually cross over it also."[24]

Word processors then began to hum. For wasn't the overlapping boundary between history and fiction analogous in one measure or other to the boundaries among all fields, whether pure or applied? Were they indeed demarcated by clear boundaries except in an administrative sense? Were liberal and professional ever-present dimensions rather than discrete spheres? Were the sites of greatest intellectual energy, whether pure or applied, situated at the points of intersection and overlap among fields rather than in their arcane, autonomous centers? If so, should we look for a new configuration of academia, at least in the classroom and curriculum, the laboratory and library, if not also in the administrative structure of the university?[25]

This line of questioning received independent reinforcement from the natural sciences. The physicist described developments in the sciences which indicate that, after a century of increasing specialization, the most promising lines of advance are converging in new joint fields such as biochemistry and biophysics.[26] While drawing attention to the potentially wide implications of the realignment that the world of science is undergoing, he however cautioned against abandonment of rigorous professionalism in method. In doing so, he reinforced the literary theorists who see value in the autonomy of discourse communities, and the social historian who pleads for strengthening not only of our intersections, but of our disciplinary and professional centers. Surrounded by colleagues whose modes of expression are markedly unlike his own, the artist stresses that the faculty seminar has manifested not only what we have in common but also what distinguishes us, yet in a way that takes the fear and antagonism out of this recognition of differences.

The convergence of all these observations forced us finally to abandon the original definition of our objective—to integrate liberal and professional education. Instead, we seek a truer, more comprehensive, and more incisive conception of the relationship.

Another form of communication had the same effect, on occasion even more forcefully than the written or spoken word.
Through the insistence of the artist, through the use that the art historian and the television writer-director made of pictures and videotapes in the proceedings, and through collective viewing and discussion of films, the seminar was deeply affected by the power of seeing.[27] Sometimes, like the drawings that our prehistoric forebears
scratched out on the walls of caves, we found that visual images enabled us to express thoughts and discover depths and dimensions
that eluded us in our usual verbal mode. The comment "I see" when
one grasps a point is more than a metaphor. Seeing is more than a
matter of grasping essentially verbal points. The visual arts have
their own observations to convey, often most potent when least accessible to verbal explanation. Visual communication contributed to
the proceedings out of all proportion to our infrequent use of it.

Still another sort of vision has molded the thinking of the seminar and pointed out fruitful ways of moving forward. Several faculty
entered the project suspicious that their professions were not taken
quite seriously. They came from nursing, composition, and drama,
and as it happened all were women. Some of the most difficult early
moments in the seminar occurred during debate on the proposal for
a course on gender and the professions. The contention that gender
affects perception as well as conduct in every discipline and profession met with stiff resistance before it won acceptance. Clear—if
unconscious—gender implications, for example in the statement
that "both engineering and science are popularly considered to be
tools of conquest, enabling man to extend his control over his environment,"[28] had to be pointed out. Appreciation of what the distinctive perceptions of women could contribute to the project came
slowly.

Yet, from first to last, the professor of nursing stressed the in-
terrelatedness of ingredients in the process of healing, and in doing
so she prefigured the eventual call for reconception of the relationship between liberal and professional education. When the director
of the project emphasized the seminar's duels and gladiatorial debate. But the woman from the Department of History pointed out
the much greater importance of cooperative group effort and elaboration of points of agreement in the seminar's growth. The professor of composition suggested the multi-faceted diamond as a better
metaphor for the proceedings than engagement in battle, and she
stressed the greater fruitfulness of opening up lines of questioning

Mark Tansey, *Action Painting No. 2*, 1984. Oil on canvas, 76″ x 110″. Collection of the Montreal Museum of Fine Arts. Gift of Mr. Nahum Gelber, Q.C. Photo courtesy of Curt Marcus Gallery.

than of hastening to assert answers. Their comments were reflective of the ways in which the women in the seminar fostered its development and advanced its understanding.

Remaining Challenges

These avenues of perception—from literature and composition, natural science, visual art, and the standpoint of gender—have led the seminar to call for a new configuration in the world of learning and teaching. Critical challenges—intellectual, pedagogical, and administrative—have yet to be met before that goal can be reached.

The primary intellectual challenge will be to discern the emerging configuration of liberal and professional education more clearly. Though we have seen enough of the conventional interpretation to convince us of its intellectual invalidity and pedagogical harm, so far we can speak with confidence mainly of how to go about uncovering the true relationship. Still, we know it will not turn out bland. It must reflect the genuinely distinctive features of the professions and the liberal arts. Sometimes they will display much in common. Sometimes they will prove complementary. Sometimes they will be locked in dialectic conflict. They will seldom prove irrelevant to each other. Yet the unique features of each will continue to require exploration.

Pedagogically, the project has not ventured beyond the format of small, seminar-style classes conducted less through lecture than through discussion based upon prior reading. Most of the participants find this format indispensable to stimulate the interrelational enquiry that lies at the heart of our enterprise. But until ways are devised to involve large numbers of students in the process, the impact of the enterprise will be minimal.

The administrative challenge will require an even more imaginative response.[29] The existing administrative division of virtually all American universities into liberal arts and professional colleges and departments is the greatest isolating force among them. To concern oneself with the intellectual or pedagogical relationships among them, however intrinsically promising, is a risky venture in which only tenured full professors can safely indulge.

There is a crying need, as a neighboring university president has pointed out, for "structures to support and reward builders of departmental [and we would add intercollegiate] bridges."[30] Demonstrably profitable convergences between fields may protect themselves by erecting programmatic tents, but without a reliable budgetary allocation and power to reach the first crucial decisions on matters of personnel their denizens must lead a nomadic existence. Administrative devices to protect and encourage young explorers in search of new convergences have yet to be invented. Are universities capable of such venturous elasticity? The enterprise of reconfiguring the relationship between liberal and professional education cannot be sustained without it.

The experiment begun at Syracuse with the aid of the Mellon Foundation has gone a considerable way. Like all explorations, what is discovered whets the appetite for the quest. Reconfiguring the relationship between liberal and professional education is an intellectual journey rather than a final destination. But that only makes the endeavor more rewarding.

Notes

1. Joan S. Stark, Malcolm A. Lowther, and Bonnie M. K. Hagerty, *Responsive Professional Education: Balancing Outcomes and Opportunities* (Washington: Eric-Ashe, 1986), xvi.

2. See chapter 4 on "The Engineering Dilemma."

3. Joan S. Stark, "Liberal Education and Professional Programs: Conflict, Coexistence or Compatibility?" in *Selecting Career Programs for College Campuses*, edited by M. A. Rehnke. (San Francisco: Jossey-Bass, 1986), 8–9.

4. Frank Rhodes, "Reforming Higher Education Will Take More Than Just Tinkering With Curricula," *The Chronicle of Higher Education*, 22 May 1985.

5. See chapter 9, "The Impact of Science on Medicine," and the appendix to chapter 18 containing the responses of some leading medical educators to the course created under that title.

6. Samuel C. Florman, *Engineering and the Liberal Arts* (New York: McGraw-Hill, 1968), 17.

7. See chapter 17, "From Specialization toward Integration: A Scientist's Perspective."

8. James M. Powell, "Professionalism and the Liberal Arts in the American University," *Liberal Education* 69, no.3 (1983), 231.

9. *Syracuse University Catalogue*, 1909–1910

10. Lawrence Weschler, *Seeing is Forgetting the Name of the Thing One Sees: A Life of Contemporary Artist Robert Irwin* (Berkeley: University of California Press, 1982).

11. See chapter 2, "The Faculty Seminar: Discourse Communities and the Quotation Marks."

12. See chapter 10, "Gender and the Professions."

13. See "Background Reading."

14. "Sillybustering" is an alternative spelling.

15. J. B. Quinn, "Managing Strategic Change," in *Strategies for Change: Logical Incrementation* (Homewood, Ill.: R. D. Irwin, 1980), 105.

16. See chapter 3, "The Phenomena of Professions."

17. See chapter 5, "The Concept of Objectivity."

18. See chapter 8, "The Concepts of Embeddedness and Enculturation."

19. See chapter 19, "Of Bridges, Ships, and Sea Dogs."

20. See chapter 12, "The Varieties of Collaboration."

21. Erich Harth, *Windows on the Mind* (New York: Wm. Morrow, 1982), 192.

22. See chapter 13, "Everyone Writes."

23. See chapter 16, "Education in a Transformed Field."

24. Suzanne Gearhart, *The Open Boundary of History and Fiction: A Critical Approach to the French Enlightenment* (Princeton: Princeton University Press, 1984), 3–4.

25. See chapter 19, "Of Bridges, Ships, and Sea Dogs."

26. See chapter 17, "From Specialization toward Integration: A Scientist's Perspective."

27. See chapter 7, "The Impact of Seeing."

28. Samuel C. Florman, *Engineering and the Liberal Arts*, 25

29. See chapter 19, "Of Bridges, Ships and Sea Dogs."

30. Frank Rhodes, "Reforming Higher Education."

2

The Faculty Seminar:
Discourse Communities and Quotation Marks

MARGARET HIMLEY

It would seem to be a simple thing to bring together for a common purpose a group of twenty open-minded, dedicated, and articulate experts from a wide range of disciplines and professions, and ask them to talk—talk about their research, talk about their courses, and talk about a collection of readings drawn widely from the diversity of fields represented among them. That is, in fact, the traditional idea of what a university is.

And it would seem to be a simple thing to expect that, after some initial discomfort and defensiveness, talk would result in a deepened understanding of each other's fields and perhaps the establishment of a shared common language, or meta-discourse. After all, as the neuroscientist put it, we should be able to find language for explaining to each other even the most difficult concepts of our fields. It is a premise in his course on the natural sciences that even the most technical concepts can be translated into language accessible to students from all majors, not just the sciences.

Indeed, the initial definition of our task together—"integrating" liberal and professional learning—suggested this notion of making whole, uniting, bringing disparate, but potentially harmonious, parts together. In that early version of the project, we anticipated fine-tuning the courses by adding readings from the professional schools to the liberal arts courses and vice versa. We would visit each other's classes and even team-teach to show how professional the liberal arts have become, how liberal the professions really are. What historical circumstance and university administrative structure had sundered, the new courses would bring together. To facilitate this model, we used the forum of the faculty seminar; obviously, we all had to talk with each other in order to bring about the integration so devoutly to be wished.

But it didn't happen that way. The very process of two years of "talk" was far more complex, central, and interesting, at least to a language researcher like myself, than this simple scenario would suggest. The initial idea of "integration" was quickly assaulted, in part because of the problems we encountered as we tried to talk—*really talk*—with each other. In the end, as in this book, the seminar participants came neither to remain particular professionals speaking strictly in their own language nor to meld into a community identity speaking in a generalist language or educator-ese. In complex ways and over time, we came to speak "in view of" each other; we speak, that is, in quotation marks.

As a compositionist, I "naturally" saw the problems we had in talking with each other partially as a result of the differences in our discourse communities. A discourse community is a group of people bound by common interests who communicate through approved channels and whose talk is regulated; for example, I belong to the field of composition, the Syracuse University Writing Program, the Himley family. It has been our individual professional discourse communities, however, that have remained salient in the talk in the seminar. Within each of these communities are shared assumptions about "what objects are appropriate for examination and discussion, what operating functions are performed on those objects, what constitutes 'evidence' and 'validity,' and what formal conventions are followed."[1] In that way, discursive practices both reflect and constitute different worldviews. In entering our different fields, we took on the particular ways of talking—the interpretive frames—of those fields.

In the early days of the seminar, perhaps as a response to the diversity of discourse communities represented in the it, *monologues* prevailed, as participants explained their research interests to each other and described the general shape and purpose of their courses. This talk was seamless, coherent in its own terms, and we listened, politely attentive, and rarely interrupted each other. We saw connections to our own fields, suggested readings that might relate to the new courses, and asked each other to come as guest lecturers to our classes. My notes from those early seminar meetings remind me of my student days when I attended lectures, writing summaries of main ideas and willing in a very real sense to suspend my own authority in order to enter into another's area of expertise. It was one way we learned about each other.

Visitors in each other's territories, we acted like tourists, checking out the landscape, listening to the new lingo, taking snapshots of famous monuments—and wishing at times we were back home.

Over time, of course, disagreements emerged and seams showed. The early disagreements tended to take the form of debate, with seminar participants taking a few moments to put forth a particular position or to rebut a different one. We continued to make self-contained statements, *mini-monologues* in a sense, and these discourse practices allowed speakers to locate themselves in terms of the ongoing discussion while only indirectly confronting each other. Situated within our own positions, we talked *at* each other, explaining, arguing, redirecting, clarifying.

Slowly, however, we got to know each other—our personalities, values, ethics of teaching, professional commitments, ways of talking. And gradually we came to care about the project in which we were engaged, care enough that we wanted to persuade others to our point of view, care enough to try at times to move the seminar in certain intellectual directions. Within the common enterprise, we became increasingly intellectually engaged and differences became increasingly visible and important.

Things began to happen. At times the discursive and interpretive diversity brought about richer understanding. When the art historian put up on a wall a slide of a Norman Rockwell painting depicting a "traditional" American Thanksgiving dinner, the professional perspectives brought to bear by the literary theorists, the cross-cultural psychologist, the drama professor, and the historians, to mention only a few, prompted a provocatively diverse, interactive reading of a "simple" visual text.

Yet at other times it was the diversity that was highlighted, and perhaps even more deeply forged. The discussion of Robert Irwin's art, for example,[2] was characterized by sharp disagreement and dramatically marked the intellectual boundaries that divided us. The discussion on these occasions confirmed the divergences between us, alienating some, aligning others.

For the seminar to proceed, we had to work at making sense of each other's perspectives and ways of talking. Talking is a collaborative activity, the communal establishment of mutual frames of reference, not just the transmittal of information. When people inhabit the same or similar discourse communities, and hence possess common understandings—when they are mutually knowledgeable— they are able to establish those frames of reference by taking for granted much of what otherwise would need to be said. The language of the art historian, for example, with its emphasis on the active role of the viewer in interpretation, is consonant with my theoretical understanding of the way in which written texts work, and thus I readily made sense of, and appropriated, the language of his field.

Such a mutual frame, of course, was not always the case, and we had to work to achieve at least some kind of shared knowledge, as experts sought to introduce novices to their fields. In a sense, we "negotiated" meaning; we worked with metaphors and comparisons to create bridges that enabled us to have some idea about what was being discussed, some shared understanding of things. Members of the seminar were willing to "de-professionalize" their discourse at times.[3] They tolerated a certain amount of semantic sloppiness in order to sustain interdisciplinary talk at all. This willingness was critical.

Negotiation of meaning across disciplinary and discourse community boundaries may be paradigmatic of all talk. In this respect, our situation is not different from that described in a simple example by the psycholinguist Rommetveit: in teaching French history in a culture in rural Africa where the concept of "president" is meaningless, the teacher negotiates or explains the meaning by referring to De Gaulle as a powerful "king" of France. We too talked to establish shared, if never fully mutual, knowledge. The vital role of the four common themes that we identified[4] may have resulted from their functioning as mutual frames of reference in which seminar participants could locate themselves and their fields as well as from a willingness to work with a kind of residual equivocation. "Embeddedness," for example, a term that was unfamiliar to us at first, provided a pivotal point in our talk, as we each tried to define the term and apply it to our different disciplines.

Sometimes even this effort at establishing shared knowledge just didn't work, with concepts or ideas sliding away, eluding some of us, confusing others. Even when two disciplines share a term, the particular meanings and uses of the term, emerging as they do in different intellectual contexts, can result in different—even diametrically opposed—meanings. "Equilibrium" was such a term for us. When the professor of nursing used the term, she was speaking against the backdrop of a medical profession dominated by a particular biomedical model of health and a piecemeal approach to healing. For her, "equilibrium" represented attention to the whole person, the psychological, social, and biological person, as well as attention to a balanced approach to "wellness." Yet the neuroscientist rejected the term, which in physics implies stasis, and hence death, and he argued the need for crisis and stress in systems to facilitate change and growth. Within discourse communities, words come populated—even overpopulated—with meanings and accents, and cannot readily be wrested from the contexts of those communities. These mark the points of frustration, closure, and boundedness that we also experienced as we talked.

In the process of talking from within my particular discourse community as a compositionist, my own discourse has become "unfamiliar" to me in ways, as I had to explain terms and ideas that seemed "natural" to me. Even to use a common phrase from my discipline—"invention heuristics"—was to call forth a whole network of meanings that would just "be there" for those who work and read in that discipline, and remained limited to synonyms for those outside the discipline. An insider would think of specific strategies, the history of those strategies in recent discussions of the teaching of writing, names of key figures, debates about the philosophical implications of the term (e.g., does it imply a particular definition of an autonomous subject, and does it carry a particular theory of knowledge as a private act?). Yet to an outsider, the term translates rather flatly into "procedures for generating ideas," ways for structuring brainstorming activities. An insider brings a knowledge and understanding—a way of locating the term—that enables her to realize a fuller meaning potential. Talking across disciplinary boundaries defamiliarized me with taken-for-granted meanings, creating gaps and silences at times, reengaging me with my own terms, raising questions.

Oddly, the seminar developed few new terms. When we worked with the concept of "embeddedness," we strove valiantly to come up with a shared definition, but the flurry of metaphors that supported that effort illustrated the difficulty in wresting a term from one context and trying to extend it to cover a range of possibilities. For example, is the embeddedness of our discipline and professions in the world like a rock in the earth, and then does the earth define the space of the rock or does the rock define itself? Is it like the confluence of tide waters? Or is it more like bridges connecting islands that all sit in the same ocean? It is indicative of how much we worked with, and worried about, that bridge metaphor that it turns up in various configurations, still not fully resolved, throughout this book.

The only term we developed that does seem to have a metafunction is "Mellonization" or "Mellonized," a word that seems to sum up the whole experience of participation in the seminar and to identify common features of the courses we created. As I recall, the term emerged in discussions about bringing new faculty into the project, faculty who had not been through the seminar and hence had not yet been "Mellonized." Yet the term gained great currency after we decided to write a book together. My speculation is that its frequency of use came about when we had a new audience. No longer just talking among ourselves, with all those differences and tensions, we were now going public, working as a group, addressing all those "others" out there. The term marks the common aspects of our enterprise. It serves as semantic shorthand for extending this effort to other undergraduate courses and for describing our experience as the first participants. It also marks closure, a process now completed.

In the last few weekends of the seminar, the talk was characterized by lots of "quotation marks," that is, by an apparently self-conscious use of each other's language.[5] The leader might say the term "process" now (one he has learned from the management faculty) *as if* it had quotation marks around it, *as if* he were marking it as half his, half theirs. I have noticed he hesitates a bit when he says "process," adding a touch of irony to his use of the term and creating a sense of artifice. Or we might directly quote someone else as we work their language into our text, as we add their voice and discourse to our own. This can be ironic, as when a seminar participant, after a particularly energetic discussion, notes with satiric dismay, "Oh, no, now we'll have to write a 'micro-theme.'" My words in another's text—a new idea, a bit of discomfort, a touch of irony, a comment offered "in view of" me. These additions, therefore, are not necessarily blended in smoothly, but rather exist in various degrees of harmony and discord, marking how we now talk "in view of" each other and illustrating how we have both accepted and resisted the authority of others.

The quotation mark effect in our talk suggests how we have transformed the initial monologues into *hybrids*, texts that acknowledge that while we are still located within specific discourse communities, we have also worked to "own" the words and worldviews of others. At times that language has harmoniously blended into our discourse, adding depth and richness and variety; at times that language conflicts and jars, adding tensions and divergences. No longer self-contained, seamless monologues, our talk is truly *dialogic* and reveals the seams, the points of overlap, the moments of conflict.

The process of "talk" in the seminar, therefore, has not been

Mark Tansey, *Secret of the Sphinx,* 1984. Oil on canvas, 60″ x 65″. Collection of Robert M. Kaye. Photo courtesy of Curt Marcus Gallery.

simple but it has been central; in complex ways and at different times we have acquiesced in the authority of others, we have taken in and "owned" their languages, we have resisted others' language and thereby discovered our divergences and differences, and we have become "unfamiliar" with our own discourse. Neither located strictly within our own professional discourse communities nor forged into a new and common one, we retain our voices even as we talk "in view of" each other.

Discursive diversity within an important common enterprise has been, I believe, a fundamental and enabling condition of our intellectual enterprise—a diversity, that is, to be seen as a critical and valuable feature of interdisciplinary work, central to the project, and not as an obstacle that should, or even could, be overcome.

This book, in a parallel way, intends to acknowledge the strong and divergent voices of seminar participants as it recounts their experiences. Two other options might have presented themselves: the book could have been completed in a more traditional (and probably easier) way as an edited collection of disparate, separately authored chapters; or it could have been written as a single-voiced text, for example by the seminar leader. We chose, instead, to truly collaborate. We collaborated on possible outlines, we circulated drafts back and forth, and we wrote together. In four long and demanding weekend meetings during the fall of 1986, we all met to critique chapters, one at a time, in detail, with great care and respect.

As a writing teacher, I have been impressed by the willingness of all the seminar participants to write in a discourse style often far removed from the kind of articles they produce within their own disciplines, and even more impressed by their subsequent willingness to submit those drafts to a very intensive peer review process. And I was most impressed with the quality of the peer reviews, the ability and the willingness of the members of the seminar to enter into the intellectual frame and discursive style of each writer and make suggestions that took that frame and style fully into account yet also pushed the writer to work his or her material with greater force or cogency. The revised chapters were *always* better, at times startlingly better—a result of the way we are also now able to write "in view of" each other.

I hope readers of this book will hear strong and different voices, some more resonant and accessible for them than others, some even disharmonious at times. I hope too that readers will see how we have acknowledged each other in both direct and indirect ways, from explicit quotations to references drawn from different disciplines to actual appropriation of others' language.

Like the seminar, this book is also a story about discourse communities and "quotation marks," about the role of discursive diversity in intellectual endeavors.

Notes

1. James E. Porter, "Intertextuality and the Discourse Community," *Rhetoric Review* 5 (Fall 1986): 34–47.

2. See above, pages 17–19.

3. Ironically, in a sense the writing faculty or consultants bucked this trend and actually became "professionalized" in and through the seminar. At the beginning, we had no real experience doing writing across the curriculum, had been "tacked on" to the seminar at the last moment, had no actual course of our own, and were defined as playing a methodological or pedagogical role in course design. The consultants were all part-time instructors, very sensitive to the difference in their rank as compared to other seminar participants. Yet writing became increasingly central, an expertise was developed, and a new language for talking about writing gained currency. The handbook on writing strategies that we produced for the project has been circulated to all instructors in the new SU Writing Program, the first extension of the project into the SU curriculum at large.

4. See chapter 3, "The Phenomenon of Professions," chapter 5, "The Concept of Objectivity," chapter 8, "The Concepts of Embeddedness and Enculturation," and pages 23–24.

5. This analysis of the seminar relies heavily upon the work of M. M. Bakhtin, a Russian language theorist. See Michael Holquist, ed., Caryle Emerson and Michael Holquist, trans., *The Dialogic Imagination* (Austin: The University of Texas Press, 1981).

3

The Phenomenon of Professions

SALLY GREGORY KOHLSTEDT

Early in the seminar I told two tales of the profession of medicine. One story was the textbook history recounted in medical schools: Using folk wisdom and their own experience, ancient world physicians, like Hippocrates and Galen, began to systematize knowledge about human physiology and disease. By the time of the scientific revolution, accumulated expertise brought physicians, surgeons, and pharmacists into specialized guilds through which their expertise was certified and their techniques and therapies expanded. After a period of confused and competitive practice in colonial America, the most well-trained (English, Scottish, and Continental born, of course) physicians gradually organized medical schools for systematic training, hospitals to centralize and define treatment, and licensing laws to protect the public from quacks. The American Medical Association worked during the last half of the nineteenth century to establish ethical standards for physicians and define specialties in such a way as to maximize the attack on diseases. Armed with munitions from biochemistry and scientific research, the physicians and researchers in twentieth-century America so successfully challenged major epidemic and endemic disease that they created a medical profession preeminent in the world.

The second story, a less sanguine tale, was drawn from the point of view of other health practitioners and a critical public: Efforts to establish good health had motivated folk "doctors" in rural communities to promote healthy habits and to heal the sick since the beginning of recorded history. Their knowledge and skill brought them power, and a few took control of both ritual and efficacious remedies. By denouncing or punishing others who practiced surgery or prescribed herbal remedies—at the most extreme branding them as witches and wizards—the physicians consolidated their authority among the ancient and medieval elites in cities and in royal courts. As hospitals and medical schools were established in the wake of the scientific revolution, the physicians gained ever more control, closing out a variety of other practitioners including midwives, and redefining such natural events as childbirth as diseases. Identifying themselves with science, some physicians oversaw major laboratories or developed surgical specialties which provided distance from patient contact, thus serving to enhance their status.[1] Despite the wealth and power of the medical establishment—gained from monopolistic practices, including the organized defeat in the United States of a national public health plan in the 1920s—actual health care deteriorated to post-crisis management. Emphasis on treating disease overshadowed concern for maintaining health (except in such cases of preventative intervention as polio vaccine, always administered under doctors' supervision), for assisting patients and their families, and for adequately distributing health care to poor people in rural and inner city areas. As a result of doctors' narrowly defined professionalism, international health statistics (using such measures as infant mortality and adult longevity) show the United States behind many other countries.[2]

Both histories can be documented and have an evident subjective element as well. Neither story, by itself, reveals the complex mix of personal motivations and economic and social forces which shaped the medical profession or any other. In both accounts we hear elements of the mythology and the critique found in all of distinctive disciplines and professions.

What history shall we tell students? Basically, we want them to understand the implications of choosing a profession—often *our* profession. Too often, if only implicitly, we recount the heroic story of pioneering individuals and high ideals. We want to reassure students, and ourselves, that our activity can bring satisfaction to the individual practitioners and benefit to society. Yet such accounts easily become self-serving platitudes. With them we risk disillusionment or complicity. We know that circumstances within, as well as outside, the professions may run counter to high ideals and good intentions. Surely our task is to warn students about the challenges they face ahead. But what if they hear us only cynically? What if they discount the possibilities offered by collective endeavor, by mutual challenges, and by individual responsibility guided through shared ethics? Describing and evaluating the state of our professions and disciplines is at the heart of the project at Syracuse.

The faculty turned briefly to the history of professions in modern western culture. Those we know and represent are more than simply occupational designations. The basic tasks and status of our work echo prehistoric roles assigned to healers and social arbiters, and the term "profession" itself carries a reminder of medieval days when the learned and religious professed certain knowledge and beliefs. What interested us most, however, was the more recent design and role of professions and disciplines as we now know them, rooted firmly in our immediate academic turf.

In order to gain a larger perspective and distance from current issues, the seminar members read Burton Bledstein's *Culture of Professionalism* and a number of shorter essays on the origins and nature of particular professions. Bledstein elaborated his subtitle, "The Middle Class and the Development of Higher Education in America," in a provocative presentation of the "ego-satisfying pretensions of professionalism" which he argued were even more important than the "raw profits of capitalism."[3] These incentives included financial security, status, self-fulfillment, autonomy, and power. We read as well from intellectual historians who alternatively emphasize that optimism regarding rational scientific investigation and planning also accounts for the elaboration of professions and disciplines a century ago.[4]

The method for gaining these multiple goals in a literate, capitalist, and democratic society has been through the creation of institutions which serve as filters for scrutinizing potential recruits, for providing credentials to those judged appropriate, and for regulating participants' behavior. Liberal education, as redesigned by Charles Eliot while president of Harvard University and by his contemporary educational reformers at the end of the nineteenth century, was divided into "major" areas of study. Some, like political economy, were quite evidently preprofessional by design, even as law and medicine were designated post-graduate degrees in a distinctively American university structure. Yet at that point the simple distinction between theory and practice was not assumed; law was advanced political theory in the classes taught by Oliver Wendell Holmes, Jr., and most students attending even small colleges were presumed to be en route to professional careers. Distinctions between undergraduate education, graduate study, and professional training were established only after considerable debate; but rationalism and standardization had brought all three into the university setting by the twentieth century.

Academic departments were developed to parallel the emerging disciplines, and both show the imprint of prominent individuals and institutional exigencies, in ways not unrelated to contemporary transitions in German, British, and French higher education. Nine-teenth-century efforts to deal with social problems scientifically led to the disciplines of economics, sociology, and political economy (later divided between political science and parts of history). Natural history became zoology, botany, paleontology, and geology, as college graduates sorted themselves out into museums, herbaria, and state and federal surveys. In a similarly self-conscious way, the physical scientists took ever more specialized occupational designations and formed organizations as physicists, chemists, astronomers, and mathematicians. If some of the terms were traditional, the meanings changed in the cultural nexus of industrialized and bureaucratized society where business and government were principal sponsors of research. Updated courses in modern languages, art, literature, philosophy, and history were identified as the humanities. Close examination of any of these young disciplines reveals the logic—and illogic—of the distinctions made by individuals about a century ago as they established knowledge and power bases, sought identifiable methods for research, and created professional associations. In distinct—but in some ways parallel—fashion, engineering, management, nursing, and a host of other aspiring professions established separate schools and then university affiliation. While their absorption remains incomplete, the tendency toward specialization has been similarly evident. Members of the seminar could recount, sometimes with humor or in frustration, historical explanations of what often seem to be quite arbitrary definitions and distinctions within their own disciplinary and professional arenas.

As the seminar reconsidered such origins, familiar categories lost some of their imperative force, and we became more free to reconsider the boundaries of our disciplines and professional clusters. The reconfigurations we contemplated seemed increasingly reasonable, given the evident fluidity of boundaries in the past. We could ask fundamental questions: What constitute the appropriate, as well as legitimate, concerns of our work lives? How do these concerns relate to subject matter and clientele? Nothing needed to be taken for granted. At the same time, none of us denied the important legacy reflected in the historically derived categories of responsibility and knowledge, or wanted to blur important distinctions. Donald Campbell's argument for more, rather than fewer, specialties had its adherents in our seminar.[5] History reminded us of the dynamic ways in which knowledge and practice develop, but it provided no road map to the future.

Boundaries, distinctions, and definitions in the disciplines and professions proved to be only a part of our concern with these historical developments, however, because as faculty we face another legacy in education itself. The emphasis on research and service (or practice) in universities established at the turn of the century tended to lower the prestige of teaching itself and of those institutions that cherish teaching as their central concern. George Santayana observed, for example, "Many of the young professors . . . are no longer the sort of persons that might as well have been clergymen or schoolmasters; they have rather the type of mind of a doctor, an engineer, or a social reformer; the wide awake young man . . . can do most things better than old people and knows it."[6] These young professors shifted the priorities they assigned to their varied tasks and to the self-image they cultivated. They established our legacy. As investigation and the production of new knowledge become primary, loyalties turn from our college and students to our specialties and our colleagues.[7] We therefore face two professional identities —often ambiguous and sometimes conflicting in their claims—one of which relates to our disciplinary or professional role, and the other to our teaching function. In both, however, we face observant, inquiring students.

They, in their turn, expect us either explicitly or implicitly to prepare them for professional lives. Involvement in the project at Syracuse reflected its members' sense of responsibility to make that intellectual, professional, and even social preparation adequate. We attempted initially to discover what was meant by frequently used terms like "professional education" and "professionalism," but grew impatient with the abstraction of the task. The goal of consensus seemed to be impractical and uninteresting. We did discover, however, some reasons for our different points of view. We also found in our pluralism that the contested boundaries among us did not necessarily fall along tidy lines of liberal and professional appointments. Equally important, we recovered general elements of mutual concern, most of them captured in Magali Sarfatti Larson's description of professionalism:

> The cognitive dimension is centered on the body of knowledge and the techniques which professionals apply in this work, and on the training necessary to master such knowledge and skills; the normative dimension covers the service orientation of professionals, and their distinctive ethics, which justify the privilege of self-regulation

granted them by society; the evaluative dimension implicitly com-
pares professions to other occupations, underscoring the professions' singular characteristic of autonomy and prestige.[8]

How individual faculty from different backgrounds deal with these
dimensions, and which ones we emphasize, varies considerably.

Faculty from engineering, management, nursing, communications, and theater accept the term "professional" quite automatically,
while those in the liberal arts tend to avoid it altogether. The latter
much prefer such specific designations as art historian or literary
theorist, and use "professional" almost exclusively as an adjective.
Uneasiness with the noun and its associations goes beyond intellectual disagreement. For some, there is ambivalence about the "special
interest" quality of professions, an elite within a democracy, as exercised through professional organizations.[9] The American Medical
Association, with its considerable influence in Washington, provides
a frequently cited example. Other faculty suggest that claims for expertise might be abused ("statistics lie") as well as used, and that specialized language too often seems intended to obscure rather than to
clarify. Faculty are also uneasy about wide variation in the status and
power of particular professions and disciplines. Defensiveness, def-
erence, and cynicism crept into conversations when we discussed
professionalism concretely, especially as we characterized doctors,
lawyers, and merchant chiefs. In nearly every instance, however,
distance—whether respectful or not—was reserved for professions
other than our own.

As we planned our individual courses, a loyalty to the discipline
or profession to which we had devoted much of our lives was coun-
terbalanced by efforts to point out the limitations, pitfalls, and need
for revision in the substance and practice of that profession. In fact,
having chosen to be teachers (albeit another profession) rather than
full-time writers, scientists, civil servants, managers, writers, engineers, actors, or whatever, faculty members feel particularly ready to
analyze "their professions" even as they transmit information and
project acceptable behavior. They recognize that professions tend to
manifest, maintain, and only occasionally challenge the norms and
values of the groups of which they are an intimate part. Those in the
professional colleges, moreover, argue that the most penetrating cri-
tiques usually come from an insider's perspective, from those who
are sufficiently experienced to measure the distance between professed ideals and actual practice and to formulate new possibilities

based on commitment to the future. Perhaps inevitably, those faculty whose fields had insecure or ill-defined professional status were most vocal about the benefits of professional standards and ethics.

Debates about just who is a professional were quickly left behind in the seminar (although few denied the efficacy of the question in daily life). In their place came exchanges regarding the changing purposes and structures of individual professions (their distinctive characteristics as well as their affinities to models of professionalism), the relationship between expert and public (and definition of that public), and the nature of knowledge and of actual practice. Professional-school faculty were most confident in describing their purposes and practices, and they provided the seminar with relevant, accessible literature concerned with such topics. Liberal arts faculty members, by contrast, revealed a curious vulnerability—despite their apparent "higher" status—because they were unable to define any exclusive domain for their disciplines.[10] Designated as at the "center" of university life, liberal arts faculty are unsure about the radius of their influence.

Discussions of professionalism—with the term seldom used—explored the horizontal and lateral interchange of practice and information. Because education was at the core of our enterprise, it was stressed over research, although we frequently reminded each other of the latter as an important, related goal. Teachers all, we described or demonstrated to each other certain fundamental elements in our work—styles in drama, approaches to art history, techniques of middle management. At that concrete level we discovered dynamics for collaboration or debate, as when the art historian found much in common with the civil engineers, or when the nurse showed how distinctive the practice and outlook of nursing was in comparison to the behavior of typical physicians described by the biochemist teaching about medicine.

The process of sharing content led, almost inevitably, to discussions about how we teach. Some uncomfortable early meetings of the seminar reminded even seasoned faculty of the difficulties in learning about fields far from their own, as well as the excitement of having new information illuminate things we already knew. Heightened awareness fostered willingness to present our varied reasons for becoming teachers, techniques for conducting classes, frustrations and worries about the effectiveness of such techniques, and determination to engage students in learning. This expressed commitment (or recommitment) to education led to the decision to collaborate on this book.

Those who decided to contribute necessarily reduced and reallocated their scarce resources of time and attention otherwise available for consulting, research, and of course teaching and advising—not to mention personal lives. In retrospect, these individual decisions involved professional identity. To paraphrase Larson's definitional categories, we agreed, first, to generate new knowledge of the relationship between professional and liberal education; second, to reaffirm mutual confidence in the possibilities and process of educating students; and third, to examine in a public way the central faculty prerogatives of defining curricula and, more fundamentally, the nature of the university. Even without degrees in education, we are indeed professional educators.

The tensions in being, simultaneously, teachers, scholars, and practitioners are not easily resolved, of course; members of the seminar know full well that tenure and promotion decisions in universities tend to discount teaching. They brought widely diverse responses to a questionnaire that asked, among other things, "Does college teaching enhance or inhibit your professional status and credibility?" For those in the liberal arts, faculty positions seem particularly competitive, even essential; indeed, an English professor claims, "I have no professional status or credibility apart from university involvement." At the same time, several faculty noted how often faculty view teaching itself, in the words of one seminar member, as a "regrettable distraction from research and writing."

In the professional schools, the responses reflected, by contrast, the existence of other employment alternatives, with faculty more often "electing" to teach. They have at some point chosen to place themselves in the special corner of their professions that directs training, and they earn a certain distinction by choosing to enter the classroom. Engineers stress the fundamental importance of a P.E. license (requiring experience) which, together with a university appointment, enlarges visibility and prestige. In art, however, "the credibility is frail, and if you let the teaching get in the way of being a serious artist, everyone sees it."

As we reflected on students and their goals, along with the future of our professions and society, the seminar became ever more conscious of the fundamental nature of its inquiry into the professions and liberal arts disciplines in modern America. The story of the academic profession, like that of medicine, has often heroic dimensions; but honest evaluation reveals as well that the professional commitment to education—and thus to the larger society—has been differently understood and not often well articulated. At the outset, the chief academic administrator of the university suggested that we might prove subversive of the status quo. He was right. Some participants in the project challenged directly the general acceptance of research as *the* primary function of an institution of higher education, and even more rejected traditional explanatory distinctions between professional schools and the liberal arts college. Conversely, the seminar reaffirmed every member's commitment to teach and to demonstrate the excitement of learning, of generating new knowledge, and of taking responsibility for what is to be learned. Through this volume, we attest to the generative force of collective, professional engagement in education.

Notes

1. Joan J. Brumberg and Nancy Tomes, "Women in the Professions: A Research Agenda for American Historians," *Reviews in American History*, 10 (1982): 288. They observe that high-status professionals do not maintain close contact with their clients. Philosophical abstraction and distance from human complications characterize elite cadres. Thus, doctors engaged in "pure" research have greater prestige than family practitioners; in legal circles, the corporate attorney has more status than the divorce lawyer; and, in departments of English, the literary critics and poets often enjoy lighter teaching assignments than writing teachers.

2. Some of these themes may be found in Paul Starr, *The Transformation of American Medicine* (New York: Basic Books, 1983).

3. Burton Bledstein, *The Culture of Professionalism: The Middle Class and the Development of Higher Education in America* (New York: Norton, 1978).

4. This was the principal focus of discussion at a Woodrow Wilson Center Conference, September 1986, on "The State and Social Investigation: An Overview," especially the papers by Michael Lacey and Mary Furner.

5. Donald T. Campbell, "Ethnocentrism of Disciplines and the Fish-Scale Model of Omniscience," in *Interdisciplinary Relationships in the Social Sciences*, edited by Muzafer Sherif and Carolyn W. Sherif (Chicago: Aldine, 1969), 328–48.

6. Quoted in Robert A. McCaughey, "The Transformation of American Academic Life: Harvard University 1821–1892," *Perspectives in American History* 8 (1974): 314.

7. Jurgen Herbst, "Diversification in American Higher Education," in Konrad H. Jarusch, ed., *The Transformation of Higher Learning, 1860–1930: Expansion, Diversifi-*

cation, Social Opening and Professionalization in England, Germany, Russia, and the United States (Chicago: University of Chicago, 1983), 196–206.

8. For an analytical, and sometimes critical, historical overview written with sociological categories in mind, see Magali Sarfatti Larson, *The Rise of Professionalism: A Sociological Analysis* (Berkeley: University of California Press, 1977).

9. The skepticism of the present generation toward the professions, as well as ambivalence toward expertise, more generally provides the theme of Thomas Haskell's "Introduction" to his edited volume *The Authority of Experts: Studies in Theory and Practice* (Bloomington: Indiana University Press, 1984), ix–xxxix.

10. This has been the subject of a number of recent editorials in *The Chronicle of Higher Education*, including Sol Sarporta, "Professors Must Share the Blame for the Humanities Decline" (24 September 1986).

Still from Werner Herzog's 1982 movie *Fitzcarraldo*. Courtesy of the Museum of Modern Art/Film Stills Archive and New World Pictures.

4

The Problem Exemplified
The Engineering Dilemma

JAMES STEWART

This chapter explores issues associated with offering a limited number of non-technical courses that conform to the Mellon project's objectives within colleges of engineering. Similar issues are germane in other professional schools, but engineering schools seem to present some of the greatest challenges to, as well to derive some of the greatest potential benefits from, improved integration of liberal and professional studies. The case of engineering offers an extreme instance of a problem that runs across the field of professional education, and it draws attention to the difficulties of integration. In particular, it makes us ask again what we mean by "depth" and "breadth" as dimensions of an education.

The offering of such courses needs to be justified in light of apparently conflicting demands placed on engineering curricula from many sides, not the least being burgeoning technology. Engineering schools promise to develop student competence in the application of modern, sophisticated, and dynamic technologies. The time in which increasingly complex technology must be mastered by undergraduates to acquire certification as engineers has remained constant for thirty or forty years at four years; in fact, it was decreased from five years to four several decades ago! Incorporating new courses in the already cramped curricula must be vigorously contested. Any new courses must not only be shown to address true student needs, but also must use students' time more desirably than at present.

The Problem

Perhaps no other profession stands to gain as much from improved integration with liberal arts education as engineering. Engineering curricula are bursting with coursework in mathematics, sciences, and engineering—all subjects that deal with a world that is understood in hard, cold, physical terms. Humanities and social sciences, which deal primarily with the human mind, are given a lower priority in engineering schools than they are in some other professional degree programs because there appears to be a stronger linkage between those professions and the liberal arts. In contrast to many other professional fields, a traditional dichotomy seems to exist between engineering problems of the definite physical world and the abstract nature of the liberal arts. Social science has obvious connections to the practices of management and advertising; art obviously relates to architecture; the humanities have strong ties to journalism and the performing arts. The ties between microchip engineering and the humanities simply are not as strong or as obvious.

Engineers also study less of the social sciences and humanities than some other professionals such as physicians and lawyers, who typically enroll in professional schools after obtaining an undergraduate degree in the liberal arts. Given the natural tendency for engineering students to de-emphasize the liberal arts, substantial numbers of engineering educators have long sought to incorporate liberal arts study effectively into their curricula. Discussions about increasing or improving the liberal arts content in engineering curricula have been common among educators and employers for forty years. The discussions continue without resolution.

There are two obvious approaches to liberalizing engineering education, and both are concerned with increasing the number of liberal arts courses in the curriculum. The first approach is to increase the length of study for the degree program to five years. This has been suggested many times during the last forty years but does not yet appear to be gaining acceptance. Even if degree programs were extended, it is not clear that merely requiring additional coursework would necessarily enhance the engineer's liberal education. Engineering students often feel, under mid-semester pressures, that their time should be spent on what really counts, and that would seem to them to be their major. Thus even the courses that are in the curricula now may not be of maximum benefit.

The second approach is to change the balance between technical and non-technical courses so that study of the humanities and social sciences receives a higher priority. The configuration of engineering curricula has been debated often by department faculty, accrediting bodies, and professional societies. Nearly all agree that students would benefit from additional study in many areas, but the typical

Table 2

Subject	Number of semester courses: typical course titles
mathematics	5 to 7 : calculus and statistics
basic sciences	5 to 7 : physics, chemistry, geology, biology
engineering science	8 to 10 : statics, dynamics, thermodynamics, fluid mechanics, solid mechanics, electrical science, properties of materials
engineering analysis and design	10 : structural and geotechnical design, water technology, environmental systems, transportation
social/human sciences	6 : free electives
computer applications	1 to 2 : programming, applications
technical support	5 to 7 : surveying, management, communication, professionalism and ethics, economics, graphics, freshman English

total number of semester courses   40 to 49

(note: 8 full semesters of study = 40 semester courses)

curriculum is jam-packed already. The curricula are intended to provide general education as well as in-depth, specialized technical knowledge required of today's engineers. Since engineers cannot do their jobs without the technical knowledge, the primary emphasis in engineering education has been on developing the background necessary to understand technology, understanding the technology pertinent to specific fields, and developing the skill and insight necessary to solve engineering problems by applying the appropriate technology. Because technology has become more sophisticated, many engineering educators feel that engineering students may now need a deeper technical background and more technical coursework to assimilate the technology than they did a few decades ago.

While engineering degree programs differ from field to field and university to university, there are several elements common to many of the curricula: mathematics, basic sciences, engineering sciences, engineering analysis and design, social/human sciences, computer applications, and support areas. Many engineering curricula are similar in some respects to the civil engineering curriculum illustrated in Table 2. The curriculum described above is fuller than it may appear because many science and engineering courses require laboratory time in addition to the normal class time. Although the curriculum seems quite inflexible, most schools manage to emphasize problems of timely or regional concern. For example, a Texas school will probably emphasize some coursework in offshore oil technology, whereas a Utah school may emphasize engineering geology because landsliding is a major problem in Utah's mountain areas. Obviously, engineering educators have no difficulty defining four years of useful study for engineering students; indeed it is easy to define five or six years.

Curriculum study, debate, and questioning are nothing new. The central problem in the debates seems to be that not everything useful can be easily incorporated into the four-year curriculum. Therefore, the debate is not over what is important, but what is *most* important. Several traditional and useful courses—such as engineering graphics and surveying—have all but vanished from most civil engineering curricula, and study of such practical subjects as geology, biology, and chemistry is rarely as detailed as some educators feel it should be. Unfortunately, therefore, adding any new courses to engineering curricula also means deleting some existing courses; and if any courses are deleted, there is already a waiting list for the space.

Given the fact that extending engineering programs beyond the current four years doesn't seem practical, increased liberal arts study by engineering students would seem to be at the expense of some technical coursework. Accrediting organizations, professional societies, and educators and administrators have not favored increasing the liberal arts content of the curricula to the extent of compromising the quantity of technical coursework. In addition, I would guess that a majority of engineering educators would favor deepening the technical content of their curricula where possible.

If liberalizing engineering curricula seems to involve subtracting from existing curricula in order to add courses, the question becomes: "How much priority should engineering studies have in the curriculum for engineering students?" In venturing an answer, the wary soul needs the skills of a campaigning politician because the question is loaded. If it is reduced to trading off technical competence against other attributes, how much are we willing to trade off? Given the fact that much of the technology today already seems too sophisticated or complex for undergraduate study, is it wise to de-emphasize technical coursework at all? If we advocate a change in engineering curricula, do we imply that engineering schools have not done a good job preparing engineers in the past? On the other hand, if the calls for liberalizing engineering education are creditable, can we be satisfied with the status quo?

Merely adding more liberal arts courses to engineering curricula may not constitute the "liberalizing" influence sought. As Cornell University President Frank Rhodes warns, the value of coursework in the liberal arts has often been overstated, and the liberal arts have no monopoly on liberal learning.[1] Unrealistic claims for the value of liberal arts study can be damaging; they may lull engineering educators into dangerous complacency. Engineering educators may hope that a few courses in liberal arts will transform their students into able writers, speakers, listeners, and socially responsible and graceful adults, but such wishful thinking may only relieve engineering schools of a sense of their own responsibility for nurturing these qualities in the students. It is fundamentally unsound to send students across campus for such important kinds of development while not nurturing them at home. This sort of thinking also permits educators to assume that students can easily transfer the concepts from their liberal arts courses to their engineering world without any transition or guidance. It is precisely the connections between the liberal arts and the professions that we desire our students to discover. Rarely, however, do universities formally encourage integrating liberal arts courses with professional studies. If the liberal arts studies really are valuable to professionals, why do educators stop short of encouraging that all-important final linkage by leaving it entirely up to the student?

Perhaps greatly improved integration between engineering and liberal arts can be attained not so much by increasing the number of liberal arts courses, but rather by making the most out of the ones that are already included in the curricula. Little has changed since the 1979 Civil Engineering Education Conference concluded that the one-eighth of the engineering curriculum devoted to study of the liberal arts "is used inadequately."[2] A linkage or transition between engineering and liberal arts is not apparent within the organization of most universities. Such a link could be essential for professional-school students to make the most of their limited study of liberal arts.

Integrating liberal arts with engineering study is not something that follows naturally from the structure of a university. The distinctions between various academic disciplines have been described as arising at least partially out of convenience.[3] It is quite rational for this situation to exist. Students and researchers within a particular discipline can agree on a common framework for their knowledge and need not revert to first principles each time their knowledge is to be advanced. By defining disciplines of study, however, we imply the fundamental irrelevance, or less relevance, of knowledge drawn from other disciplines. Perhaps as a result, the distinction between liberal arts and engineering is much stronger at the university than in the world into which our students graduate. Does the structure of a university, broken into units on the basis of academic disciplines, somehow discourage students from even looking for relevance outside their own discipline or major?

Need for Liberalizing the Curriculum

While there certainly is no consensus, calls for liberalizing engineering curricula have been frequent and compelling. Vild argues that the public holds engineers more accountable for their projects today than a few decades ago and that the critical examination of ideas characteristic of the liberal arts may have more significance to engineering practice than in the past.[4] In short, the distinction between purely technical and purely nontechnical issues may not be as readily accepted by today's public as in the past. Engineering students should study the humanities and social sciences because such study enhances their awareness of, and sensitivity to, other people. We want engineers to foresee and be responsible for the far-reaching consequences of their work.

A second reason for liberalizing engineering education is that liberal studies utilize and refine communication skills, skills that are very important in most types of engineering practice. Writing and discussion are emphasized to a much greater degree in liberal arts than in other portions of an engineer's curriculum.

A third compelling reason for liberalizing the curriculum has nothing to do with social consciousness or improving the engineer's ability to do his or her job. It is simply that liberal study can be interesting and rewarding, and it is pertinent to personal life. Students may want to sustain their study and enjoyment of the humanities and social sciences even after they leave the university—that is, if it all seems to have some value to them.

There is, moreover, another way to look at the imperative for integration. It is not simply a matter of humanizing the engineer, but of more fully acknowledging the ways in which the engineer's activity is an essentially human activity. Technology and engineering are uniquely human. They didn't spring up as unwanted weeds, but were planted and cared for by human beings. The interrelationship between technology and engineering and the humanities is much stronger than we might first believe.

Liberal Arts for Engineers

A key issue to address is: "In what form should engineers study liberal arts?" Should their study be limited to what may be of tangible value in engineering practice? Erich Harth makes an important point later on in this book when he states that "it would be a disservice to the students to omit the mention of black holes (to pick an example) just because future physicians or engineers are not soon likely to run into one."[5] Tailoring and compartmentalizing curricula to immediate needs would narrow important intellectual horizons. While "humanities-for-engineers" courses offer a seemingly expedient and efficient way to address the special problems posed by the limitations of a four-year engineering curriculum, courses of this type may not provide the liberalizing influence that is desired.

The second issue is: "Can the number of technical courses be pared back in the engineering curriculum to make more room for further study of liberal arts?" Perhaps the in-depth examinations and applications of specialized technology currently included in undergraduate education should be deferred to graduate study. Many students enrolled in engineering colleges will be employed in nuts-and-bolts engineering for only a few years, if at all. Many students view engineering school as a springboard into management or other careers that utilize a broad technical, but not particularly specialized, background. Students from bioengineering programs are increasingly and successfully applying to medical schools. Other engineers go on to graduate school or will receive "retraining" on the job. Most will recognize the need for, and seek, continuing education to update their knowledge.

These changing career patterns are related to the way engineering as a field has changed. Historically, engineering sprang up as two disciplines: military and civilian, or civil, engineering. The two branches of knowledge had many obvious things in common, but they also had different perspectives on the world and addressed different problems. With expanding technology, engineering has splintered to encompass more than 100 fields today. Each practitioner usually specializes in only a tiny portion of a field.

These changes in both the nature of the engineering career and the structure of the field suggest that it may be time for increased specialization on the part of undergraduates. Why struggle to squeeze so much into a fairly general curriculum that may not be used? Reducing the breadth of the engineering curriculum may provide the opportunity for adding non-technical courses.

Such a proposal is quite properly resisted within the profession. The engineer's job is to explore and choose the appropriate technology for a particular application. "Bridges" may be a powerful metaphor for an educational discussion, but for an engineer, bridges are also quite real. They *must* stand; at stake are human lives. It would seem wise, therefore, not to compromise the engineer's technical background. Nothing is more important than that the engineer be competent to select the appropriate technology to solve a particular problem—that *is* engineering. Breadth of knowledge is important in this regard. Engineers have to be able to respond to the world in the ways in which it presents itself, and these ways are often diverse and changing. The latest technology today may be obsolete tomorrow. Preparing engineers with backgrounds that are narrow is short-sighted, since they may need to adapt to unforeseen technologies in the future. A broad background provides a base that can be adapted easily. Nevertheless, the difficulty in maintaining the current degree of breadth seems to indicate that, sooner or later, undergraduates may be forced to specialize to a greater degree than they do at present.

It is worthy of notice that most engineers out of school less than five or six years will say they wish they had had a more in-depth technically oriented education. After a few more years, they typically feel that they would have benefitted from more management training. After twenty years, they often feel they should have had more exposure to the humanities. The changing career patterns can only accelerate this tendency. If we are not preparing students for a long-range future that requires continued learning, we are failing them. The immediate future of most engineering graduates will be as a specialist on a team of specialists. In this situation, what is needed is competence in their specialty. The clear risk of specialist teams is that communication will break down and important considerations fall through the gaps between the specialties. The solution to the specialist risk is probably not so much increased technical engineering competence as it is being alert to the situation and remaining open to things of importance outside one's specialty.

Proposal

I began by suggesting that education in engineering presents, in an extreme form, the problem of "depth and breadth" that underlies any talk about the integration of liberal and professional education. As this issue is normally conceived, there is neither room nor any compelling motive to offer non-technical courses of the Mellon kind within an engineering school. But the profession tells us over and over again that there is something that educators should be doing that we are not, and this should suggest that the depth and breadth issue, as we are accustomed to address it, is badly posed. The breadth that engineers need is not general and simply "humanistic." It is particular, and arises out of the particular shape of our activity. The problem engineering has is indeed not different from that of the Mellon project in general; it is a problem about how to make particular, more or less specialized, practices and bodies of knowledge responsive to the larger context in which they are put to work. The Mellon seminar has consistently refused to trade off specialization for generality. In the particular case of the engineering curriculum, this view may lead to a call for greater specialization within undergraduate education in order to create the room for greater attention to the limitations and consequences of that inevitable specialization. Increased specialization without this attention would seem to pose some insidious new problems.

Early in the Mellon project, there was a temptation to think of the liberal arts as offering a gateway to the professions. What I want to suggest here is the opposite: the course to be taught within engineering schools should be thought of as a gateway out of, rather than into, the profession. Since academic units have grown narrow and specialized, it is hard to envision any existing units as the sole foundation or gateway *into* any other. The gateway out, however, doesn't lead so much out of the profession as it does *beyond* the artificial constraints that exist in any discipline. Perhaps a course designed along these lines could also serve as a capstone to establish some otherwise unmade connections between the students' liberal and professional studies. Offered to juniors who have had exposure to the study of the sciences, engineering, and the humanities, it is the perfect opportunity to prepare students to look past the artificial walls that have been built around each profession or discipline.

Adding a single course of this type to engineering curricula does not seem to be a major hurdle. However, as discussed above, any additions to the curricula will be difficult to incorporate. A clear need for such courses has been demonstrated, but the practical questions about inserting them into the curricula have not been addressed, since they will vary from department to department. One important detail is that faculty interest and spirit is essential to the success of such a course. Also, since the goals of such a course can be approached from so many different directions, each course would surely need to be tailored to meet the special interests and talents of the faculty in charge.

Finally, such a course needs to be offered from within the engineering schools by engineering faculty, perhaps in collaboration with faculty from the liberal arts. The foremost reason for offering such a course through a professional school is that it is an essential component in the preparation of a true professional. The true professional is more than a competent specialized worker. A second reason of almost equal strength for offering such a course within professional schools is to draw on the professional-school faculty. Only engineering faculty can establish urgent and credible connections—in the minds of many engineering students anyway—between things that are called engineering and things that are not. Engineering faculty have the most reason and the greatest resources available on campus to identify issues that are important to their students. Clearly, no other academic unit has as much responsibility for, or as great an interest in, the graduate engineer as the engineering school.

The goal of the Mellon project at Syracuse is to examine linkages between the liberal arts and studies and practice in the professional schools. The formal establishment of these linkages is all the more important in view of the tendency of the organizational structure of a university to obfuscate them. Students' discoveries of the linkages is not an end or a goal so much as a conduit for future professional and personal growth after graduation.

Notes

1. Frank H. T. Rhodes, "Reforming Higher Education Will Take More than Just Tinkering with Curricula," *The Chronicle of Higher Education*, 22 May 1985.

2. William E. Saul, "The 1979 ASCE Civil Engineering Education Conference," *Journal of Professional Issues in Engineering* 109, no. 2 (November 1984): 127–35.

3. Donald T. Campbell, "Ethnocentrism of Disciplines and the Fishscale Model of Omniscience," in Muzafer Sherif and Carolyn W. Sherif, eds., *Interdisciplinary Relationships in the Social Sciences* (Chicago: Aldine, 1969), 328–48.

4. Kathleen A. Vild, "The Civil Engineering Degree: Education or Training?" *Journal of Issues in Engineering*, 101, no. 1 (January 1984): 25–30.

5. See Chapter 17, "From Specialization toward Integration: A Scientist's Perspective."

II

Objectivity

Preface

PETER T. MARSH

This section and the next revolve around concepts that run through and help to shape every field of learning, whether in the liberal arts or in professional colleges. The opening chapter in each of these sections sets its conceptual theme, and is followed by chapters of course description and accounts of aspects of our project that play on that conceptual theme. We hope in this way to convey the persistent interweaving of courses and concepts, and the interconnecting of central concepts within courses, which characterized our enterprise and propelled it forward.

Common denominators can prove uncommonly interesting. Higher education is virtually synonymous with thoughtful consideration of objects. It involves a conscious interplay of subjectivity and objectivity. Faculty and students engage in systematic examination of fields of thought and action, attentive both to their process of analysis and to the object to which they apply it. This is as true in professional colleges as in the arts and sciences. One of the great rewards in combining liberal and professional education is awareness of the interlocking range of processes of subjective and objective analysis.

After exploring each other's fields in search of intersections, linkages, and overlaps among them, the seminar was quick to identify objectivity in this sense as a concern common to every field of education. It is, accordingly, the theme of Section II here. Each discipline and profession is defined as much by the way its members seek, and the value they place upon, objectivity as by the objects that they choose to study.

Objectivity is most commonly associated with the "pure" arts and sciences, and the definition of the idea is usually left to philosophers. Yet, true to the spirit of our project, the issue was first brought up in our seminar by a professor of journalism, Cleve Mathews. His concern with this theme is of long standing, first aroused by the debate over the reporting of the Vietnam War. In the opening chapter of this section he defines the concept of objectivity by describing the

69

genesis of our seminar's discussion of this theme. He recounts the earlier heated exchange on the issue among his fellow journalists, places that debate in a philosophical context, and indicates the contribution that attention to this issue can make throughout the world of learning.

Subjectivity is the reverse side of objectivity, its implicit other dimension. It is a source of truth about the observer as well as the lens through which the observer sees. That point underlies the next chapter (6). Written by a cross-cultural social psychologist, Marshall Segall, it describes a course that he developed for our project. His mandate was to fashion an introduction to the social sciences that would address the distinctive concerns of an undergraduate clientele drawn predominantly from the university's professional colleges. Wishing to come up with more than a cosmetic response to this mandate, he created a course on the determinants of personal identity, for among those determinants professional affiliation was bound to bulk large.

The resulting course epitomizes much that our project seeks to bring about. All the themes of common concern that our faculty seminar identified as running through each discipline and profession arise naturally in this course—not only objectivity, but also professionalism, gender, the impact of skills on those who acquire them, and the cultural embeddedness of the group memberships that shape a person's identity. These themes are examined with the aid of social science theory. The subject matter is brought home to the students by focusing on that most absorbing of objects—themselves. What social, cultural, and personal determinants have shaped their individual identity? How has their identity influenced their choice of intended profession? How is that profession likely, in turn, to shape their identity?

The concluding chapter of this section deals with one of the forms of communication that we employ to gain objective and subjective understanding of our world and of ourselves. Given the composition of our faculty seminar, we made more use of visual art than of music—the most evocative, but ambiguous, form of human communication. We paid conspicuously little attention to mathematics, for though it possesses greater representational clarity than any language and is capable of being understood by people regardless of their native tongue, it is still largely unintelligible to the innumerate majority among us.

Inevitably, we relied upon written and spoken English to gain entry into each other's disciplines and professions. But common language is as elusive as common sense. Disciplines and professions are distinguished and shaped as much by how their members analyze and talk about their objects of study as by the objects themselves. In attempting to fathom their chosen objects and convey their discoveries to each other, the practitioners in each discipline and profession form a partially autonomous discourse community. The challenge to which our seminar and project attempted to rise required each of us to talk from the community of discourse in which he or she was most comfortable to those in other discursive communities. Chapter 2, "The Faculty Seminar: Discourse Communities and Quotation Marks," has described how we responded to that challenge.

Repeatedly during our proceedings, some of the participants compared our enterprise to Akira Kurosawa's classic film, *Rashomon*. The story of one set of events—a rape and murder—is recalled and rationalized from four points of view: the wife who was raped, her murdered husband, the murderer, and a woodcutter who saw something of the crimes. The "true" story remains a mystery, obscured by the "truth" that those who tell the story reveal about themselves. Whenever our seminar generated differing, seemingly irreconcilable, interpretations of a particular subject (object) that we had all examined, we tended to speak of "the *Rashomon* effect." When eventually we viewed *Rashomon* together, the film reproduced this effect by coming across differently to each viewer.

Though we assume that works of art are intensely subjective creations, viewers tend to stand back and observe them more objectively than written texts. For whatever reason, while our seminar normally relied upon words to acquire understanding of each other's perspectives, visual images enabled us to *see* what words failed to convey at critical junctures. Written by Gary Radke, an art historian who specializes in the Italian Renaissance, and Stephen Melville, a literary theorist who has devoted considerable study to the "texts" that art provides, the final chapter of this section assesses the significance of these occasions for our enterprise.

The visual artist in our project, Stephen Zaima, contributes to this volume, as he has to the seminar, primarily through pictures. Although a less frequent contributor than some to our verbal exchanges, when he spoke his words demanded attention as good captions do. To fathom his captions we needed to think of the visual images that might have prompted them. Doing so only increased their impact. Even so, translation between these two forms of communication is not easy, as the seminar discovered in seeking to extend its collaborative activity to the selection of pictures for this book. The ones eventually chosen are not meant simply as illustrations of the verbal text. Each picture is reproduced within a border to remind the reader that it is an object in itself and should be interpreted within its own frame.

Mark Tansey, *Robbe-Grillet Cleansing Every Object in Sight*, 1981. Oil on canvas, 72″ x 72¼″. Collection, the Museum of Modern Art, N.Y. Gift of Mr. and Mrs. Warren Brandt.

5

The Concept of Objectivity

CLEVE MATHEWS

The exhilaration of the seminar arose from discussion of important issues in our respective fields and of concerns about how to get students to understand such issues. We peered more deeply than ever before into the heart of each other's disciplines. Our sense of success in reaching one another across boundaries could be attributed to two factors: confidence, perhaps naive, that our perceptions of each others' discourses were valid, and realization that each field possessed an integrity and uniqueness that could engage those in unrelated fields.

While not articulated, these two factors may have led to the emergence of themes that recurred throughout the seminar. One was an insistence on justifying statements as a means of clarifying scholarly interpretations of one body of knowledge to those in other fields. As an audience we could accept subjective interpretations by credible scholars, but as interactive colleagues discussing bodies of knowledge across boundaries, we strove for objective discourse. Thus, one theme became objectivity.

A second theme was closely related to objectivity. It arises from the fact that the content of each of our fields exists as a substantial body in the world. Such content can best be understood in its context. Within its context it is an object asserting its existence, resisting integration, but amenable to up-close understanding. This quality led to the theme of embeddedness[1] as a perspective for the mutual understanding of our fields.

As the journalist participating in the seminar, I saw in the efforts by participants to perceive one another accurately and clearly a manifestation of concern for objectivity. No doubt, I saw it because of my own interest in a topic that has been attracting attention from media scholars. Nevertheless, I suggested that objectivity be placed as a topic on the agenda of the seminar because it seemed to be important for communication between the professional schools and the liberal arts college. Beyond that, it would provide valuable perspectives for my own understanding of objectivity, which also seemed a goal of the project.

Objectivity subsequently became prominent in the agenda. To no one's great surprise, responses to it were divergent, beginning with a lack of agreement about what objectivity is. It clearly meant different things in different fields, depending perhaps on the questions various disciplines seek to answer. Objectivity seemed more important to some fields than to others. To some it was a principle, to others an instrument.

The intriguing result of the discussions was seeming agreement that each discipline and profession had an objectivity-subjectivity validation element, however defined, as part of its vision of itself. A sense emerged that this element provided something common to all the fields, even though it might differ in emphasis and application in each.

One reason the concept of objectivity seemed valuable was that it offered a way for students majoring in one field to perceive something basic in other fields related to, albeit different from, basic elements in their own. By considering the debates or tensions in a field over objectivity and subjectivity, students could sense the quality of a body of knowledge or practice in the field even though their courses touched only its surface.

The question of objectivity was raised most insistently for the seminar by artist Robert Irwin and historian Thomas Kuhn, whose views were set forth in seminar readings.[2] The two men did so by contesting objectivity. It is not surprising that Irwin, presumably more concerned with conveying feelings than facts, should reject objectivity. But Irwin persistently insists on reasoning his way—slowly, deliberately—to his artistic expressions. At times, he seems determined to eliminate any arbitrary or superfluous elements that might bias one's perceptions of his art as he strips away all imagery from the unmediated "phenomenal presence" that he says an art work is all about. If this leads to presenting an empty room as an exhibit, it nevertheless succeeds in forcing people to ask what it's all about. Yet Irwin ends up rejecting the "logic" of the scientist that cuts the world into slices and doesn't deal with its overall complexities. He accepts, instead, the approach of "reason," which intuitively grapples with the situation as a whole. He finds hope in those who work "beyond the techniques of their disciplines," which seems to be his warning against the constraints of objectivity.[3]

Kuhn is concerned with explaining the development of science, and he is more complex than Irwin is in his view of the logic of science. He sees science progressing through the replacement of one body of theory that is unable to account for a serious anomaly by another body of theory that can account for it. Kuhn calls such a body of theory a paradigm. The new theory attracts a community of scientists committed to articulating and applying it. Within that community of scientists, an objective kind of logic prevails in the development of the paradigm's potential. But science progresses through the rise of new paradigms in a series of discontinuous steps brought about by breakthroughs that displace or resolve anomalies troubling earlier paradigms. The logic of normal science does not permit effective communication between paradigms. A scientist "converted" to one paradigm cannot accept all the explanations acceptable in another. This incommensurable quality vitiates the traditional function of objectivity, which is to enable any scientist to make an independent check of some other scientist's assertion of truth.[4]

The views of Irwin and Kuhn are forms of idealism, in tune with a good deal of modern thinking from Immanuel Kant to today's phenomenologists. Objectivity to such thinkers is an unobtainable ideal, and trying to live up to it may not be the proper thing to do. Since it is an ideal, it can be applied only through imperfect means, which may cause more harm than good.

Objectivity encounters less criticism from those who operate as realists or empiricists. To them objectivity serves more as an instrument than as a concept. It is defined by one of Kuhn's critics, Israel Scheffler, as "fair control over assertion," and he sees commitment to such control as the basis of the scientific attitude of impartiality and detachment. Scientists, Scheffler says, are no more naturally impartial than anyone else, but the scientific habits of mind reflected in such objectivity are compatible with passionate advocacy, strong faith, intuitive conjecture, and imaginative speculation.[5] So objectivity provides a way for preventing error that might arise from more subjective factors.

The debate between idealism and realism has a long and sophisticated history, and our seminar did not try to pursue it. Yet the issues of that debate cropped up in various forms as the disciplines encountered one another. A warning against falling into the trap of dualistic analogies was raised in an article by Richard A. Shweder circulated to members of the seminar. It warned of simply accepting the dichotomy that one can either "tell it as it is" or find the answer through "divine" revelation.[6]

Shweder said good writers of ethnography are casuists who take the perspective of others and thus get outside themselves. Perhaps journalists, seeking to reach their audience more effectively by putting themselves in their readers' and viewers' places, tend to become casuistic. Yet in conveying their pictures of the world, implicitly framed by rights and wrongs, they find objectivity a comfortable, credible way of validating their information.

I said before that a look at the debate over objectivity could provide students with a sense of the quality of knowledge of a field. Let me offer such a look at the debate in the field of journalism.

The turbulence of the 1960s, first over civil rights and later over Vietnam, brought to a head reactions that had been long developing among journalists to what was seen as a formulistic kind of automatic objectivity. A decade earlier, Senator Joseph McCarthy had exploited journalistic routines that validated controversial information by attributing it to a credible source. After all, a United States senator was a newsworthy source, and attributing unfounded charges to him was all that was required by traditional objectivity. The press subsequently sought to avoid the trap revealed by McCarthy by modifying the objectivity routines to encourage reporters to quote participants on both sides of an issue in the same report, if possible.

The 1960s put even this modified view of journalistic objectivity under great strain. Reporters, contending with deceptive information issued by official sources and with special interests dramatically thrusting forth their own visions, sought to tell the truth as they saw it. Sometimes that truth was quite subjective. The mainline press resisted subjective reporting.

The classic view of journalistic objectivity was restated in a modern form on October 7, 1969, by A. M. Rosenthal, then managing editor and later executive editor of *The New York Times*. In a memorandum to guide his reporters and editors in dealing with the pressures of the Vietnam period, he called for preserving "the basic character of the paper." He told the staff that the newspaper's character rested on:[7]

> The belief that although total objectivity may be impossible because every story is written by a human being, the duty of every reporter and editor is to strive for as much objectivity as possible.
>
> The belief that no matter how engaged the reporter is emotionally he tries as best he can to disengage himself when he sits down at the typewriter.

The belief that expression of personal opinion should be excluded from the news columns.

The belief that our own pejorative phrases should be excluded, and so should anonymous charges against people or institutions.

The belief that every accused man or institution should have the immediate right of reply.

The belief that we should not use a typewriter to stick our fingers in people's eyes just because we have the power to do so.

The belief that presenting both sides of an issue is not hedging, but the essence of responsible journalism.

While saying that "our business is facts," Rosenthal asserted that "a social movement, a change in life styles, a trend in music or art, an emotion spreading among people, can be as real a fact as a speech or a parade." He said he was not talking about cold, dry reporting, just fair reporting.

"The nature of *The Times*," he concluded, "rests on what can be demonstrated, what can be reported, dissected, analyzed, rather than on what can simply be labeled or characterized or caricaturized."

If Rosenthal represented the establishment view, perhaps Hunter Thompson dramatized the alternative view. Writing in *Fear and Loathing on the Campaign Trail* about his objectivity, he said:

Well, my doctor says it swole up and busted about ten years ago. The only thing I ever saw that came close to Objective Journalism was a closed-circuit TV set-up that watched shoplifters in the General Store at Woody Creek, Colorado. I always admired that machine, but I noticed that nobody paid much attention to it until one of those known, heavy, out-front shoplifters came into the place . . . but when that happened everybody got so excited that the thief had to do something quick, like buy a green popsicle or a can of Coors and get out of the place immediately.

So much for Objective Journalism. Don't bother to look for it here—not under any byline of mine; or anyone else's I can think of. With the possible exception of things like box scores, race results and stock market tabulations, there is no such thing as Objective Journalism. The phrase itself is a pompous contradiction in terms.[8]

Not all the critics of traditional objectivity were so extreme, but many sympathized with Thompson's views.

Anthony Smith, in *Goodby Gutenberg*, saw objectivity as partly a response to the chaos in the international political sphere. He said, "It fostered the collection of information on the basis of a specific diction, which restricted the definition of a statement to that which could be assented to by all."[9]

Smith's example of an objectivity suitable to the times was that of Michael Herr. In Herr's book *Dispatches*,[10] a collection of his reports from Vietnam, Smith found that "one can see something of what has endured of the new strains of reporting: a deep commitment to straight facts and background, suffused with the passions of an individual who feels free to use his emotions as a guide to the event while holding back from pressing opinions of a political kind—the reporter offering his experience as part of his material without prejudicing accuracy or objectivity."[11]

A current example of reporting of the Thompson-Herr kind is that of Jimmy Breslin. *Newsweek* wrote of him in the spring of 1986, "Breslin tries to get the details right, but generally believes that a contest between a particular fact and the absolute truth (as he defines it) is not really any contest at all." The magazine said Breslin admitted some details in a report he filed about the Three Mile Island nuclear accident were wrong, but he insisted "the absolute truth of the column was overwhelming."[12]

A major complaint by the young reporters of the Vietnam era was that traditional objectivity supported the status quo and thus was not really objective. Press historian Michael Schudson notes in his *Discovering the News* that the critics charged the establishment journalists with being political, whether they intended to be or not. "Their political impact lay not in what they openly advocated but in the unexamined assumptions on which they based their professional practice and, most of all, in their conformity to the conventions of objective reporting." Schudson says tradtitional objectivity has become not an ideal, but a mystification. "The slant of journalism lay not in explicit bias but in the social structure of news gathering which reinforced official viewpoints of social reality."[13]

The "social structure of news gathering" has proved a fruitful field for media sociologists trying to find out what causes journalists to do what they do. The dogma of objectivity quickly aroused the interest of these sociologists. Herbert Gans found wide-scale doubts about objectivity in the 1960s and 1970s, but attributed the persistence of claims of objectivity to the need to protect journalistic credibility and to the fact that journalism is a low-cost kind of information gathering. Both reasons are basically commercial. In the first case, credibility is seen as essential to holding the audience that is the ulti-mate source of revenue. In the second case, the media have to rely on knowledgeable sources and other information collectors because it would raise the cost of news too much to develop the expertise and the capacity needed to gather the information on a timely basis themselves.[14]

Additional reasons for the traditional form of objectivity were detected by other media researchers. Gaye Tuchman asserted that objectivity was a strategic ritual designed to protect journalists who must make numerous quick decisions about the quality of their news. The speed with which the news becomes stale prevents the journalists from determining the accuracy of their information, so they attribute it to their sources as a way of validating it.[15]

E. Barbara Phillips developed this line of thought, and con-tended that daily journalism encourages a lack of expertise and promotes a non-systematic, copying-machine kind of concrete infor-mation.[16] This supports the distinction made much earlier by Rob-ert Park that journalistic information merely provides "acquaintance with" facts rather than "understanding of" them.[17]

The reliance on sources implicit in journalistic objectivity has be-come a key part of current theories that the sources and the media collaborate to construct the picture of reality that is presented to the audience. This is the conclusion to which a model by an early champion of objectivity, Walter Lippmann, has led. He asserted that the media contribute to the picture of the world that resides in the heads of the public.[18] But this phenomenon is frequently offered as a reason to reject the idea of objectivity because the reality that is constructed results from the special interests of those constructing it. The term "reality," of course, is not really reality, but instead a fabri-cated kind of ideal in the sense that it exists in the minds of mem-bers of the public. So the long debate between idealism and realism emerges anew in a special formulation at the center of today's world of media theory and research.

Students will find similar debates going on in other fields. In literary criticism, for example, Terry Eagleton's *Literary Theory: An Introduction*,[19] and such works as Raman Selden's *Criticism and Ob-jectivity*,[20] could sensitize the students to the depth and diversity of the elements that contribute to meaning. Selden, in fact, finds the objectivity of historical criticism growing out of a "structural plural-ity" of forces that interact to determine the meaning of a message. While these forces are not randomly independent, their numerous conjunctures give rise to an overdetermination of meanings that

Duane Michals, *This Photograph Is My Proof*, 1974. Photograph. Courtesy
Sidney Janis Gallery, N.Y.

makes the "true" meaning of a text indeterminate, one among many possible interpretations. This results in a complexly structured discourse that Selden finds more suitable for giving an objective reading than a subjective one.

The conjuncture of forces at the receiving end of the message also acts to determine the meaning. We operate in a world of perceptions, which might cause some to accept the view of philosopher Ludwig Wittgenstein that objectivity is the acceptance of appearances. If, as to Wittgenstein, the world is an expressive phenomenon rather than a logical, causal one, then the stance of objectivity loses its anchor to objects, the link responsible for the very term itself.[21]

Phenomenologist Edmund Husserl places the fact-world of time and space "out there" in brackets beyond judgment. Asserting that objects and events cannot be apprehended in neutral fashion in any case, he follows purely subjective processes, rejecting the testimony of others in confronting the givenness of experience in "an unremitting assault on the peak of certitude." He insists on shifting the focus of attention from specific fact to essential and universal qualities.[22] Husserl argues that while reason can demonstrate the truth, it cannot persuade people that truth is desirable. Only by an intentional act of will can a person choose to bring value and truth together.[23]

Scholars engrossed in the debate over ethical behavior of the media draw on the phenomenologists' position to make their arguments. Theodore L. Glasser argues that objectivity makes it difficult for journalism to consider ethical questions. Leading off a series on objectivity in *The Quill*, the publication of the Society of Professional Journalists, he writes: "Since news exists 'out there'—apparently independent of the reporter—journalists can't be held responsible for it. And since they are not responsible for the news being there, how can we expect journalists to be responsible for the consequences of merely reporting it? What objectivity has brought about, in short, is a disregard for the consequences of newsmaking."[24]

What stronger argument for exposing journalism and other students to debates in various fields about objectivity? Perhaps they might then be in a better position to answer a question raised by an engineer in our seminar's discussions: "Is objectivity always better?" If they can't answer the question, maybe they would at least recognize that Husserl's intentional act of will for bringing value and truth together is too often absent.

From a different perspective, the realists' side of the debate over objectivity appeals to the empirical tradition of journalists, but journalists have not probed this argument very deeply. In fact, Glasser blames the journalist's "naively empirical view of the world" for the "burden of objectivity," but he seems to be putting more emphasis on the "empirical" than on the "naively."[25]

Social realists find no crucial distinction to be made between facts and values. Tronn Overend even argues that there is no fundamental distinction between ethics and the social sciences. Overend says ethics can be seen as a branch of social enquiry concerned with mapping out the empirical character of good and evil.[26] The approach in such an analysis is descriptive, rather than the prescriptive one common in studying ethics. Such issues as freedom and responsibility, not to mention obligation, are eliminated as characteristics of ethical facts.

Realists like J. Anderson, author of *Studies in Empirical Philosophy*, conceive their practice of objectivity in terms of disinterest. This is brought out by their rejection of advocacy and insistence instead "on the facts, to expound and expose, let the results be what they may."[27]

A current journalistic formulation that approaches this view of disinterest was given by James Boylan, professor of journalism at the University of Massachusetts at Amherst, in reviewing Dan Schiller's *Objectivity and the News* for the *Columbia Journalism Review*. "Objectivity," he wrote, "has gradually come to be understood not only as an impersonal, 'balanced' style of newswriting (which is the commonplace, or newsroom, sense of the word), but also as representing the broader claim of journalism for its position in society, the one that speaks for the general interest."[28]

This came close to saying that the body of knowledge to which the profession of journalism applies its skills is not journalism, but the bodies of knowledge in the other disciplines. The profession of journalism may not, then, be a profession unto itself, but a form of professional practice configured to tap into the other disciplines and professions while asserting a claim to serve the general interest of the public by disseminating timely, though superficial, information arising from those fields. Superficial here does not mean unimportant, but rather is closer to meaning adequate for satisfying public expectations.

Boylan's formulation places establishment journalism somewhere between the disinterest advocated by the philosophic realists and the interest implicit in consciously collaborating to construct a mediated reality. His position may fall short of drawing a clear guideline, but it acts to move journalism somewhat beyond any auto-matic balancing of opinionated statements to a perspective based on the journalists' understanding of society's interests.

The understanding of society's interests is furthered by the cross-disciplinary education that served as a goal of our seminar. The fact that such an educational process took place among the faculty members participating in the seminar is encouraging. It bodes well for the belief that students would benefit from courses designed to illuminate the elements that link liberal and professional education.

Objectivity can be one such element. By examining the ways various disciplines validate the truth of the bodies of knowledge they build, students may avoid an objectivity trap that threatens the pro-fessions. Alvin W. Gouldner warns of this trap in an article ad-dressed to sociologists, but his warning might well apply to the other fields.

"Professions," he writes, "do not tend to see value commitments as questions of personal commitment but tend, instead, simply to treat the values they transmit as non-problematic givens." The re-sult, he says, is that "the growth of professionalism means the substi-tution of a routine and banal code of ethics for a concern with the serious kind or morality on which alone objectivity might rest."[29]

Gouldner's concern about the professions' tendency to bury the truth-revealing queries that encumber the efficient practice was re-flected in the seminar discussions. Peter Marsh, as discussion leader, summed up the difference between disciplines and professions as to objectivity. "The question of objective criteria," he said, "is much closer to the surface in the disciplines."

Students in the professional schools may thus encounter those basic criteria of objectivity more readily in their liberal arts courses than in the professional courses that emphasize practice. The courses designed by the seminar participants, including those to be taught in the professional schools, may encourage students to apply such criteria across the boundaries between fields.

The topic is one that arouses interest. In the course developed in the seminar for the School of Public Communications, the students demonstrated that interest. Sharon Hollenback, my colleague in the school's television and film department, and I jointly taught the course in the fall of 1986. She mentioned that I had done a chapter for this book designed to probe a bit into objectivity and that I had expressed doubts about the concept as practiced by journalists generally. We then tried to pass on to the topic scheduled for the day, but the students would not let us.

"So what did you conclude objectivity is?" one asked. Sharon smiled as I danced around the question. Although I squirmed under the questioning, I was pleased by the rather passionate kind of inquiry it revealed. The fact that I could not come up with a satisfactory answer did not dismay the students. They seemed, in fact, to look on the inquiry itself as one for them to possess. We had agreed earlier in the course that freedom is redefined each generation by the way people use it. Objectivity seemed to fall into a similar category. And the students were ready to work out their own meaning of objectivity by putting it to the same kind of practical test.

This experience made me feel that objectivity is a subject that can be examined critically and feelingly by students in all fields. It reflected the experience of the seminar, which came to see objectivity not as the path to truth, but as the means, varying among fields, for improving the mutual understanding and respect among disciplines and professions.

Notes

1. See chapter 8, "The Concepts of Embeddedness and Enculturation."

2. Lawrence Weschler, *Seeing Is Forgetting the Name of the Thing One Sees: A Life of Contemporary Artist Robert Irwin* (Berkeley: University of California Press, 1982). Thomas S. Kuhn, *The Structure of Scientific Revolutions*, 2nd ed., enlarged (Chicago: The University of Chicago Press, 1970).

3. Wechsler, *Seeing Is Forgetting*, 137.

4. Kuhn, *Structure of Scientific Revolutions*, 198–207.

5. Israel Scheffler, *Science and Subjectivity*, 2nd ed. (Indianapolis: Hackett Publishing Co., 1982), 1–2.

6. Richard A. Shweder, "Storytelling Among the Anthropologists," *The New York Times Book Review*, 28 September 1986, 1, 38–39.

7. The author of this chapter was a member of the *Times* staff at the time.

8. Dr. Hunter S. Thompson, *Fear and Loathing on the Campaign Trail '72* (New York: Popular Library, 1973), 47–48.

9. Anthony Smith, *Goodbye Gutenberg: The Newspaper Revolution of the 1980s* (New York and Oxford: Oxford University Press, 1980), 168.

10. Michael Herr, *Dispatches* (New York: Alfred A. Knopf, 1977).

11. Smith, *Goodbye Gutenberg*, 183.

12. Jonathan Alter, "The Two Faces of Breslin," *Newsweek*, 12 May 1983, 74.

13. Michael Schudson, *Discovering the News: A Social History of American Newspapers* (New York: Basic Books, 1978), 162–63.

14. Herbert J. Gans, *Deciding What's News: A Study of CBS Evening News, NBC Nightly News, Newsweek and Time* (New York: Pantheon Books, 1979), 82, 186.

15. Gaye Tuchman, "Objectivity as Strategic Ritual," *American Journal of Sociology*, 77 (January 1972), 660–70.

16. E. Barbara Phillips, "Approaches to Objectivity: Journalistic versus Social Science Perspectives," in *Strategies for Communications Research* (Beverly Hills: SAGE, 1977), 68.

17. Robert Park, "News as a Form of Knowledge," *American Journal of Sociology* 45 (March 1940): 667–86.

18. Walter Lippmann, *Public Opinion* (New York: Penguin Books, 1946), 20. The book was originally published by the MacMillan Co. in 1922.

19. Terry Eagleton, *Literary Theory: An Introduction* (Minneapolis: The University of Minnesota Press, 1963).

20. Raman Selden, *Criticism and Objectivity* (London: George Allen & Unwin, Ltd., 1984), 156–57.

21. Henry LeRoy Finch, *Wittgenstein—The Later Philosophy: An Exposition of the Philosophical Investigations* (Atlantic Highlands, N.J.: Humanities Press, 1977), 190.

22. Maurice Natanson, *Edmund Husserl, Philosopher of Infinite Tasks* (Evanston, Ill.: Northwestern University Press, 1973), 60.

23. Ibid., 180.

24. Theodore L. Glasser, "Objectivity Precludes Responsibility," *The Quill* (February 1984): 13–16.

25. Ibid.

26. Tronn Overend, *Social Idealism and the Problem of Objectivity* (St. Lucia: University of Queenlands Press, 1983), 190.

27. J. Anderson, *Studies in Empirical Philosophy* (Sydney: Angus & Robertson, 1963), 287. Cited by Overend, 195.

28. James Boylan, "Infancy of Objectivity," *Columbia Journalism Review* (September/October 1981): 61–63.

29. Alvin W. Gouldner, "The Sociologist as Partisan: Sociology and the Welfare State," *The American Sociologist* 3 (May 1968): 113–16.

6

Individual, Social, and Professional Identity

MARSHALL H. SEGALL

Introduction

Observing students cross a campus between classes, we can almost unfailingly categorize them into "majors" simply by noting
dress styles, speech patterns, objects being carried (soft green book-
bags by some, large flat rectangular portfolios by others), and other
profession-specific modish displays. Like freshly incised facial scars
on tribal initiates, these signify what the students are in process of
becoming.

What are they becoming? Engineers, managers, physicians, and
sportscasters, to be sure, but more—much more. To become an engineer is to attach some new content to one's personality, in effect to
become a somewhat reshaped person who views the world from a
particular perspective, attaching more importance, significance, and
salience to certain experiences than to others. To become a sports-
caster is to do the same, but the importances, significances, and sa-
liences will be different. Within every professional group there will
be individual differences, but superimposed on these individualities
will be commonalities shaped by the professions.

In the seminar, we believed that we must somehow address this
fundamental social psychological phenomenon in our social science
course. The seminar considered alternative ways to link professional
training needs with exposure to social science concepts that would be
genuinely relevant to professional training. We examined an earlier
version of an honors course in social science. It had been well regarded by students, but had been designed before we began our
search for ways to link professional and liberal arts education, and it
did not appear to serve this program. The original course covered
several important works in the various social sciences, treating them
critically from the perspective of a philosopher of science, to give

Still from the 1932 movie *Horse Feathers* with the Marx Brothers. Courtesy of the Museum of Modern Art/Film Stills Archives.

the students some solid understanding of social science. The new course, to reflect the seminar's findings, had to be more student oriented. It would convey important social science content, but that would not be its primary purpose. We decided to design a course that would frontally attack the issues that the seminar had identified as critical to our enterprise—professionalism,[1] craft,[2] objectivity, and embeddedness[3]—and that the social science techniques and content involved would be a means to that end, rather than ends in themselves. The course would permit students to discover that, as they acquire the skills, craft and artistry attached to their chosen professions, they are also absorbing culturally embedded values that govern how they view the world. Identity then became the central theme of the course.

We decided to focus on the transformation that students could, should, and often do undergo when they enter into programs of higher education and training. Gradually acquiring skills, techniques, and craft, they are likely not to remain the persons they were when entering the university, for the acquisition of such tools carries with it much personal baggage. It is as if freshmen, who are relatively undifferentiated, become gradually more clearly distinguishable persons. What makes them so, to others, and to themselves, is heavily rooted in the attitudes, values, and ethos attached to the professions and careers to which they aspire—into which they are, in effect, being initiated.

Thus, higher education, particularly as it affects our current students—most of whom have professional orientations and aspirations—has potentially profound effects on the very core of their selves, their beings, their identities. We decided that these impacts must be examined; students ought be armed with expectations regarding the enculturation they face, prepared to defend themselves against effects on their persons which they might wish to avoid, or, equally importantly, to accept knowingly those which they might welcome. At least they should be assisted in understanding what might happen to them as they choose one career path over others. The main goal of the course on identity is to lead students into a deliberately self-conscious examination of the process of becoming.

Course Description

The course is designed to attract students prepared to question how they are being shaped by their undergraduate experience. The catalogue entry reads:

"This course will focus on the multiple identities which reflect the diverse and often cross-cutting memberships that all persons enjoy; viz., age set, gender, family, ethnic group, community, public, society, institution, organization, occupational group, and (less obviously, it is sad to note) humankind as a whole. Social science treatments, both theoretical and empirical, and brought to bear on concepts relating to personal identity, showing how groups both socialize and enculturate their members, who acquire, through role learning, new behaviors, attitudes and values. Special attention is given to professional groups and their "cultures" since the primary goal of the course is to help professionally-oriented students to place their emerging professional identities within relevant socio-cultural contexts."

The content, format and style of the course all take into account four issues of common concern to the "Syracuse experiment": professionalism, craft, objectivity, and embeddedness. These issues emerge in different ways in each of our courses. How do they look in the context of a course on identity?

Professionalism

The perspective offered by Rhodes[4] on professional education sets it apart from vocational training, and instead insists that it be concerned with how the profession and its associated values shape the quality of individual life.

Since the content of the course is the individual as shaped by his or her memberships, especially professional membership, professionalism is at the core of the course. And since the beliefs we each hold are often rooted in our membership groups, in a fundamental sense our identities are formed—at least informed—by them. Thus, as noted by Haskell, one's beliefs (such as his in Darwinian theory, which provides a mode of discerning reality which a fundamentalist creationist rejects) are "a crucially important part of my sense of who I am and where I stand in relation to others in my culture."[5]

The course conveys an understanding of the professional membership influences on identity through readings, writing activities, and class discussions with guest speakers. Readings include autobiographies of people in various fields (chosen by the students in accordance with their own professional aspirations). These are read with an eye toward discerning the values held by the individual which may have been predisposing (leading to a choice of profession) and those which may have been shaped by the process of becoming and being a member of a particular profession. What has it meant to a person who devoted a life to a profession to be a professional? How might the person have shaped the profession, and how might the profession have shaped the person? This is often the stuff of fine autobiography, and we hope it will excite our students to apply the questions—albeit in the future subjunctive—to themselves.

To encourage this line of thought, we will have them prepare their own autobiographical analyses of their positions on selected contemporary social issues, again with an eye toward how these beliefs have been shaped by their group-related experiences to date, and how they might be compatible with (or dissonant from) views they are likely to be encouraged—explicitly or more subtly—to incorporate during socialization into a profession.

To assist the students in analyzing the stories they are creating about themselves, social science treatments of professional enculturation (for example, a study of changes in beliefs among medical students in the course of several years in medical school) are presented for class discussion. Similar material is provided by inviting colleagues from the professional schools to discuss what it is "really like" to be an engineer, manager, nurse, artist, or physician. It would, of course, be arrogant for the social scientist to attempt to describe the culture of professions without relying on those who are the best informants for any culture—those who belong to it but who are nonetheless significantly marginal to it. The professionals who have chosen to teach in the professional schools, who know the profession both as doers and analysts, will continue to shape this course by suggesting readings that deal with identity-related issues in their fields and by enriching discussions of such readings with personal observations and accounts of their own personal/professional identity formation.

Here I must digress in order to tell a story that reveals much about the process of course development propelled by the seminar. For almost a year, I continued to think of this course as my course, and of its developmental problems as ones that I had to solve. Yet, as one of the arts and science professors in the group, I was never shy about suggesting to my professional school colleagues what I thought was needed in a professional school course by way of an injection of liberal learning. I was slow to realize that the integration of professional and liberal education was a two-way street. Midway through the seminar, as that became embarrassingly clear, I could turn to the professors of nursing, journalism, drama, engineering, and management and say to them that I recognized them as my key informants, without whose help my treatment of their fields could prove to be as unrecognizable to them as some ethnographies are to the "natives" purportedly described in them.

Craft

The skills and technology characteristic of particular professions are, of course, not central to this course. Highly pertinent, however, are the implications of the craft for persons who acquire it. With craft comes an outlook on life. No experience is passively received, all perceivers participate actively in their perceptions of what is out there. Like Plato's prisoners in the cave, our prior experiences shape our current ones. That we have been trained as historians rather than journalists, engineers rather than artists, or physicians rather than nurses, leads us to apply our craft to what (or those whom) we confront. What we would do to, or with, any object contributes to the definition of that object. In that sense, the portion of our identity that derives from our craft defines not only ourselves but our world. Surely the novelist uses some experiences from the supermarket in writing stories, while the economist molds them into theories of consumption, and the nurse into concerns about nutritional habits.

To make apparent this link between craft, identity, and worldview, the reading and writing assignments focus attention on examples of professionally rooted perspectives. Students will be confronted by the physician's perception of the patient as a vessel of pathology, and the nurse's perception of the same patient as a person to be healed, and encouraged to ponder which, if either, is the more valid image.

Objectivity

This course is more concerned with the limits of objectivity than with objectivity per se. We strive to understand how what we are, or believe ourselves to be—in short, our identity—interacts with efforts to "be objective." We try to show through example that each profession, each discipline, each role, has attached to it a way of judging or deciding that includes certain *techniques* for approaching objectivity. Some forms of objectivity are shared subjectivities of a profession. While a fact may be indisputably a fact, professions vary in their selection of facts thought best to depict, mirror, or represent reality. To become a professional means, in part, to acquire that profession's normative rules of objectivity. Thus, the psychometrically oriented psychologist will acquire respect for, and hence believe in, the validity of IQ scores, the advertiser will feel comfortable with the findings of market research, the physician with CAT scan readings, and so on. In all such cases, that facts are at hand is not in question; what they mean must surely be.

We undoubtedly will consider in this course how each profession has a discipline that tends to ensure objectivity. But, in addition, we know that we must try to demonstrate how in each profession objectivity is only one of the values pursued. Creativity, insight, and intuition—both earned and learned—are combined in both general and profession-specific ways with objectivity in order to arrive at valid judgment, intelligent decision, and effective action. Once again, we make selections that are the subjective aspect of our craft. Our predilections for selection are an important part of our identity. They reflect values and beliefs rooted in professional membership and in other social sources. These values are partly shared by all members, and partly unique to each individual member. The readings, writings, and class discussions try to show the complex interaction between objectivity and truth as variously influenced by particular group memberships.

Embeddedness

That no profession (or discipline, or role within one) is an island is a central theme of the project at Syracuse, and the most central one of this course. Relations, connections, and embeddedness are perhaps what the course is really about.

As Benno Schmidt remarked in his inaugural address as president of Yale University (20 September 1986):

> There is a central truth about liberal arts education and that is, that studying what is outside us in an open, curious, even playful way can give us two indispensable gifts. One is happiness. And the other is the gift of empathy.
>
> Liberal education should prepare us for a lifetime of such vulnerability and risk. Or, as Eliot put it in the "Four Quartets," a life in which "the pattern is new in every moment and every moment is a new and shocking valuation of all we have been." Our education in the end prepares us not only for our professions, but for the two-thirds of our life that is not about our jobs, our work, our status. But about dailiness. About inwardness. About our capacities for affiliation.

Concern with culture ought to be injected in all undergraduate courses, for culture is what is with us daily. How our jobs are embedded in our lives and how our lives are shaped by our jobs are only two questions that relate to the interaction of our profession and our culture. Others concern the impact of the culture on the profession, the impact of the profession on the culture, and the impact of both on us. Issues of affiliation and empathy are part of this story. Do I become a social worker because I am pained by the plight of the poor? Can I retain that empathic pain once I become a social worker, attached as much to the helping profession as to the helped?

The overarching theme of the course is that each individual is surrounded by a complex series of intersecting and overlapping social spaces. The individual is part of a family, of an age cohort, of a community, of an ethnic group, of a biological sex, and of many interest groups, communities, publics, and geopolitical collectivities, all of which provide cultural guidelines to shape attitudes, beliefs, values, and, quintessentially, personal identity.

Among these spaces are the professions to which we belong. That they, too, are embedded in culture is indisputable. The form that professions have taken and the ways in which they will change in time are products of cultural influences. The way they have been allowed to grow has been culturally conditioned. In a manner analogous to Darwinian evolution, professions must possess characteristics of systemic fit, and they must change continuously in order to optimize their cultural adaptiveness. Hence their rules, their standards, their norms, indeed the very craft that defines them and that gives them their uniqueness, must be consonant with the values of the wider culture of which they are a part. As a consequence, the culture of any profession must mirror the culture in which it was born and nourished. And just as every individual is shaped by culture but remains always a potential shaper of that culture, so professions both are shaped by, and shape in turn, their culture.

This complex process has effects that are obvious and effects that are difficult to discern. Among the less obvious effects are the ways in which cultural values provide the most fundamental assumptions that underlie each profession. These fundamentals are seldom explicit, but no less real or fundamental for that. What, for example, would the professions of management, advertising, and mass communications be in a society that was not market oriented? That these professions, as we know them in industrialized societies, must take as given some of the values of such societies is manifest in their most fundamental assumptions. That these professions may either reinforce or alter the values of the society of which they are a part is beyond doubt, and that they do both is probable.

To achieve some understanding of the cultural embeddedness of the individual and of the groups—especially professions—of which he or she is becoming a part is the principal goal of this course. To approach it, the professions of interest to the students are examined structurally and functionally, searching for the reflections of the culture in them. We try to find the ways in which cultural values both enrich and constrain the profession, inhibit and encourage innovation and creativity, and fail or succeed in reshaping the society. The search employs as data base a series of readings in part selected from the books and papers chosen by the members of the faculty seminar for their own mutual edification. Many of these papers are revealing with respect to embeddedness, as much in what they do not say as in what they do.

Additional Concerns

Concern with gender:[6] Gender is arguably the single most potent source of identity. Gender roles, attitudes surrounding sex, gender limitations on selection into professions, and differential approaches to performance and assessment of men and women in particular professions are quintessentially salient issues in this course. To deal

with gender issues, men and women students are encouraged to
confront them in themselves and in their attitudes, and are alerted
to gender-related differences in the autobiographies which they
both read and write. In this regard, several autobiographies of
women are featured in the readings. Seminar colleagues identified
readings by social workers, anthropologists, photographers, physicians, politicians, performers, and numerous other professionals;
only some of them were famous, but all were women, each with
a provocative story to tell about being a woman in her particular
profession.

The social science contribution: Whatever else happens in this
course, taking it should inform all the students about social science
as a set of disciplines and as a perspective on the world. Toward this
end, that perspective is infused through reading and discussion of
several kinds of literature including theoretical works on identity,[7]
social learning theory,[8] roles,[9] and socialization and enculturation,[10] as well as specific works on particular cultures, including our
own.[11] Also, as noted earlier, the class reads and discusses sociological analyses of the cultures of particular professions. Some empirical
techniques of the social scientist are considered, including survey
techniques and attitude questionnaires. Chief among these is the
particularly relevant "who am I" procedure, which the students complete during the first meeting of the class and continually revise as
appropriate. Thus, they have an opportunity to learn something
about social science *per se*, while employing it to learn about themselves and their chosen professions. If learning about social science
is not the central goal of this course, it must be one of them because,
as the members of the faculty seminar agree, communicating to students what we find exciting about our disciplines, and how they
might come to experience this excitement for themselves, is one of
the best ways to infuse education with the liberal arts tradition.

The role of writing: Since the course focuses on identity—a preeminently personal construct—and I am actively urging the students to examine themselves in the light of their various memberships, I am asking them to make of themselves a text and to search
for how it has been written and how it is in process of revision. I
have been taught to do this by the writing teachers who participated
in the seminar.[12] To manifest that text, students do several writing
tasks, including responding periodically to a "what am I" questionnaire, and writing and updating an autobiography. Through reading logs, they digest social science readings on theory, and through

class magazines they document each others' opinions on various controversial issues. In their final paper, they apply the theories of identity they have learned to their own autobiography, with a special section on "why I am becoming a _____" and "why I could never be a _____." The final paper is meant to be somewhat argumentative and show appreciation of social science theory by dealing, for example, with how Skinner might understand me and why I either agree or disagree.

Efforts are made to convince the students that they are writing mainly for themselves and each other, and that my role as instructor with respect to their writing is to help them more than to judge them. Only the final paper is graded. The students are encouraged to write to each other rather than to the instructor. They are also encouraged to view the writing exercises not as discrete, but rather as cumulative, with issues dealt with repeatedly in increasingly enriched form.

Conclusion

Part of the pedagogical challenge of this course is to assist students in integrating three rather different kinds of material in their writings—theoretical works about identity formation, case histories of other persons, and their own insights into themselves. But this is a challenge that must be accepted, since I wish to exploit their natural concern with themselves in a way that does not deteriorate into narcissistic ventilation. The ideas which the students bring to their writing and class discussions from their own experiences will be compared, contrasted, challenged, or reinforced with ideas they find in the assigned readings.

Still, this is an unabashedly personally oriented course. Rather than deny or ignore the pervasive concern of undergraduates with themselves, this course spotlights it. Doing so entails risk, but one that seems eminently worth taking. The understanding that could emerge if students are encouraged and allowed to relate themselves to disciplined thinking that others have done about themselves is worth seeking. To seek this kind of understanding—to find ways to help aspiring professionals frame answerable questions about what it may mean to them to become a professional—is to help them participate in the interrogative pause that should be the signature of all the courses that have emerged from the Mellon Foundation seminar.

Notes

1. See chapter 3, "The Phenomena of Professions."
2. See above, page 23.
3. See chapter 8, "The Concepts of Embeddedness and Enculturation."
4. Frank H. T. Rhodes, "Reforming Higher Education Will Take More than Just Tinkering with Curricula," *Chronicle of Higher Education*, 22 May 1986, 80.
5. Thomas L. Haskell, *The Authority of Experts* (Bloomington, Ind.: Indiana University Press, 1984), x.
6. See chapter 10, "Gender and the Professions."
7. Erik H. Erikson, *Identity: Youth and Crisis* (New York: Norton, 1968). Also Carol Gilligan, *In a Different Voice* (Cambridge, Mass.: Harvard University Press, 1982).
8. Albert Bandura, *Social Learning Theory* (Morristown, N.J.: General Learning Press, 1971).
9. Bruce J. Biddle, *Role Theory: Expectations, Identities and Behaviors* (New York: Academic Press, 1979). Also Erving Goffman, *The Presentation of Self in Everyday Life* (Garden City, N.Y.: Doubleday, 1959).
10. Marshall H. Segall, *Cross-Cultural Psychology* (Syracuse, N.Y.: Orange Student Books, 1979).
11. B. F. Skinner, *Beyond Freedom and Dignity* (New York: Bantam, 1971).
12. See chapter 13, "Everyone Writes."

7

The Impact of Seeing

GARY M. RADKE and STEPHEN MELVILLE

When the seminar first convened, it seemed obvious that our activities would consist of reading, writing, and talking. That's what we had done as graduate students, and that was what we continued to do in most of our classes. None of us flinched—or at least none of us felt that we dare flinch—when the project director asked us to suggest readings for the seminar. His announcement that the meetings of the seminar would revolve around a discussion of those readings seemed quite sensible. This was going to be a relatively safe, genuinely academic enterprise. Most of us, after all, assumed that education was inherently textual and linguistic. Why else were we so concerned about perceived weaknesses in our student's abilities to express themselves in writing? Why did we usually look askance at a course syllabus that was not heavily weighted with readings? And why did we go to the expense of setting up discussion sections for so many of our large lectures? We not only believed that education was inherently textual and linguistic, we almost seemed to be saying that it was exclusively so.

But as the faculty seminar proceeded, we began to discover the inadequacy of viewing education this way. It all started when one of the civil engineers arranged the viewing of a film about the Brooklyn Bridge. He was convinced that the film could *show* us more about the bridge than he could possibly *tell*. And indeed, this moment of visual encounter allowed a good number of us to see, as if for the first time, the aesthetic dimensions of an engineering feat.

Then the art historian, uncomfortable with the way all discussions about the assigned readings had followed a nearly identical format, decided to engage us visually. Instead of prefacing the discussion of Michael Baxandall's *Painting and Experience in Fifteenth-Century Italy* with information about the author or an explanation of why we were reading this particular book, he set up a slide projector. Much to the initial horror of the painter in our midst who, like many, probably thought that glowing images of Renaissance art

99

were going to emerge from the lens, we confronted an image of Thanksgiving dinner by Norman Rockwell. The actor in our midst recalls the experience this way:

> The illustration was one so familiar to some of us who were over forty as to represent virtually an icon of America. In the background a sweet-faced, work-worn elderly woman holds a turkey-laden platter which she is about to place on a holiday-decorated table. Around the table (which rushes to the foreground of the illustration) apparently sit her grown family, their spouses and children clearly regathered for the celebration. Some of the participants look smilingly at the matriarch and patriarch, others at the magnificent bird or at each other, and in the extreme foreground one young wag grins straight out, gesturing perhaps to another family member outside the frame, perhaps at us to join the festivities.
>
> One would have thought that an image so hackneyed and conventional would hardly have excited a ripple of comment, much less controversy. In the hubbub of response that followed, it soon became clear that we were literally not seeing the same thing . . .
>
> Moreover, our observations were not only consistent with, but clearly attributable to, the particular perspective of our individual professions or disciplines. The social psychologist commented on his unease at the representation of the archetypal American family as quintessentially Midwestern and WASP; the historians in the group linked Rockwellian Americana in general with the political climate of the '40s; the art historian pointed to our common tendency to take a photographic record of an offset press illustration based on an original painting for the original work; the artist spoke of the tenuousness of the original's claim on the honorific "art"; and I responded principally to the dramatic elements of character, action, and staging implicit in the work.

What the Rockwell poster did, then, was invite us to see each other more clearly and to engage in our own work of cultural archaeology. Both the ease and the difficulty of the discussion seemed exemplary, highlighting the mixture of readability and opacity within which we live, and pointing very strongly to the continuity between high art and popular culture that became one of the essential themes of the humanities course.[1] As Baxandall uncovered barrel-gauging as a practice informing both the production and appreciation of Renaissance painting, so we uncovered the pervasive influence of advertising in ours, how its conventions both reflect and, in part, control the very structure of our society.

Norman Rockwell poster, *Freedom from Want*. Courtesy Library of Congress.

Fascinated by what we heard each other seeing—yes, seeing, almost more than saying—we continued the discussion. The Thanksgiving scene became palpably more opaque as its strange image of ethnic narrowness (its image of America as a purely Christian and northern European melting pot) became increasingly visible. As might have been expected, there were a number of members of the seminar who had actually grown up, in effect, inside such pictures. But there was some shock for them in learning that others had spent their youth angrily outside and excluded by its frame. Those others were both unable and unwilling to see or read any invitation in it. For some this discussion started, and for others it gave greater urgency and explicitness to, questions about what it means or how it is possible to live with—within or without—such images. What had at first seemed so univeral an icon of America, of the way in which all American families could celebrate what the poster called "Freedom from Want," turned out to have a potent exclusionary quality as well.

And the possible irreality of the scene also turned out to be manifesting itself quite visually. The closer we looked at the poster, the more we were aware of its odd willingness to put forward a picture of "family" that was singularly empty of reasonable detail. It was a rich image whose details led off into myth rather than into the particularity that they at first seemed to offer. The family so clearly visible very quickly became an "apparent family," and our relationship to it—our willingness to see or respond to the youngest member's gesture—became increasingly problematic.

At the same time, this exercise helped us to see what we held in common. We were all, it turned out, much more intensely visual than we had thought. And upon reflection, we realized that so is our culture. Faced with videotapes from the Mary Tyler Moore Show (which we viewed in a later session with one of our colleagues from the School of Public Communications[2]) or other illustrations by Norman Rockwell, many of us ceased to be specialists in management or nursing or literary theory, and became the viewers that in so much of our lives we are. Watching a movie or looking at an illustration for an advertisement, we automatically tapped into a considerable body of experience, competence, and intelligence we hold to an extraordinary degree in common, but which we frequently do not count as intelligence or competence.

It seems fair to say that the visual objects we considered embody some of the tightest connections between our various disciplines—

and brought equally to light some of the widest divisions. Viewing and discussing a television commercial made for Mobil Corp. during the oil crisis brought this into high relief. The rather lengthy ad juxtaposed the Alvin Ailey dancers as chattering jungle animals, characterized as being unduly critical of the oil industry, against an animated wise old owl who was the embodiment of an enlightened industry that cleaned up its spills. The commercial was praised as a first-rate piece of work by some—it was distinctly "artsy" and told its message in a unique way—and denounced as racist by others, who were particularly offended by its portrayal of the jungle and the choice of black-faced animals as fools. The argument it provoked on the role of advertising and cultural representation became a reference point for a great many discussions that followed. And the questions it raised about the relation between effect and intent, text and subtext, became increasingly important to us.

Les Blank's movie *The Burden of Dreams*, suggested by the painter and the film critic among us, turned out to be still more provocative and controversial, earning for its central figure, the German film-maker Werner Herzog, the epithet "unprofessional"—strong language in this group. The discussion that followed broke up only under the pressure of hunger and thirst, and turned around two points of particular interest that had remained submerged through much of the seminar. The first is the economic bottom-line notion of "professional" that most professionals disavow when asked to produce a definition of professionalism, but which surfaces very quickly under certain circumstances: to have spent *that* much money *that* wastefully, to have undertaken so large a project with so little or such shoddy preparation—that was unprofessional. The fact that the conflict here is between an extremely romantic view of art and an equally hardheaded view of business is not enough to make it go away. The question of how much waste or bad luck a profession can allow itself to tolerate seems to go to the heart of our current practices.

It certainly goes to the heart of the pedagogical questions around which the project at Syracuse is formed: What is the proper economy of an education? What counts as a squandering of educational resources and what as the yielding of an adequate return? (Could waste count? This would be to claim that we in academia live in an economy organized by something other than mere economics.) That these questions should have arisen with such clarity, even starkness, around a work of visual art—in, that is, a cultural site in which the relation between "liberal" value and professional commodity is hotly contested—does not seem accidental. At several points over the two years of the project, the representatives from Visual and Performing Arts spoke of a sense of feeling themselves to be a part of the project only under false pretenses; one of the things this discussion made clear is that those pretenses are false only if professionalism is just a name for sound capitalist economic practice. This subtext of professionalism, we would have to say, remains a central and, for the present moment at least, an unresolved issue.

The Les Blank movie also raised the question of objectivity in ways that outran our discussions of that concept. It did so primarily by making inseparable the issues of reportage and creativity. Blank's film is peculiarly intimate with the movie that is its object. Within Blank's film, Herzog plays the role of the character that Fitzcarraldo plays in the movie[3] that Herzog is making and Blank documenting, so the line between what is documentary and what fiction becomes at times exceedingly fine. This intimacy allows *The Burden of Dreams* to embody a compact meditation on the notion of objectivity. In a sense, the film can be said to address and challenge our tendency to separate the objectivity of knowledge from the making of objects. By and large, we were not successful in seeing this at the time, being content to accept the documentary objectivity of Blank's film and to debate the rights and wrongs, success or failure of Herzog's object, without pushing to put these two senses of objectivity in contact with one another. It was as if to some degree the one sense blocked the other. For us, Blank's film was transparent. We saw only *through* it; we did not *see it*. We had lost it as an object.

The play between objectivity as some even-handed, clear-seeing, logically constrained, empirically sound way of standing toward the world, and objectivity as something apparently simpler and more like the having or forging of an object has traversed many of our discussions. It was certainly at home here. The contrast between an epistemologically oriented, more or less "scientific" stance toward the world, and one that is oriented to questions about the disciplinary construction of objectivity and the interpretive demands that follow therefrom seems increasingly central to our discussions. It establishes a difference that coincides with neither the liberal/professional division, nor with the division between the sciences and the humanities.

To the extent that our project did not tend toward the construction of a common language, this awareness of the variability of vision became an important resource for conversations that turned frequently on the trading of images and metaphors. This had both major and minor consequences in our teaching. An English professor and a historian in our group report that while they previously had conducted their courses completely verbally, they now find themselves using the blackboard or overhead projectors, and there has been a good deal of movement between courses by visiting lecturers who bring visual materials from their disciplines (art history, film, advertising) to others. Even more significant is our increased willingness to find film and video to be a pedagogical resource of considerable importance for courses in all fields, not just something to fill a class period when the professor is absent or when large numbers of students are likely to have started their mid-semester break a few days early. These are the kinds of materials that engage students and which, when thoughtfully approached and openly discussed, teach us all a great deal.

Still, the long-run consequences of these visual adventures upon courses, students, and faculty seem difficult to gauge at this point. As we have moved on from the initial project of creating courses to writing the present book, we have continued to struggle with the visual element. It seemed clear to us that there had to be a visual component to the volume, and certain images that had been particularly significant for us—the Rockwell Thanksgiving scene, for example— needed to be included. But we wanted more than illustrations of what had proved provocative for us; we wanted some visual images that might engage the reader, too. So we asked the artist in the seminar to amass a group of images for our consideration. We also decided that we wanted to organize another film viewing, in this case of Kurosawa's *Rashomon*, which only a few of us had seen but which, because it told the story of a single event from four very different points of view, had been adopted in our discussions as a kind of insistent model for how we had attempted to tell our story to ourselves.

Both experiences turned out to be deflating. When we screened the movie we were somewhat surprised to find how far our image or memory of it was from the actual fact of the movie. And when we gathered to consider the proposed set of illustrations there was a hush of repressed embarassment as most of us found ourselves incapable of reading our artist's message, which, standing upon his artist's visual prerogative, he quite rightly refused to explain in verbal terms. It was only on a second try, after the artist sought out images that were provocative but had a more literal connection to some of the themes of our texts, that seminar members began to appropriate them as adjuncts to certain chapters. We had failed to write a communal visual text, but we were quite content to read single images in our own ways and place them as purposefully ambiguous and provocative signposts within many of our texts.

There is probably something still to be discovered here about the terms of the various histories that brought us together. We have, in general, a greater consciousness of the visual dimensions of our lives and world, and here and there we have found places where a given course can make use of material that might not have seemed so pertinent before. But most of us must rely upon words, even while our stance toward language has been quite altered by this experience. We can no longer espouse total faith in the textual and the linguistic, and we have learned that the altering of our faith in language is continuous with our discovery of the extent to which we are bound within particular discursive communities and situations.[4] How far we may be able to liberate ourselves from these bounds, and in what ways we may have to be content with living within them, is yet to be determined. In any case, it is clear to us that we need to do more of this kind of thing as the project at Syracuse continues. Faced with visual objects, we find ourselves more frequently than not in touch with vital strands in our culture, already crossing the boundaries we talk about.

Notes

1. See chapter 14, "The Liberation of the Humanities."
2. Sharon Hollenback, who contributes the following note: "The Mary Tyler Moore Show", excerpt, from "CBS: On the Air", retrospective shown 26 March–1 April 1978.

In this sequence from the show which ran from 1970 through 1977, we see the way social messages were integrated into the entertaining situation-comedy format. The contrast here is between the first show in which Mary is hired by Lou Grant to be an associate producer, and the situation some seasons later when she asks for equal pay with the man who held the job before her.

3. Sharon Hollenback, who contributes the following note: Les Blank and Maureen Gosling, *Burden of Dreams*, 1983, distributed by Les Blank/Flower Films, El Cerrito, California.

This is a documentary about the making of Werner Herzog's *Fitzcarraldo* in the remote areas of the Amazon. The rubber baron, Bryan Sweeney Fitzgerald, called Fitzcarraldo by the native Peruvians and the Spanish-speaking rubber barons with whom he associates in Iquitos, Peru, is often laughed at, but his goal is to build an opera house in this remote location and import singers such as Caruso. He'll make a fortune by opening a tract of land for rubber, but the land is inaccessible. So he concocts a scheme to take a steamer up one river, pull it over a mountain, and then gain access to his land through the river on the other side.

Herzog met unbelievable obstacles in making *Fitzcarraldo* during its several years of creation. Native Indians burned the original location; Jason Robards quit because of illness after 40 percent of the film had been shot; Mick Jagger left because his concert commitments didn't allow for the extended shooting schedule; accidents, disease, and stranded steamships plagued the film. The central metaphor of the film is a real 320 ton steamship being hauled up a steep incline with the most primitive equipment. Everything in the film requires tremendous effort because Herzog wanted locations, natives, shops, dangers to be real.

Blank and Gosling's documentary delves into the making of the film by focusing on Herzog's intent and the workings of his mind. Like Klaus Kinski who plays the lead character, Herzog becomes obsessed with the entire project and the extremes to which this artistic endeavor will lead him. The documentary offers fascinating insights into this one instance of filmmaking. In 1985, North Atlantic Books published *Burden of Dreams*, which includes the screenplay of the documentary, journals kept by Blank and Gosling, and essays on both the feature film *Fitzcarraldo* and this documentary about it.

4. See chapter 2, "The Faculty Seminar: Discourse Communities and Quotation Marks."

III

Embeddedness and Enculturation

Preface

PETER H. MARSH

No instance of the interweaving emergence of concepts and courses in the Syracuse experiment is clearer than that explored in this section. Though it begins with a chapter that sets its conceptual theme, that theme first surfaced in the seminar during its discussion of one of the courses described in the following chapter, and the theme in turn left a deep conceptual mark on the rest of the courses that the participant faculty were developing.

The need to understand the social and cultural context in which every particular discipline or profession must be pursued is widely recognized. The social science and humanities course requirements of every professional college and the general education core requirements common at a good many universities have been framed, in large part, to meet that need. Yet these arrangements implicitly accentuate the distinction between the student's major field of interest and its context, all the more invidious a distinction when the major is in the student's intended profession and its context is relegated to the liberal arts. The intimate relationship between the two is rarely addressed directly because each course is taught by a specialist in the field, who tends naturally to treat it as central rather than contextual, and in any case would find it difficult to address the contextual interests of a diverse student body and still remain true to the subject at hand. Our sense of the seriousness of this pedagogical dilemma deepened as we came to appreciate that the lines of intersection among the disciplines and professions are not of marginal, but of central, importance to them, that each field is constituted as much by these intersections as by its particular subject matter.

We began to acquire conceptual tools to move beyond the distinction between context and central field of interest midway through our seminar during discussion of "The Impact of Science on Medicine," the course which H. Richard Levy, an enzymologist, was developing and describes in chapter 9. In a host of ways, this course emerged as a model of the curricular developments we wish

111

to encourage. It deals with concerns of one of the major pre-professional groups of students in the arts and sciences in a manner that exemplifies some of the best traits traditionally associated with liberal education. Over the years, Levy has taught biochemistry to numerous pre-medical students, but in this course he had to venture well beyond his field of expertise in order to respond to the interest of such students in medical science and practice. Used to dispensing information through lectures, he found a seminar-style format of reading and discussion indispensable to stimulate the reflective enquiry that his new course required. The spirited way in which he plunged into the venture and the warm endorsement that it received from leading educators in medical schools[1] encouraged the rest of the seminar in their cognate endeavors. And the intellectual content of the course prompted searching thought about our entire enterprise.

The course focuses on the paradoxically empowering, yet dehumanizing, impact that science has had on medicine. That focus led Stephen Melville, a literary theorist, to put forward the idea of embeddedness to account for this and similar seams of creative paradox that we were uncovering in each discipline and profession between its claims to autonomy and its dependence on other spheres of concern for effectiveness.

The idea was refined and its potential significance was expanded when Marshall Segall, a cross-cultural social psychologist, fused it with the concept of enculturation, the recognition that every pattern of thought and action is shaped profoundly by the culture in which it arises. The resulting combination of concepts promised to do much to clarify the pervasive interrelationships that we were discovering among the disciplines and professions. From that point, we were drawn toward the conclusion, evocatively expressed by Stephen Melville and Marshall Segall in chapter 8, that what finally counts about all of our island-like subjects is the ocean in which they sit, the waters of which connect them.

This is a controversial conclusion which some members of our seminar do not fully accept and which others among the faculty in their home colleges would emphatically reject. In management, for example, some professors, implicitly dismissing the concept of enculturation, insist that business is most successfully pursued when it concentrates singlemindedly on profits. Most would be content with contextual courses in the arts and sciences that simply make the relevance of their subject matter to the concerns of management clearer. Some members of our seminar would agree with that general stance. Others are willing to carry the concept of enculturation farther, insisting, for example, that students of public communications need to appreciate the peculiarly American character of the media in the United States.

It is with the more radical implications of the concept of embeddedness, emanating as it does from literary theory, that a sizeable proportion of the participants in the seminar would take issue. Literary theorists are willing to "deconstruct" not only the study of literature, but also their own discipline or profession, profoundly impressed with the extent to which it is constituted and needs to be reconstituted by interaction with others. Still, without going that far, our entire seminar has been stimulated by the intellectual and pedagogical ferment that has been thus precipitated. It has kindled among us and in the new courses an awareness that the interactions at work among the varied disciplines and professions are far more extensive and important than we initially imagined.

All spheres of life and work are molded by social culture, race, class, and gender. That fact can be passed off as a truism of secondary significance. Examining the depth to which these forces influence each avenue of thought and action, however, produces sometimes heated controversy. It is tempting, as educators, to take refuge from these storms by concentrating on teaching students the generally accepted precepts and subject matter of their chosen disciplines and professions. That temptation comfortably reinforces the familiar division of undergraduate education into self-contained subjects.

Though we did not envision it at the outset, it seems natural that the course on "Gender and the Professions," described in chapter 10 by Sally Gregory Kohlstedt and Delia Temes, should have been created in our project. It is the one course we have developed that deals with a force that runs through all professions and disciplines. As such, it highlights a cardinal defect produced by the departmentalization of the existing undergraduate curriculum. What college or department should the course be assigned to? Because Kohlstedt and Temes, the creators of the course, come from the departments of history and English, it is now housed among the arts and sciences; but it could just as well be in a professional college. The universality of its concerns does not deprive it of intellectual bite. On the contrary, the course prompts students to call upon some of the sharpest conceptual tools of the liberal arts, and it addresses issues of ethical, theoretical, and personal importance in professional life.

What other courses of this kind and quality can be created? The question is easier asked than answered, but no less pressing for that. A comparable course on race, color, and ethnicity in the professions is not hard to envision. Socioeconomic class might prove harder to deal with as incisively, in part because all members of the faculty are members of the professional middle class. Nonetheless, the function of the professions, including the liberal arts professoriate, as agencies of middle-class assertion and vehicles for upward mobility, needs to be recognized and understood by those who aspire to join and benefit from them.

Part of the new configuration of the undergraduate curriculum that we envision will consist of horizontal courses dealing with concepts, themes, and forces that run through, or shape, all fields of learning. Another will consist of courses that examine the points of convergence emerging with increasing frequency and significance among the disciplines and professions. Conjunctions such as those that have given rise to biochemistry and biophysics[2] are not peculiar to the natural sciences. The boundaries among the various social sciences have never been sharply defined, and overlapping among them is endemic. Points of intersection are occurring still more widely between various disciplines and professions, creating unusual but fruitful connections among spheres hitherto deemed quite remote from each other.

Typical of these developments is an intersection in recent years between visual art and literature, each making use of the symbolism of the other. Still radically exploratory, the conjoint movement can be defined so far only in terms of the past that it is rejecting; hence it calls itself on the one side postmodernist, and on the other poststructuralist. This movement is the subject of the newest course to be created in the project, developed by Stephen Melville and Stephen Zaima, from the departments of English and Studio Arts, who outline it in chapter 11.

Teaching about this subject annihilates a boundary between the liberal arts and professional colleges. The course must involve liberal arts faculty from a literature department and professional faculty from the School of Art. Neither can serve as adjective to the other's noun, for the subject is drawn equally from the two sides. Nor is the course a bridge between their two island-colleges. Subject matter common to the two constitutes this island; their colleges form the surrounding water. How many other islands of this sort await exploration? How often does the contemporary organization of American higher education discourage the search?

Notes

1. See the appendix to chapter 18.
2. See chapter 17, "From Specialization toward Integration: A Scientist's Perspective."

8

The Concepts of Embeddedness and Enculturation

STEPHEN MELVILLE and MARSHALL H. SEGALL

As the seminar progressed, a new concept—embeddedness—began to be developed independently of earlier established interests in gender and culture. It emerged out of attempts to think about questions of objectivity in the disciplines and professions. In time we came to see that embeddedness and cultural concerns were closely intertwined, sharing a common interest in forcing acknowledgment of the complexity of context.

The university curriculum divides the world into discrete subjects reflecting distinct objects or professional activities. We wanted to build into that system of distinctions an active and effective awareness of the fuzzy, overlapping, and thoroughly contextual nature of boundaries of the real world. Yet we did not intend to lapse into intellectual fuzziness by simply asserting the relevance of context and then abandoning the effort to make something of it.

Embeddedness proved to be one of the most vexed and troublesome concepts in the project, if also one of the most fruitful. Meant to underscore the critical power of interdisciplinary analysis, whereby serious consideration is given to contextual effects (not treating them as merely contextual), the concept pointed us toward an appreciation of the ways in which thinking within the framework of any discipline or profession is shaped, limited, constrained, or enriched—often unconsciously and invisibly—by influences impinging from outside itself.

Insights from Literary Theory

The notion of embeddedness originated in an attempt to generalize issues that are acute in contemporary literary studies. After an extended period of focus on the integrity and autonomy of works of

116

Posters announcing Akira Kurosawa's 1951 film *Rashomon*. Courtesy of the Museum of Modern Art/Film Stills Archive.

literature, literary scholars have become newly aware of the need to admit the rootedness of any such work in what is, after all, its world. The effects of this awareness on students of literature have been manifold, but prominent among them has been the increasingly detailed admission that context is what texts have, not accidentally but essentially. Its effects are therefore neither excludable from any adequate treatment of a text nor adequately dealt with as simple additions to it. Literary studies are thus increasingly sites of interdisciplinary research and of research into the grounds and necessity of the interdisciplinary enterprise in general.[1]

Although educational doctrine has traditionally acknowledged the relevance of context, that acknowledgment has been, for the most part, unsophisticated and inconsequential. Disciplines and professions alike claim to be well-founded and self-regulating practices, reciprocal linkings of objects and principles, within an essentially closed discursive structure. There is general agreement that context is a good thing, and most educational programs enforce some kind of contextualization upon students. In the study of English, for example, the context requirement may be satisfied by work in history or linguistics, in advertising it may be satisfied by work in economics or other social sciences, and so on. Such "related subjects" requirements are understood to be broadening, perhaps "humanizing," but they leave it to the students to do the actual relating; it is doubtful whether they often succeed.

Our concern focuses on the relations themselves, and reflects an emerging belief that what finally counts about each island-like subject matter is the ocean in which it sits, and the waters connecting them. These moving bridges not only link one island to another but do much to give each its particular shape and history.

Those scholars and teachers who, in increasing numbers, find themselves driven to interdisciplinary work frequently find that their interest goes deeper even than this picture of context allows. Their interest in the outsides of their disciplines is not accidental to the structure of the discipline itself, but somehow essential. The interest is peculiar because it arises as an exploration of the foundations of the discipline and yet achieves itself only as a transgression of the norms and limits of that discipline. Pursuit of the disciplinary object leads to a space in which that object may itself cease to exist.[2] There is no discipline without an outside that is more than simply exterior to it and in which it is intimately rooted; at the limits of a discipline, one's work is to engage the embeddedness of that discipline in its outside. This is contextualization with a bite; it does not broaden except as it questions—and questions radically.

Insights from Cross-Cultural Psychology

Insights from cross-cultural psychology come to a closely related point by a different route. A central theme of this field is that human behavior is meaningful only when viewed in the sociocultural context in which it occurs. Behavior as observed in a particular eco-cultural setting is often called "human nature" by laypersons and by all too many culture-bound psychologists. Instead, such behavior must be viewed not only as a reflection of human biological potential but also as a product of two classes of experience—socialization and enculturation—the substantive contents of which vary dramatically across cultures. Without this starting point, one could not possibly understand either the uniformities or the diversities in the behavior patterns of the human animal.

All social animals, including the human, are subject to socialization. We alone are also subject to enculturation. Both of these processes must be understood if we are to have even the most fundamental appreciation of the whys of human behavior. Socialization is understood by the cross-cultural psychologist as an active and often conflictual process taking place between a learner and a socializing agent. It assumes the availability of choices, and its outcome is, ideally, correct choice-making. Enculturation, by contrast, occurs without interpersonal or social conflict in a field that offers no alternative. When one learns through enculturation, one learns simply what there is to be learned. When a child struggles with an older sibling who offers behavioral guidelines and insists they be followed, we have an instance of socialization; but what is struggled over and how the struggle is carried on probably reflect enculturation. First employed by Herskovits, this term refers to all of the learning that occurs in human life just because of the limitations in each society on what is available to be learned.[3] What a child learns to be worth struggling for must be a part of the cultural content of that society. The manner in which the child expresses a desire for it will be determined by prevalent attitudes toward the expression of desire. The child will learn these as much by emulating others as by being taught deliberately by them. Whenever we learn by observation, even in a relatively unconscious way, any part of the content of our society—content that has been culturally shaped and limited during preceding generations—enculturation is occurring.

Although all human beings are enculturated, with effects obvious to the social scientist, enculturated individuals are usually unaware of how much of what they do reflects the process. No person is likely to be aware of how much he or she has learned from a society without knowing what was unavailable in the society to be learned. This leads to the apparent paradox that persons who are most thoroughly enculturated are often the least aware of their culture's role in molding them.

Much of what people learn about their society is learned without direct, deliberate teaching. We all learn particular ideas, concepts, and values simply because of the differential availability of ideas to be learned. We learn, for example, what is music and what is noise. What people learn to identify as music depends primarily on what is there—previously labeled as music—to be learned. Similarly, in every society a high percentage of the people would agree on what is worth fighting for. Such values are widely transmitted, both directly and indirectly, and are learned very well because they are hardly ever questioned.

So it must also be with disciplines and professions into which newly recruited members are enculturated. Once accomplished, the enculturation process can produce ethnocentric adherents, unaware of the roots of the doctrines, values, and norms to which they adhere. Paradoxically, the more enculturated they become, the less they appreciate either the sources of their beliefs or the effects those beliefs, when acted upon, may have on the surrounding world. Worse, perhaps, they may be unaware of alternative beliefs or, if aware, disdainful of them.[4]

We return then to the proposition that, at the limits of one's practice, one's work is to engage the embeddedness of that discipline in its outside. Not to do so is to ignore the profound effects of culture. The true sources or causes of a phenomenon are likely to be overlooked by an observer who is oblivious of his own culture, and serious interpretive error can result.

One might think here of the limitations imposed upon psychoanalytic theory by its containment within the culture of nineteenth-century Vienna. Thus did Sigmund Freud possibly err when he attributed male adolescent hostility to sexual jealousy directed toward father (a sometimes mother's lover) rather than to resentment of discipline (much more consistently administered to boys by their nineteenth-century Hapsburgian fathers). Had Freud been aware of anthropological data from the Trobriand Islands, showing in an avuncular society (where uncles discipline, while fathers love mothers) that adolescents have nightmares in which uncles but not fathers suffer, we might have been spared the Oedipus complex.[5]

The lesson of cross-cultural psychology is that to stay within a single cultural context and study human behavior is to risk asserting pan-cultural universals that are in fact culture-bound overgeneralizations. Psychologists increasingly recognize the ethnocentrism of their own discipline in its earlier forms. Work by a newer breed of cross-cultural psychologists is at the cutting edge of psychology precisely because it focuses on its own outsides.

Embeddedness and the Professions

In the professions, the notion of embeddedness seems most usefully thought of in terms of a certain inevitable excess of effect: consequences that belong to a practice are suppressed or overlooked in the professional pursuit of that practice. Advertising, for example, is the communication of a message. It has done its work well when it succeeds in that communication by making a brand more visible. But it achieves that success only within a culture whose materials are its means; and so in communicating its message it invariably also endorses, contests, or extends that culture. However incidental that effect, it is one advertising cannot avoid exerting. No rhetoric of persuasion goes without a rhetoric of tropes—veerings from the displacements of literal sense—and the advertiser is, willy-nilly, a forger of our culture.

A sharp disagreement emerged in the seminar regarding the claim that advertising influences the society in which it functions. The professor of advertising, while agreeing that society influences advertising, denied vigorously that the reverse was true. "I would say," he asserted, "that the influence of society on advertising is about ten times greater than the influence of advertising on society."

He rephrased his argument in terms of advertising's "feeble effects on consumer behavior," citing evidence such as: (1) the failure of 95 percent of new brands, (2) studies showing that the creative content of campaigns has no influence on their effectiveness, (3) data showing the marginal yield of extra sales generated by advertising to be smaller than the marginal cost of the advertising itself, (4) the lack of correlation between sales drop and reduction in advertising, as in the case of cigarettes following the 1971 cessation of advertising on television, and (5) the "almost invariable failure" of advertising to increase total consumption of a product field, as opposed to brand share. He noted that advertising influences the cultural values of the society to a far smaller degree than does television entertainment. What advertising does when it works best, he concluded, is "hold up a mirror to society."

To these assertions we responded that advertising and entertainment on television are entangled, and that we were not claiming that either has a greater effect on society than the other. Further, we considered the data pertaining to brand success, market share, and the like as questions internal to the ordinary practice of advertising, and not as pertinent to our central point as our colleague in the field considered them to be. Whether advertisements sell particular products or not, we reassert, they sell a version of America.

This argument forced us to restate our central theme. Our claim is simply that advertising, like programming on television, is one of the central sites of self-representation in our culture. This representation is not neutral (as the mirror or window metaphor would claim) but active; it either endorses or contests (and more often the former) the images that it takes from, and returns to, the culture.

While the professor of advertising believed the matter to be subject to settlement by empirical data, we argued that it could not. As the concept of enculturation implies, we said, "America (and this includes expressions of America in advertising and other rhetorical objects) makes Americans; that this cannot be falsified doesn't mean it isn't true." Finally, we concluded that even if it were granted that advertising "merely" reflects the culture, that is an act with effects all its own.

We have presented this disagreement here in some detail because it is one of the best examples we can offer of the vigorous discussions which occasionally emerged in the seminar. It serves also to underscore a central point of the present chapter, namely that each of us, when speaking from inside a particular field, is prone to minimize its embeddedness.

Similarly, the engineer is, on her own ground, simply a solver of technical problems, but every actual technical solution is inevitably also an act of human engineering. Thus, the interstate highway system in the United States, built ostensibly for military defense, made possible and encouraged suburban growth. It helped to establish a terminus for "white flight," and set the material stage for the decay of inner cities, all of which fed into the accompanying deterioration of race relations.

In each of these instances, we see particular practices that out-race the professional intentions which inform them and by which they are justified. In this light, the notions of objectivity upon which the profession depends serve only to sever the relation between professional intent and material effect. To insist that the engineer only designs the machine or that the advertiser plays only upon desires that are already there is to deny the essential responsibility of the profession, not to itself but to its outside. By contrast, to insist upon this connection is to acknowledge the embeddedness of every professional act in its material culture.

It follows from this that professional training, whether in an English department or a college of engineering, cannot be simply an introduction to the principles and practices of the profession but must also—and perhaps most importantly—be an introduction to a criticism of the effects and material conditions of the profession.

The general claim underlying a focus on embeddedness is that the abstraction through which a discipline or a profession establishes itself as autonomous is essentially violent, and that the marks of that violence will be found within the practice as a seam or system of seams,[6] where the exclusions on which the profession depends are readable within it. Plato excludes poetry from the *Republic*, and in so doing engenders a regime of sense in which philosophy can be king; but philosophy cannot cease to be written and its every text betrays it to poetry—none more so than Plato's own. It is, one might say, only our willingness to fall in with Plato's exclusion that makes these texts the "obvious" property of philosophy rather than literary study. To read philosophy—as opposed to doing its work of argument while ignoring the conditions under which that work unfolds—is to recall it to its founding violence and to revise radically its claim to autonomy. One task of fundamental reflection upon our practices would then be to find and make visible such seams.

Embeddedness Revealed: Science and Medicine

Among the professional courses developed through the project at Syracuse, the one that perhaps best spotlights the seams between the profession and its cultural context is the course for pre-medical students on the relation of medicine to science.[7] This is a relation that we tend to think goes without saying; medicine would not be medicine without science, it just follows from it. But when we try to speak of that relation in detail, we find ourselves suddenly engaged in a deep critique of medicine, caught up in philosophy and history and anthropology.

The course opens up for examination one of the seams through which medical knowledge and practice is constituted. The critique cuts deep enough to force every student in the course to question whether to continue toward that profession, yet it also uncovers the fundamental object of medicine in such a way that the student may well choose to go on. And presumably that student who will become a physician knows him- or herself to have an interest—a permanent, objective, medical interest—in what lies outside the norms and limits of his or her professional training and its internal images of objectivity. This is an interest that cannot be quieted or dispelled by the invocation of the professional delimitations of responsibility.

The course says more than that there would be no medicine without science. It considers the possibility that science and its technological offshoots not only inform medicine, but constrain and distort it. The course makes the student consider that science and technology reflect a broader culture, and that medicine informed by science and technology is not the only conceivable medicine. It suggests that medicine as a profession has a culture of its own, with hard-to-bend rules governing doctor-patient relationships, norms governing physicians' modes of behavior, and economic considerations tied to the broader culture in which the profession exists. The course demonstrates as well that the conduct of medicine impacts, in its turn, on that broader culture.

The course works to make doctors who are not simply "liberally educated," but who know themselves to have an abiding interest in what lies outside the norms and limits of the profession itself. It is the ambition for all the new courses that such interests should be discovered and encouraged until they can resist being dispelled by any merely professional assertion of boundaries. In a deep sense there are no such boundaries. Nor is the outside outside.

The Interface of Embeddedness and Enculturation

The focus of embeddedness is thus on the structure and internal limits of particular practices—on the ways in which the contextual fact of the world gets inside and disturbs merely disciplinary or professional considerations. The natural rhetoric of embeddedness produces figures of rupture and transgression. But it is also possible to stand outside of such practices and ask about their meaningfulness in terms of the sociocultural context in which they occur. To do so entails speaking about the bridges that lead to and from practices that tend to conceive of themselves as autonomous. Cross-cultural comparison offers a particularly effective way of making visible the world that enables, facilitates, and determines particular practices. In focusing on the process of enculturation we look toward the world in which our practices are embedded rather than at particular practices insofar as they are marked by that embeddedness.

The more enculturated participants in such practices become, the less they can appreciate either the sources of their beliefs or the effects those beliefs may have upon the surrounding world. Theirs are "natural" ways to act. If we return to the example of the interstate highway system, the concept of enculturation focuses our interest on all the forces in our society—the value of individual freedom, the right of individual ownership, the interest of a competitive market—that make the car a privileged form of mobility and so produce an interstate highway system as the "natural" solution to a problem that another society might, with equal "naturalness," address through the development of a rail network and yet another with a system of exclusively military transportation.

Within the humanities, we might similarly be led to inquire into the way in which an art historian "naturally" takes one range of artifacts within a culture as falling within his purview and excludes another such range within the same culture. The questions one will then ask will be on the order of: Is there any sense to a phrase like "primitive" art? What is it in our culture that makes "art" available to us as a natural category within the world? Which objects from other cultures which we designate works of art are seen by their own members as simple objects of daily use? The student of painting ought to be inspired to wonder why we so commonly enclose paintings in rectangular frames, a phenomenon that is clearly rooted in our carpentered, Western culture. The question is easily opened through cross-cultural comparison; opening it leads to further questions about the limits of painting and our central interest in its delimitation—embeddedness.

Issues of gender offer particularly powerful access to the work of enculturation. Is our rather casual distinction of male and female professions (engineers and nurses, "hard" scientists and "soft" hu-

Still from Les Blank's 1982 film *The Burden of Dreams*. Courtesy of the Museum of Modern Art/Film Stills Archive and Les Blank—Flower Films. (Blank's film documents the making of Werner Herzog's *Fitzcarraldo*.)

manists) a reflection of some simple biological fact, or of a somewhat more complex economic fact, or of a very complex cultural coding that has consequences of its own for the shaping of the norms and rationales of disciplines and professions? When one asks how disciplines and professions are engendered, the answers can lead, critically, to the heart of those practices. In some of these instances, historical investigation may well play the role we have suggested for cross-cultural comparison. This suggests a new and deeper interest for the traditional courses in the history of a profession that have been the main places where attempts have been made in the past to create some humanistic penumbra for professional education.[8]

Recalling the pre-medical course, to employ the notion of enculturation in it is to insist upon the role that the larger culture plays in determining the self-evidence of the linkages between medicine, technology, and science. It is also to suggest that medicine, while embedded in a culture, itself *has* a culture. And, finally, it is to suggest that medicine has its own enculturating effects on its surrounding culture.

What holds for the pre-medical course applies to all courses. The pedagogical faith that underlies what we have come to see as the complementary notions of embeddedness and enculturation is that while every course that teaches the skills of a particular discipline or profession must teach them in the conviction that they are valid, so too these same courses ought to throw that claim of validity into sustained question and doubt.

The claim we assert via the concepts of embeddedness and enculturation is that the abstraction through which any discipline or profession attempts to establish itself as autonomous is essentially invalid. Disciplines, professions, and particular practices all behave, to a high degree, like cultures, and they too produce ethnocentric adherents, unaware of the roots of the doctrines, values, and norms they espouse.

Whatever the insights and achievements of any discipline or profession, they are never untroubled nor without cost. If we conceal this, we fail as educators. An awareness of the real depth of context must inform the entire undergraduate curriculum.

Notes

1. The focus on the integrity and autonomy of the literary work is, to a large degree, the achievement of American New Criticism and is closely linked to the bundle of views described as "formalist" in the visual arts. These two tendencies are central to most descriptions of modernism. The critique of this position has roots in an amalgam of Marxism and tendencies in contemporary Continental philosophy. The particular focus on relations between "inside" and "outside" is perhaps most closely associated with the work of the French philosopher Jacques Derrida, whose coinage "deconstruction" has gained considerable currency as a general term for efforts to undo the exclusions upon which idealisms like the New Criticism depend.

2. Thus, for example, Martin Heidegger defined his philosophic task as the destruction of philosophy, understanding that full pursuit of a disciplinary object must lead to a space in which the object itself ceases to exist. Similarly, Derrida coined the word "deconstruction" to name a logic whereby he works at once within and without philosophy. In view of the links argued here between the notions of embeddedness and enculturation, it is worth noting that Derrida sees his philosophic project as, in part, a critique of ethnocentrism, and that his own early work was informed by a growing awareness of languages, like Chinese, the unity of which is not spoken but written.

3. Melville J. Herskovits, *Man and His Works: The Science of Cultural Anthropology* (New York: Knopf, 1948), 39–42. Note the resonance of this formulation with assertions like Ludwig Wittgenstein's that "the limits of my language are the limits of my world" and with a range of Marxist theories of ideology which see as ideological the misrecognitions consequent upon the "natural" recognitions fostered by the categories of any culture.

4. The seminar found instructive the ideas of a pioneer cross-cultural psychologist/epistemologist, Donald Campbell, who wrote of "the ethnocentrism of disciplines" as "symptoms of tribalism . . . in the internal and external relations of university departments, national scientific organizations, and academic disciplines." Donald T. Campbell, "Ethnocentrism of Disciplines and the Fishscale Model of Omniscience," in Muzafer Sherif and Carolyn W. Sherif, eds., *Interdisciplinary Relationships in the Social Sciences* (Chicago: Aldine, 1969), 328.

5. As Campbell and Naroll have noted, "Freud validly observed that boys in late Hapsburgian Vienna had hostile feelings toward their fathers. Two possible explanations offered themselves—the hostility could be due to the father's role as the disciplinarian, or to the father's role as the mother's lover. . . . Freud chose to emphasize the role of the mother's lover. However, working only with his patient population there was no adequate basis for making the choice." Donald T. Campbell and Raoul Naroll, "The Mutual Methodological Relevance of Anthropology and Psychology," in Francis L. K. Hsu, ed., *Psychological Anthropology*, rev. ed. (Cambridge, Mass.: Schenkman, 1972), 437. Our point here is not that Freud necessarily made the wrong choice, but that he lacked the necessary data to make that choice on empirical grounds. Without data from a society in which the roles of boy's disciplinarian and mother's lover are not confounded, as they were in Vienna, Freud could only make a guess.

It should be noted that the authors of this chapter are divided on the implications of the cross-cultural data for psychoanalytic theory. Characteristically, the literary theorist is less willing to dismiss Freud's insights than the psychologist! The former sees the real impress of anthropological data on psychoanalysis to be the kind of complex and abstract theory that emerged after 1950 in France. Still, we agree that Freud's unawareness of anthropological data is a good example of ethnocentrism. It is also worth noting that some post-Freudian retheorizations of psychoanalysis make the Unconscious a paradigmatically embedded object.

6. The word "seam" is chosen here in part because of its particularly rich implications. On the one hand, it points to a cut that has been healed over and remains visible as such, or a ragged tear within a fabric that has been stitched over but is not part of the whole cloth it binds together. On the other hand, it points toward a geological sense, a place in a rock formation where something has slipped or where "alien" matter has been extruded into the formation. Both images point toward a unity that is essentially marked by rupture and a relation to something other than itself.

7. See chapter 9, "The Impact of Science on Medicine."

8. The course "Gender and the Professions" developed within the program was in fact conceived by a historian. See chapter 10, "Gender and the Professions."

9

The Impact of Science on Medicine

H. RICHARD LEVY

During the second half of the twentieth century, science and technology have had an unprecedented impact on medicine, resulting in the eradication of diseases that were once the scourge of man, and making possible feats of healing undreamed of previously. While these triumphs of Western medical science are widely acknowledged and admired, there is, at the same time, a pervasive sense of the erosion of the patient-doctor relationship. Gaining increasingly refined insights into the mechanisms of ever more diseases, physicians appear to have lost sight of the individual persons who harbor them. This phenomenon is hardly new, having been recognized and deplored repeatedly for more than 100 years.[1] Recently it has, once more, stimulated widespread discussion of the role of the educational process in distorting physicians' values and attitudes, diminishing their concern for patients as unique individuals with problems that may result from complex interactions among biological and non-biological factors.

As professors in the natural sciences, what and how we teach our students helps to shape future physicians. If we have participated in making possible the triumphs of medicine, we have also contributed to the disillusion that surrounds its very core—the encounter between patient and doctor. It is our task, therefore, to search for ways in which the educational process may help to resolve this paradox.

Much has already been written on this subject. The Association of American Medical Colleges recently issued the *GPEP Report* that provides a number of conclusions and recommendations regarding the education of physicians.[2] One is that physicians' undergraduate education must encompass broad study in the humanities and in the social as well as the natural sciences. Colleges have stressed this need for some time, encouraging or requiring those pre-medical students whose curriculum is heavily science-oriented to supplement it with a substantial number of courses in the humanities and social sciences. In another approach to broadening the education of physicians,

Thomas Eakins, *The Gross Clinic,* 1875. Oil on canvas, 96″x 89″. Photograph courtesy of the Jefferson Medical College of Thomas Jefferson University, Philadelphia, Pa.

many medical schools now include humanities electives in their programs.[3] Locally, the Syracuse Consortium for the Cultural Foundations of Medicine, a cooperative program of LeMoyne College, Syracuse University, and the State University of New York Health Science Center at Syracuse, sponsors a variety of courses and seminars and facilitates research in the medical humanities.

A paradoxically complementary conclusion is that medicine is not scientific enough. This argument, far from denying the importance of humanism in medicine, or from failing to recognize its absence in many of today's physicians, deplores the narrow purview of science as currently conceived, excluding its applicability to the human domain. The fact that the clinical encounter constitutes personal involvement of physician and patient does not place it outside the realm of science, but merely excludes it from a classical view of science, one that has been extraordinarily successful, to be sure, but that has had to be expanded in the twentieth century. In this view, training our doctors to be scientific physicians—allowing for a contemporary and more encompassing view of what consitutes "scientific"—would help dispel the dichotomy between science and humanism as it applies to the interaction between physicians and patients.[4]

Worthy and important as these approaches are, each is likely to achieve only limited success. In college, pre-medical students are typically and single-mindedly oriented toward gaining admission to medical school, and therefore regard the "broadening" courses as irrelevant to their goal.[5] In medical school, the pressures of the scientific and clinical curriculum generally preclude the reflection necessary for humanities courses to have their desired effect.

A key conclusion of the *GPEP Report* is that one purpose of physicians' education is to enable students to acquire "values and attitudes that promote caring and concern for the individual and for society."[6] Specific recommendations on how this can be achieved focus on the role of the medical school. It is clear, however, that an individual's values and attitudes are shaped from early childhood on. Indeed, the *GPEP Report* states in a section on "Emerging Perspectives": "Medical education must enhance understanding, kindness, empathy, integrity, intellectual curiosity, and humaneness. *The student must possess these qualities before entering medical school*" (my italics).[7] During their undergraduate education, students are exposed to numerous experiences that mold their values and attitudes, including formal course work and interactions with their peers and professors. Their participation in a course that promotes caring and concern and engenders reflection about complex and paradoxical issues pertinent to contemporary medicine is likely to be particularly fruitful at this period in their lives, and affords an additional approach toward broadening future physicians that should complement those strategies currently in use.

I have developed a course, "The Impact of Science on Medicine," that attempts to do this. Directed primarily toward pre-medical honors students in their junior and senior years, it currently addresses the following topics:

1. A historical perspective of medicine, placing past medical practices and thinking in the intellectual, cultural, and scientific context of the time. The focus is not on the history of medicine, but on the constancy of medical problems and physicians' goals in the face of changing scientific concepts and technological innovations. An important aim of this section is to provide a perspective that will enable students to view contemporary thinking and practices in a context that reflects today's cultural forces, dominated by science and technology, and as part of a continuum rather than as ultimate solutions of perennial medical problems.

2. The impact of scientific and technological advances on the development of clinical science, the practice of medicine, and the physician-patient relationship. The influence of basic research on medical treatment and thinking is illustrated by several examples, from James Lind's experiments on scurvy in the eighteenth century to recent studies on sickle cell anemia—a "molecular disease." Also examined is the evolution of the scientific method and its influence on the development of clinical science. Technological advances, such as the stethoscope, the x-ray machine, and the chemical analysis of body fluids are discussed, emphasizing the fact that their application had effects far beyond the enhancement of physicians' diagnostic acuity. This section also includes an examination of science and technology gone tragically awry through an in-depth analysis of the long-term effects of diethylstilbestrol (DES) ingestion on pregnant women and their children exposed to this drug *in utero*.

3. The relationship between science and medicine as disciplines and professions, and an examination of the similarities and differences in their aims and methods. Given that contemporary medicine uses "scientific methods," does that make it a science? What is "scientific thinking" and when do physicians apply it? What is meant by "the art of medicine?" Do physicians employ different modes of

thinking when they make a clinical diagnosis and when they interact with a patient at the bedside? Examination of these questions helps to illuminate the tensions that permeate medicine today.

4. The prevailing model of Western medicine, the biomedical model, and other models, particularly the biopsychosocial model.[8] This section, which provides a summary of many ideas encountered in the other sections, focuses on the problematic relationship between medicine and science as commonly perceived. The biomedical model rests on the assumption that diseases are the manifestation of one or more biological abnormalities in the patient. Spectacular advances in the application of biochemistry and related disciplines to medicine have led to the success of this reductionist approach to the diagnosis and treatment of many diseases. The biopsychosocial model, emphasizing the complexity of human beings and the multitude of interactions among the various levels of their being that comprise this complexity, postulates that persons may be ill because of malfunctions at any one of these levels or of the interactions among them. It seeks scientific understanding of the person who feels ill, whereas the biomedical model searches for scientific explanations of the disease he might harbor.[9]

This course has several aims and goals. First, it serves as a bridge between the humanities and social sciences on the one hand and the natural sciences on the other, by virtue of its perceived relevance to medicine. That is, topics from the humanities and social sciences that are discussed bear directly on scientific and medical issues, thus helping to quicken student interest. Second, it provides a reflective pause in the midst of these students' science-oriented curriculum, enabling them to examine viewpoints, attitudes, and ideas at a point in their education when they have more time and inclination for reflection than they will have in medical school. Third, it sensitizes them to human values in their approach to medicine. Because they have had considerable exposure to science and know that contemporary medicine is heavily based on science, their discovery that the effects of science and technology on medicine have not been uniformly beneficial has a strong impact on them. Fourth, it provides a historical perspective, described in the course outline above, helping to liberate future physicians from the temporal and cultural blinders that we all acquire naturally as individuals and that physicians develop unconsciously as they become enculturated within their profession. It is my hope that in this way they may be helped to develop empathy, a quality that we deem to be especially important in a caring physician.

Two recurrent themes that have engaged the faculty seminar —objectivity[10] and embeddedness[11]—have also been featured in this course. One of the transformations that medicine underwent in the seventeenth and eighteenth centuries was the increasing reliance placed by physicians on objective observations of their patients, at the expense of patients' subjective descriptions of their symptoms.[12] This trend was furthered by the availability of an increasing array of instruments and techniques, from the stethoscope in the early eighteenth century, to CAT scanners and NMR [Nuclear Magnetic Resonance] imaging in the late twentieth. Increasingly, physicians relied on "objective" numbers, furnished by sophisticated analyses of bodily tissues and fluids, for their diagnoses. This shift of focus in the clinical encounter, in the context of the triumphs of scientific research on the mechanisms of diseases, emphasized the value of objectivity in medicine. But diagnosis and treatment of the patient inevitably call into play physicians' judgment of all available information on their patients. Not all of this can be derived from the numbers provided by instruments—no matter how sophisticated—but must include the physicians' observations of, and engagement with, the patient. The exclusion of such interaction from the realm of objectivity has been sharply criticized.[13]

"The Impact of Science on Medicine" is also constantly involved with embeddedness. By examining the relationship between science and medicine, students necessarily view medicine's embeddedness in the surrounding culture that validates its aims and practices. This should enable them to become aware of the enculturating effects of the profession they are about to enter, and thus sensitize them to the constraints these effects could place on their effectiveness as physicians.

This course is not concerned with transmitting facts so much as stimulating reflection. The manner in which the material is presented, and the way in which students are evaluated, must be compatible with the goals of the course. Students are expected to read extensively—four books and thirty-five articles the first time the course was offered—and to come to class prepared to engage in a probing discussion about these readings. They are encouraged to bring issues from widely divergent disciplines and experiences to bear on these discussions. They use a variety of formal and informal writing strategies to help them reflect on what they have read and to develop a critical stance toward the issues and assumptions embedded within the disciplines of the sciences and the profession of medicine. The role of the professor as the facilitator for this kind of learning is best discharged not through lecturing, but by encouraging open, searching discussion. It is essential, therefore, that the professor be an active participant, willing to share reflections, experiences, and uncertainty, and to encourage the expression of widely diverse views and opinions. It is equally essential that the evaluation of students be based not on their mastery of facts and concepts, but on the broadening of their outlook and their sensitization to some of the dilemmas of contemporary medicine.

How does this course fit into the project at Syracuse, with its general aim of addressing the interface between professional and liberal education? Most pre-medical students at Syracuse are matriculated in the College of Arts and Sciences, and are therefore presumed to be receiving a liberal education. The curriculum and orientation of these students, however, generally resembles those of students in the professional schools. For example, a biology major at Syracuse typically takes a minimum of seventy-three credits (out of a total of 120 required for graduation) in the sciences and mathematics. These are supplemented by a minimum of twelve credits each in the humanities and the social sciences, to help the students gain a liberal education. In general, however, there is little connection between these courses and their science courses. Furthermore, none of these courses, or any of their science courses, is likely to engender reflection about medicine, or to raise many of those issues discussed in "The Impact of Science on Medicine." Clearly, this course does address the interface between professional and liberal education, and, like some of the other new courses, it invites us to reconsider the "liberal" nature of some of the curricula within the College of Arts and Sciences.

Although the course is directed primarily toward pre-medical honors students, it should be of interest to others. One of the students who took it the first time it was offered was a biology major planning to do graduate work in biochemistry, and she found it highly relevant. I hope in the future students from journalism, public affairs, or other disciplines will participate in the course. Class discussions would be enhanced by the contributions of students with widely diverse backgrounds and viewpoints.

The development of this course and the articulation of its aims did not, of course, arise full-blown at the beginning, but involved much stumbling, uncertainty, and revision—processes that are still going on and will continue. While I was teaching it for the first time, many aspects of the course concerned me greatly. First, the format of the course caused me continual apprehension. Accustomed—through many years of teaching courses on biochemistry and enzymology—to organizing, dispensing, and explaining a large body of facts about which I had considerable expertise, I had great misgivings about how to deal with material that I myself was just beginning to discover, and that was largely comprised of ideas and opinions, subject to varying and contradictory interpretations. How would I retain control of the class? What would happen if the discussion faltered and I had no ideas for its revival? What would happen if I were unable to answer students' questions?

While these fears were legitimate, the openness of the format proved to be a positive feature of the course. The discussion was always lively and never in need of artificial resuscitation. The evaluation of the course by one of the students included this comment: "We leave class having discovered something new—with Dr. Levy as the *guide*, not the informer." This was especially satisfying to me as it confirmed that my approach was on target.

Second, I was apprehensive about the use of various writing strategies, suggested by the writing consultants.[14] Students wrote four short papers and one long one. They prepared and circulated drafts to all the participants and then revised in accordance with comments from me, the English instructor, and the other students. Brief in-class writing was used to formulate and sharpen ideas prior to or during discussion. Students maintained informal journals, in which they wrote responses to their readings and any ideas that developed from these or from our class discussions. They took turns at preparing summaries of our class discussions and distributed them at the next class meeting. In this way we developed an ongoing outline of what transpired during the course. Most of these strategies were new to me. I was not comfortable, at first, evaluating them because it required much more subjectivity than I use in my other courses. This work became easier, however, as the semester progressed and as I became increasingly aware of what I was trying to evaluate.

Another concern related to the perception of the course in medical schools. This was fueled by a faculty member—one of the pre-medical advisors—who believed that the word "medicine" in the course title would arouse suspicion or antagonism in the minds of physicians and admissions officers examining an applicant's transcript, and who was not inclined, therefore, to recommend the course to pre-medical students. Discussions with an admissions officer at the local medical school, however, quickly dispelled this concern. Moreover, correspondence with several distinguished medical educators, to whom I sent course descriptions at the end of the semester, suggested that the course would be regarded favorably by medical school faculty.[15]

While these developments are encouraging, and while the responses of those students who took the course were positive, it is too early to say whether the course can achieve its intended aims. Clearly, a few students taking a single course will not solve a pervasive dilemma of contemporary medicine. The ultimate worth of the course will depend on the extent to which its students can bring a heightened awareness of the issues confronting contemporary medicine to their future practice as physicians, and also on the degree to which it stimulates other educators to provide different approaches.

Notes

1. George L. Engel, "Physician-Scientists and Scientific Physicians: Resolving the Humanism-Science Dichotomy," *American Journal of Medicine*, 82 (January 1987): 107–11.

2. "Physicians for the Twenty-First Century," Report of the Panel on the General Professional Education of the Physician and College Preparation for Medicine (*GPEP Report*) (Washington, D.C.: Association of American Medical Colleges, 1984). [The full report appears in the *Journal of Medical Education* 59, no. 11 (November 1984, pt. 2.) 1–208.]

3. Eric J. Cassell, *The Place of the Humanities in Medicine* (Hastings-on-Hudson: The Hastings Center, Institute of Society, Ethics and the Life Sciences, 1984).

4. George L. Engel, "Physician-Scientists and Scientific Physicians."

5. This is one of several perceptions that premedical students have regarding their short-term goal (gaining admission to medical school) that militates against their long-term goal (becoming good physicians). One of the recommendations of the *GPEP Report*, to improve communications between medical school and college faculties regarding admissions criteria, should help to correct such misperceptions.

6. *GPEP Report*, 1.

7. *Journal of Medical Education* 59 (November 1984): 67.

8. George L. Engel, "The Need for a New Medical Model: A Challenge for Biomedicine," *Science* 196 (1977): 129–36.

9. Michael A. Schwartz and Osborne Wiggins, "Science, Humanism, and the Nature of Medical Practice: A Phenomenological View," *Perspectives in Biology and Medicine* 28 (1985): 331–61.

10. See chapter 5, "The Concept of Objectivity."

11. See chapter 8, "The Concepts of Embeddedness and Enculturation."

12. Stanley Joel Reiser, *Medicine and the Reign of Technology* (Cambridge: Cambridge University Press, 1978).

13. George L. Engel, "Physician-Scientists and Scientific Physicians."

14. See chapter 13, "Everyone Writes."

15. See the appendix to chapter 18, "Evaluating the Experiment: Micrometers and Elephants."

10

Gender and the Professions

SALLY GREGORY KOHLSTEDT and DELIA C. TEMES

A course entitled "Gender and the Professions" was not on the original agenda of our project. Rather it emerged, tentatively, during the early months of the faculty seminar as we explored basic definitions of professionalization and tried to relate this phenomenon to a liberal arts setting and to the experience of students in professional schools. Fundamental to the very definitions of professions and disciplines are the practices involved in transmitting expertise, providing credentials, and allowing access for new talent (or indeed recruiting the best possible talent). These activities also represent a cluster of values intended to enhance opportunity and self-realization for individuals in a democratic and competitive society. Yet these well articulated goals are often very distant from real-life results—most evidently when sex, race, ethnicity, class, and other social variables are taken into account.

The seminar faculty initially showed considerable discomfort themselves when gender issues were discussed; race issues seldom came up but elicited similar responses. A range of explanations was posited when the group discussed hypothetical situations faced by men and by women in various fields, and yet the group—perhaps because some members thought the topic unimportant and others feared the result—did not push the discussion to real debate. When we experienced such intellectual and personal anxiety and uncertainty, however, sometimes particularly fruitful discussion and innovative planning occurred. In this case, a subset of the seminar held a series of meetings, discussed several options for integrating the gender question into the courses already being planned, and finally settled on constructing a new course.

Two related but distinct concerns emerged immediately in the group discussions. How are men and women represented—in simple statistics and in terms of their images—in various professions, and what does representation mean for the individuals who enter them? Does the fact that some professions (or professional settings)

140

Walter Sanders, *Young Girl Studies Her Image in the Mirrored Section of a Gar-den Wall,* 1942. Photograph. Walter Sanders, Life Magazine © Time Inc. Reprinted by permission.

have more men and others more women mean that the professions themselves are somehow gender-typed, making law, for example, seem more masculine and elementary teaching more feminine? The "Gender and the Professions" course became an extension of seminar discussions, pursuing questions whose substance fitted in intimate ways with some of the other new courses and providing an alternative to others where such issues were not discussed. Questions about expertise and appropriateness revealed that the proposed course was unsettling, even controversial. The historian's experience teaching the history of women and coordinating the Women's Studies Program, however, persuaded her that it was possible—even exciting—to envision a class on this complex and still relatively new (in academia, at least) subject whose texts require discussion, debate, and deliberation.

The course, as it emerged, immediately crossed boundaries between the liberal arts and the professional schools. We intended to probe basic theories of gender, using a variety of methods and subject matter, and at the same time to acquaint students with personal and practical dimensions of professional life. It should be, we believed, neither a women's nor men's studies course. Taught by a historian and a writing specialist with a background in literature, the course relies on methods of analysis typically found in the humanities and the social sciences; students are expected to read literature, reflect on statistical data, and search for philosophical distinctions.

The rich array of content suggests that future faculty could be drawn from other fields and disciplines, and also that they would have to search beyond their ordinary boundaries for texts, data, and interpretation. As in any "Mellonized" course, the prerequisite in the faculty should be a basic expertise, in this case on gender issues, along with a commitment to expand established scholarly interests into neighboring—and even occasionally alien—arenas. "Gender and the Professions" is intended to be handed on to other faculty. No one anticipates that the "second generation" of the new courses can be precisely the same as the first; faculty create courses distinctive to their expertise and interests. The more fundamental question is whether each new faculty member should somehow be initiated into the discussions which so engaged the original faculty and provided them with a fresh content and context. As it happens, "Gender and the Professions" will be taught the second time by two "outsiders." They have had access to all the materials used in the previous course, and one has studied with one of the previous faculty members; yet the new pair of faculty will give the course an independent configuration inevitable without the influence of the Mellon-sponsored faculty seminar.

The initial course focused on professional life, studying systematically the skills and standards designated by leaders in particular fields (medicine, law, education, nursing, and library science), and identifying distinctions, such as the relative balance between experience and education required in different professions. Readings —usually essays from history, sociology, economics, literature, and women's studies—are used to explore the complex, troubling, and pervasive ways in which gender (like other social categories) cuts across professions and is part of their embeddedness in culture. Because the emphasis is on gender (that is, the identification of certain personal, and by inference institutional, characteristics as being either masculine or feminine), readings from women's studies are an essential complement to the many sociological accounts of professionalization based on male experience. There is also limited literature available on men working in female identified fields. Feminist research typically considers both men and women and offers striking, innovative, sometimes conflicting, ways to understand culture. Readings from women's studies and professional literature reveal the complex ways in which women's professional activity is determined by, and yet distinguishable from, that of male models. The self-selection of women into the class and the availability of texts skewed this first course effort toward women, but that imbalance will be redirected as the student constituency and scholarship change in the future.

The goals of "Gender and the Professions" are multiple. They relate to the understood aims of the University, of the Mellon project, and of the professions themselves. Students are to be taught to think critically and analytically about the world of work and the causes and effects of gender stereotyping. Learning to understand themselves as people, recognizing the effect that being male or female has in certain situations, and being able to shape their own responses to stereotypes—such skills equip students for the decisions they will have to make throughout their working and personal lives. Knowing something of gender and other molding influences in the professions enables entering young professionals to chart their possible career courses, their strategies for overcoming obstacles, and their larger commitment to the ideals which frame the future possibilities of their professions. To be effective (as the course "Individual, Social, and Professional Identity" argues[1]), everyone's personal agendas should be set in a social and humanistic understanding of our past and our current situation. Such understanding seems particularly important for those who aspire to leadership, because they are the ones who must be able to comprehend their profession as it exists in a particular time and place, and yet be able to anticipate the effects of new knowledge and new social configurations in a future still undefined. Forward-looking leaders may find alternatives to flawed or outdated institutions in neglected paths of the past, in other cultures, in imaginative projections about human potential, as well as in an appreciation of the complexity of professional life.

The course began with a challenge to students' notions of what is "given" with regard to the professions and to gender. The intention has been to challenge myths and facile understanding about how knowledge and work life are structured. Burton Bledstein's *The Culture of Professionalism*[2] analyzed the nineteenth-century origins of professions in the United States and explained certain motives for establishing the institutions as well as standards and precise boundaries of such professions as medicine and law. In a different but related way, the history of higher education revealed just who could be educated, in what ways, and to what purposes, as professionalization became a fundamental aspect of American culture over the past hundred years.[3] A chronological approach permitted the students to explore how professions exist in culture and what changes have —and have not—occurred. History provided one mechanism (comparative studies of different cultures might provide another) for tracing the cumulative, connected, and contextual pattern of professional development.

Students quickly discovered that the vocabulary and behavior of professionals revealed personal as well as idealistic motives. Thus they could probe some reasons why advocates of professionalization usually value formal education (credentialling) over experience, objectivity over subjectivity, and centralization and homogeneity over diversity; and they often discerned the gender identity (masculinity) in such goals. In ways parallel to our faculty seminar, "Gender and the Professions" was tantalized by evidence that experience, subjectivity, and diversity are regaining attention and credibility in various professions as they move away from their nineteenth-century positivist origins.

The class then studied a number of materials from anthropology and literature intended to examine and clarify fundamental assumptions about sex differences and, relatedly, gender roles. Discussion concentrated not only on the range of behavior of men and women but also on the reasons for, and reactions to, research being done on these subjects. Margaret Mead's *Sex and Temperament in Three Cultures* served as one such important and controversial source.[4] Students read personal accounts of professionals, examined some reasons for the relative "silence" of women, and considered what they might tell of themselves.[5] Language became an important means of discerning how knowledge and behavior shape, in profound ways, what are often dismissed as the work-a-day aspects of professional life.

By the end of the course, students were reading literature on professions today. Using Evelyn Fox Keller's biography of Barbara McClintock, for example, they examined how personality and research experience connected in that biologist's Nobel Prize-winning work on genetics.[6] Using such sources, students reevaluated the claims of objective knowledge[7] and discovered many signs of reaction against both the claims and usage of narrowly defined expertise. From management faculty, for example, came new evidence about the success of collaborative, sensitive, intrusive styles that modified earlier theories regarding authority and control in middle and upper management. The class members read, with healthy skepticism but a sense of genuine inquiry, about the possible "feminization" in professional settings today.[8] They also examined the meaning of such psychosocial constructs as androgyny and gender identity.

As we came to contemporary issues, students were ready to apply their new ways of thinking about the professions and even themselves. "Gender and the Professions" offered juniors and seniors, already well along in their majors, a chance to step outside a well-defined program and return prepared to think more specifically about their future plans. A final project closely tied to their individual professional goals helped make the course material relevant in a personal way. A woman intending to go into sportscasting had striking success writing to a dozen women broadcasters asking them in a brief questionnaire how they had entered the field and what had happened to them as they encountered team players, colleagues in the newsroom, and even fans who believed that men could do the job better. Her respondents showed humor, offered strategies, and gave her the inevitable good advice that hard work combined with a strong sense of identity and clear personal goals were essential for success. After her presentation, the group discussed the strategies

—conformity, resistance, and social change—of men and women confronted with stereotypes, and also gauged the costs and benefits involved in implementing what were risky alternatives. This led us to ponder such fundamental concepts as equity, as well as the political and economic realities operating in contemporary society.

Students in this course wrote almost daily.[9] Equipped with a three-ring binder and looseleaf paper, they maintained reading logs, kept journals, and wrote their reflections at the end of each class. The writing specialist was, throughout, a close collaborator,[10] helping plan the course, making concrete suggestions about writing assignments (including micro-themes and short writing projects in class), and evaluating student work. Because she shared all aspects of the class, knew the content well, was familiar with the individual students, and met with them in planning their major project, she was able to evaluate their written work. Comparing our responses to student texts gave us a unique opportunity to examine and discuss our evaluation techniques and criteria.

Her engagement was evident and stimulated the classroom discussion, particularly when we found ourselves in disagreement and entered debate. Distributing authority, however, was essential. Teaching is a little like driving a car. You have or think you have ultimate control over the vehicle and its occupants. Luckily we had sufficient mutual respect that neither of us ever slipped into the position of "backseat driver," questioning the other's authority or judgment—that would have been unnerving at best, intolerable at worst. Together we designed essay examinations to encourage creative thinking. We asked students to assume roles, to write for a highly specific audience, and to justify arguments. Occasional lectures (by faculty and guests) along with the readings provided a common core of knowledge to expand students' ability to comprehend, challenge, and communicate information and ideas within the course. The achievements of individual students[11] were evident in their more engaged and serious responses to the readings in their log over the course of the semester,[12] an apparently growing commitment to their fellow students in the course, and an improved style and confidence in their writing (and necessarily therefore, in their thinking). Our collaboration seemed to make the classroom more open as well; our mutual enthusiasm and our occasional disagreements encouraged student engagement.

The course developed out of the faculty seminar and gave something back to the seminar by examining an issue which cuts across all our curricula. There were a number of important discussions in which the faculty seminar wrestled with issues of boundary determinations (when is someone inside or outside the circle of knowledge or expertise?) and with the issue of objectivity. From some of our reading in feminist literature came useful ways to deal with the particular as well as the abstract, to see integration and complexity in place of tidy delineations, and to value the "truth" of subjective (intuitive) observations. All of these played, as well, into seminar discussions of embeddedness, objectivity, and ways of knowing.

Like race and ethics, to mention two other important topics, gender has a place in all our courses, whether they are rooted in the professional schools, in liberal arts disciplines, or in new "Mellonized" courses. There should be ways to develop a number of cross-course strategies for addressing such issues. These might include general forums to which a number of classes are invited, debates and collaboration between students housed in rather different professional and disciplinary arenas, and shared resources such as films or major outside speakers.

Studying gender issues reminded those of us in the course that our choices about life and work are made in a context which does not always equitably encourage options. Fortunately our sources and classroom discussion also revealed strategies by which individuals and communities have expanded opportunities and maximized talents to their mutual advantage.

Notes

1. See chapter 6, "Individual, Social, and Professional Identity."

2. Burton Bledstein, *The Culture of Professionalism: The Middle Class and the Development of Higher Education in America* (New York: W. W. Norton, 1978).

3. Among the readings assigned were selected essays from Sharon Lee Rich and Ariel Phillips, eds., *Women's Experience and Education* (Cambridge: Harvard University Press, 1985), and Helen Lefkowitz Horowitz, *Alma Mater: Design and Experience in Women's Colleges from the Nineteenth Century to the 1930s* (New York: Knopf, 1984).

4. Margaret Mead, *Sex and Temperament in Three Societies* (New York: 1929; Quill Paperbacks reprint ed., 1980).

5. A particularly good discussion emerged from reading Tillie Olsen, "Silences in Literature" in *Silences* (New York: Delacorte Press, 1978), and Virginia Woolf, *A Room of One's Own* (London: Hogarth Press, 1929; reprint ed., 1984).

6. Evelyn Fox Keller, *A Feeling for the Organism: The Life and Work of Barbara McClintock* (San Francisco: W. J. Freeman, 1983), and her *Reflections on Gender and Science* (New Haven: Yale University Press, 1985).

7. See chapter 5, "The Concept of Objectivity."

8. Elinor Lenz and Barbara Meyerhoff, *The Feminization of America: How Women's Values are Changing Public and Private Lives* (Los Angeles: J. P. Tarcher, 1985).

9. See chapter 13, "Everyone Writes."

10. See chapter 12, "The Varieties of Collaborative Experience."

11. It is difficult to generalize here because the class was small and students showed progress in different ways.

12. For examples, see chapter 13, "Everyone Writes."

On Seeing and Reading

STEPHEN MELVILLE and STEPHEN ZAIMA

Several years ago, when Barbara Kruger was visiting the College of Visual and Performing Arts, she showed a number of examples of her recent work. These were the kind of thing that one easily recognizes as "postmodern"—not abstractions, not even paintings, but highly finished montages of photographic image and text. One might be tempted to attach them to the interest in collage and the relations among material, representation, and fragmentation that seems recurrently to animate and perhaps characterize modern art. But the more direct attachment would be to the ways in which advertising and related activities have appropriated collage; indeed one frequent description of Kruger's work is that it acts to appropriate to art the condition of modern media.

Sitting before these images, most of the audience revealed on their clothing the now-familiar spattered emblems of the modern painter's studio. This kind of work was new to this audience, as was the image of the artist that accompanied it. A year earlier a lecture on photographic appropriations had been met with outright hostility from a number of students, but this time the response was more interested. Someone in the audience asked Kruger how she had come to be making these things, and she said something to the effect that she had been doing a very different kind of work, that it hadn't really satisfied her, and that she had stopped for about a year and done some reading. She mentioned specifically the writings of Jacques Lacan, a French psychoanalyst and a pivotal figure within the tendencies often referred to as "poststructuralist."

Our course was perhaps inevitable from that moment. "Seeing, Reading, and Interpretation" arises from, and responds to, a very specific set of historical circumstances—a particular convergence of activities within the contemporary artworld, with some part of the range of studies currently lumped under the heading "literary theory." This convergence has ramifications which not only weave together our own individual involvements with painting and criticism,

Barbara Kruger, *Your Gaze Hits the Side of My Face*, 1981. Photograph, 60″ x 40″. Photograph courtesy Mary Boone Gallery, N.Y.

but which reach also into traditional art history and into media studies. Engaging with postmodern visual practices, one enters a field that is dispersed and invisible within the official structure of the university; establishing a course capable of addressing the issues raised by this activity demands transgressing departmental boundaries, school limits, and the overarching separation of liberal and professional education.

It is characteristic of the high modernist impulse that it separates mediums from one another in order to preserve and display their particular values and integrities. On this view, the experience of painting should be purely visual or optical; it is a painterly failure for a painting to so constitute itself that it might be appreciated in some other terms—taking on, for example, something approaching the freestanding objectivity of a sculpture. It would be a similar failure for painting to allow itself to become an object no longer of pure vision but of something like reading. Indeed, on the usual account of these things, it is the German writer G. E. Lessing's separation of the visual and the readerly, the spatial and temporal, in his *Laocoon* of 1766 that opened the way to modern art and aesthetics, and put an end to the "confusion" of temporality and visual presence assumed in, for example, traditional allegorical painting. This aesthetic position is not separate from the development of the modern university—whether we think of its emergence in nineteenth-century Germany or its consolidation in twentieth-century America[1] —and it is thus hardly surprising that exploring its rejection in contemporary art cuts across the grain of the institution in which we work.

"Seeing, Reading, and Interpretation" begins by examining the modernist position as it is developed in the writings of Clement Greenberg and others, as it is perhaps exemplified in the American art of the 1950s and 1960s, and as it is at issue in the poetic and critical writings of figures like John Ashbery and Frank O'Hara. In the past two decades much of this position has come under sustained attack in the practice of contemporary artists, many of whom draw upon such media-linked modes as photography and video, and many of whom take an active interest in questions of "readability" or "textuality" in their work. A number of these artists have also taken an active interest in contemporary literary theory insofar as it offers them a way to address their attempt to understand anew their position as artists. For its part, literary theory has an increasing awareness that its critical stance toward received notions of literature and literary study implies a need to reexplore such closely related fields as visual art and its criticism. At the moment it is clear that English and literary theory—psychoanalysis, Continental philosophy, semiotics, and the like—are being "heard" by the artworld; it is a question for us and for our class how far this exchange is reversible.[2]

This situation offers a special opportunity to bring together two quite diverse groups of students—"critical" and "creative," "literary" and "visual," "professional" and "liberal"—and two equally diverse teachers to explore together the limits and interdependencies of the processes we distinguish as seeing and reading. Given the scope and tendency of current artworld practices, we hope to draw in a certain number of students from the S. I. Newhouse School of Public Communications. Within this diversity we can draw out, in new ways, a range of questions that cannot be interestingly asked within the simple confines of any single program.

Photography, to take one central example that recurs throughout the work considered in the course, seems to present both a fundamental challenge to painting and a privileged object for literary theory within the range of the visual arts. Why should this be? What does the emergence of this mode of reproduction often described as "automatic" do to our notions of literal and non-literal representation? Does it, as some have argued, put an end to the project of visual art, or does it harbor resources for its continuation in a different register? Is a photograph an object that demands reading in a way the modernist image either does not or claims not to? Exploring, if not answering, such questions demands a double attention both to what is being made out of photography in contemporary art and to the relatively autonomous investigations enabled by much recent literary thought about the status of representation, literal meaning, and the like.

These explorations open, in turn, beyond themselves into a reexamination of, for example, the ways in which we tell the story of modernism and its ending, overcoming, or continuation: How does postmodern visual practice lead us to see—perhaps to read—Pollock outside the terms of modernism? How far does the photograph repeat or extend the lesson of Duchamp's readymades, and how might it then lead us to think about the institutional context of art that those works seemed to expose? (There is here a more general question that surfaces for us repeatedly: What is "the artworld"? How is one to take this expression of professionalism in comparison to such expressions as "the industry" or "the profession" that are

used by other practices?) The questions opened by the postmodernist orientation to photography can also be turned around to become
questions about the nature of literature: What, for example, is one
to make of Henry James's choice of photographs as the means to illustrate his work, and the subsequent meditation on photography,
writing, and revision that organizes the preface to *The Golden Bowl?*
How might this compare with Blake's interest in the visual preparation of his poems?

Postmodernism and poststructuralism alike claim to represent a
fundamental break with, and radically critical stance toward, the
past, and both demand a deep restructuring of the field of our practices. The range of questions they conjointly open is thus considerable, and the examples given above represent but one possible way
into this thicket. Other works and other angles of entry find other
paths—through considerations of the notion of an image, through a
renewed interest in the duplicities made visible by psychoanalysis,
through feminism, or through consideration of the applicability of
central literary theoretical notions (for example, the proposition that
"all reading is misreading")—to the perhaps very different objects
that are paintings, photographs, performances. (We do talk about
"seeing as," but the notion of "mis-seeing" is likely to strike us as obscure and forced unless we take it to mean "mis-recognition," and
even then it may not strike us with the same force the literary theorist claims for the notion.)

The course can hardly pretend to be any systematic rehearsal
of all this; instead it works through a series of clustered examples
drawn from visual arts, literature, art criticism, and literary theory
(there is no problem here about finding material, only about deciding on what out of all that is available will make it into the course
and what must await another offering). To a high degree, all we can
do with these examples is work to formulate the problems they pose
and the questions they raise in the hope that by so doing we are
working toward a map of the field in which both of us are now required to find ourselves and which outraces the normal terms of individual professional self-understandings. In this sense the airing
and exploration of differences, misunderstandings, and overlaps are
conceived as essential elements in the course dynamic; in the complex overlapping of the two regions of artistic production and literary theory, it is not and cannot be clear in advance that we understand each other—even, and perhaps most essentially, at those
moments in which we use the same words (the classroom is then a

site for the exercise of seeing and reading as well as for thinking about it). As we question and engage each other, we hope the students similarly will come to question the limits of their own orientations, disciplines, and practices. In the long run, we hope that they will come to see what may at first appear to be a marginal moment of "cross-fertilization" as central to, and centrally contestative of, the fields from which they come.

Such a movement between center and margin, inside and outside, has been one of the major concerns of the project at Syracuse, and is perhaps best seen as an aspect of the notion we have discussed as "embeddedness." Modernism, whether in visual art or in literature and its criticism, traded alternately on a radical, idealist identification of seeing and reading (to see a picture was quite simply to read it; to read a lyric was to see the poem) and on their radical disjunction (each art had its own proper medium; "literariness" was neither a desirable nor a justifiable feature of a visual work). The tendencies called postmodernism and poststructuralism jointly reject such collapsing of the problem of seeing and reading and insist instead on the complexity through which these two terms are entangled with one another; our course is a teasing at the threads of relationship—binding and separating—that modernism worked to cover over.

The historical element in this description of the course is unavoidable. There is no abstract problem about seeing and reading for us to address because the object—human vision—is itself essentially historical, social, and cultural. The moment that interests us is one in which pursuing the linguistic embeddedness of vision has come to seem imperative. "Seeing, Reading, and Interpretation" reflects upon a very real and complex crossing of boundaries that is already a part of the world and that can barely be addressed at all within the normal structures of the university; it means to be a step toward an examination of practices that are emerging against the grain of the institutional distinctions that separate Arts and Sciences, Public Communications, and Visual and Performing Arts. How long this site will be open and how much can be done in it are open questions—questions that all of the Mellon courses must welcome to the extent that they are aimed against the mistaking of historical and cultural situations for substantial objects. And this suggests a deep need for alertness to the shifting moments within our culture, and a corresponding openness to a shifting, perhaps somewhat shifty, curriculum—a teaching willing to be uncertain of its ground and take its chances as they are offered.

Stephen Zaima, *Portrait Artist in Front of New York Public Library,* 1986. Photograph.

Notes

1. Literary scholars interested in poststructuralism have increasingly turned their attention to an examination of the relations between modernist aesthetics and the institutionalization of the literary canon and its study under the rubric of "English." See, for example, the introduction and first chapter of Terry Eagleton, *Literary Theory* (Minneapolis: University of Minnesota Press, 1982), or Peter Hohendahl, *The Institution of Criticism* (Ithaca: Cornell University Press, 1982). Similar research has been pursued in France with respect to the disciplining and nascent professionalization of philosophy in the German university. See, for a readily available, if not very well developed, consideration of such matters, Jacques Derrida, "The University in the Eyes of Its Pupil," *Diacritics* 13, no. 3 (Fall 1983).

2. Certainly within the world of literary theory there are those who argue that what is called "theory" is in fact the freeing, for better or worse, of criticism to a suppressed creative and aesthetic potential inherent in it. See for exemplary discussions: Elizabeth Bruss, *Beautiful Theories: The Spectacle of Discourse in Contemporary Criticism* (Baltimore: Johns Hopkins University Press, 1982); Geoffrey Hartman, *Criticism in the Wilderness: The Study of Literature Today* (New Haven: Yale University Press, 1980), chapters 8 and 10 especially; Gregory Ulmer, *Applied Grammatology: Post(e)-pedagogy from Jacques Derrida to Joseph Beuys* (Baltimore: Johns Hopkins University Press, 1985); and Harold Bloom, *The Anxiety of Influence: A Theory of Poetry* (New York: Oxford University Press, 1973).

IV

Learning and Teaching

Preface

PETER T. MARSH

The Syracuse experiment was designed to create courses to make the mutual bearing of the liberal and professional components of the curriculum manifest to undergraduates. The essential task of the faculty seminar was pedagogical. While the seminar devoted more of its energies to its own intellectual enquiry than to "syllabustering"[1] — the discussion of course outlines — it did so in order to learn what to teach. At the same time, individually or in small groups, the members of the seminar set to work devising new courses or reenvisioning existing ones to satisfy the objectives of the project. Aside from devices to encourage writing in the courses, the seminar did not concern itself explicitly with how to teach. After all, the participants had been chosen because of their distinction in teaching as well as scholarship. Yet the presence of twenty faculty with different talents in keeping with their varied fields of study turned the seminar indirectly into an enterprise as much on how as on what to teach. Every faculty member commits himself to a lifetime of learning as well as teaching, but usually in an ever more precisely defined field. Being brought together to learn and teach about the mutual bearing of fields of study transforms teaching as well as learning.

Collaboration is the key to the transformation: always collaborative learning, often collaborative teaching, and sometimes collaborative writing. Most university faculty live solitary professional lives, conducting their individual research or standing alone before groups of students. They are amused at the naiveté of outsiders who remark on how wonderful it must be to participate in the lively exchange of ideas in a university. Politicians and businessmen do their most important work in groups and communicate with each other mainly through discussion. Task forces and committees have much less importance in university life. Scholars communicate with each other mainly at a distance in print, exchanging papers or reading and reviewing each other's books. But the intellectual and pedagogical price paid for this isolation is high. We have only begun to appreciate the enormous rewards that can accrue from collaboration. It is indispensable if universities are to understand and convey an understanding of the bearing of the islands and intervening seas in the world of learning upon each other.

This section opens with "The Varieties of Collaborative Experience," appropriately the most collaborative chapter in the book. Drawn together by Delia Temes who, as part of the team of writing faculty in the project, worked with four courses involving six faculty as well as many guest lecturers, the chapter includes contributions from historian Sally Gregory Kohlstedt and civil engineer Samuel Clemence on their creation of a course in his college, from Gerardine Clark in the School of Drama, and from Marshall Segall in social psychology. In basically narrative sequence, the chapter comments on the stages and extensions of the collaborative activity.

When two faculty work together designing a course, presenting it, and supervising coursework, the students' sense of participation in a community of learning is heightened. The relationship between the faculty members is a demanding one, and it tends to work best where the lines of responsibility are clearly drawn. Where it works well, it leaves a valued impress on the participating faculty that extends beyond the course they teach together.

Collaborative learning among the faculty universalizes that effect, whether they teach in teams or alone. The need for liberal arts and professional college faculty to learn from each other if they are to teach about the relationships among their fields of interest is surely obvious. The dividends of the seminar that we convened for this purpose proved even greater than we initially foresaw. As the participants impressed themselves and their varying perspectives on each other, we found ourselves entering our separate classrooms mindful as never before of those perspectives. We began to think of them in presenting our particular subjects to our students, who responded with quickened attention when the new perspectives we now had in mind coincided with their own interests. Furthermore, though all of us prided ourselves on being good teachers and would not have sought instruction from each other about teaching, we found our inventory of teaching methods and sensitivities greatly enlarged by exposure through the seminar to the different approaches of our colleagues. Faculty seminars are needed to serve yet another purpose. Inevitably, as those who have created courses in the project leave to take up other assignments in their colleges, successors will have to be found to take over. They will not be able to do so well without participating in a seminar that renews, and hence extends, the process of mutual learning described in these pages.

The one set of teaching techniques that we examined directly had a profound impact on every aspect of our enterprise. In chapter 13 Margaret Himley, a professor of composition, describes the methods to encourage "writing across the curriculum" which she and her assistants introduced into the project. This aspect of our enterprise gave rise to the most uniformly successful form of team teaching between liberal arts and professional college faculty in our enterprise.

The final two chapters of this section focus on individual courses in our project. Each has its own story to tell. Those who enter an interdisciplinary and interprofessional enterprise put their individual disciplinary and professional commitments at risk. While they hope that the experience will enhance rather than compromise their loyalty to the field that drew them into the academy in the first place, they still fear enfeebling distraction from, and dilution of, the scholarly activity that continues to inspire their minds. The story that Gary Radke, an art historian, tells with compelling simplicity in chapter 14 should help to allay that fear and encourage the hope. His particular assignment in the project was to redesign the introductory honors course in the humanities, keeping in mind the concerns of students from professional colleges as well as from the arts and sciences. He tells of how this charge, far from debasing the course, instead brought out its humanistic worth. Involvement with professional education can enhance humanism in the humanities! Like any good story, this one leaves us looking for others in the same vein. Could similar tales be unfolded in the other divisions of the arts and sciences?

The courses developed through our project in professional colleges have approached its objectives in a variety of ways. The course entitled "The Conceptual Foundations of Management" adheres closely to the project's original intent in examining the historical and conceptual bases of that profession. "Technology and Its Practitioners" deals at length with the sociohistorical context of engineering. The course in nursing looks at "Images of Healing" conveyed through the fine arts and in the experience of our own and other cultures as well as in the health care professions.

An alternative approach has been adopted for the courses in the S. I. Newhouse School of Public Communications and the College of Visual and Performing Arts, both of which embrace a diverse range of professional interests and are in some ways more closely akin to the liberal arts than is the case, for example, of engineering. Instead of drawing attention directly to the arts and sciences, the courses developed in each of these two schools have sought to accentuate the liberally reflective dimensions of its interests by exploring fundamental issues of common concern to the cognate professions and occupations that its students hope to enter.

Translating these intentions into concrete courses is not easy. It is all very well to talk in approving generalities about relating liberal and professional education. But how do we do so college by college and course by course? In a fine match between subject matter and approach, Gerardine Clark, a professor of drama, helps to answer this question with regard to the visual and performing arts in chapter 15 by describing the process that she went through to develop the course "The Creating Mind." The questions that she helps her students to ask in seeking to understand the creative process—how do you come up with an idea, in this case artistic, and then how do we go about conveying it?—are like the questions that faculty need to raise and respond to in creating courses in other professional contexts. What are the fundamental or intersecting concepts in the profession that the course should explore? How can you engage undergraduates in the exploration? The process of course creation that Clark describes may be demanding but is, as she indicates, still more rewarding.

12

The Varieties of Collaborative Experience

DELIA C. TEMES, SAMUEL P. CLEMENCE,
SALLY GREGORY KOHLSTEDT, GERARDINE CLARK, and
MARSHALL H. SEGALL

That the project would involve collaboration seemed inevitable given its charge of finding ways to integrate professional and liberal learning. We did not imagine, however, the range of collaborative activities that we would be drawn into as a result of participation in the faculty seminar. Collaborative teaching seemed the most obvious and logical way to link professional and liberal learning; but rather than being simply the end product of collaborative activity, the team teaching and "syllabustering"[1] unintentionally set in motion a collaborative learning experience which became so addictive that, reluctant to let go of our new-found resource, we elected to continue it through collaborative writing. Teaching, learning, and writing, the central activities of all professional academics, were not new to any of us at the beginning of the project, but collaboration in each of these areas profoundly changed the way each of us practices our own profession.

Team teaching was among the first attempts at collaboration. A transportation manager and an organization manager from the School of Management designed and taught "Conceptual Foundation of Management," and a historian and a civil engineer created "Technology and Its Practitioners." Though both teams found the teaching experience enriching, they suggest it be approached carefully. The success of the endeavor depends not just on the flexibility of the team members, but on some complementary aspects of their disciplines. The historian and the engineer address in detail both the challenges and the rewards of team teaching:

> Collaborative teaching carries all the challenges, rewards, anxiety, and excitement of dealing with the unanticipated. Probably experienced faculty with a degree of self-confidence and readiness to hear other points of view on a familiar subject matter and to learn

something which may not be of direct relevance to their other work are best equipped to attempt it. The classroom is no place to convert a colleague with a different outlook—although variations in interpretation heighten student attention and sharpen even firmly held opinions. It is tough work to collaborate, but like many kinds of hard work it brings its own rewards.

The more disparate the disciplines of the collaborators, the greater the effort required to adjust perspective. The fact that we knew each other through committee work and chose to design a course together certainly increased the possibilities of a successful project. As it turned out, a historian of American science and a civil engineer have had quite different educational and work experiences, and team teaching required a great deal of effort and understanding to reach a functioning relationship. Yet, in some ways collaboration across college lines may be easier than across the boundaries between neighboring disciplines. Knowing that we had to overcome substantial differences in expertise and in teaching methods, we relaxed our usual expectations to listen closely to each other. We quickly learned that even general comments about whether lectures are appropriate or how to best evaluate students were understood quite differently by each of us. The very distinctions between our usual practices, however, made the team enterprise more intellectually challenging and interesting. While we anticipated learning matters of substance during the semester, we found we also discovered fresh approaches to teaching.

In the first time through the course, we divided responsibilities quite explicitly. The engineer, who had travelled worldwide and had studied and photographed ancient structures from Peru to Egypt, lectured during the early weeks of the course. He used a variety of visual materials—slides, overhead projections, and blackboards full of sketches, words and data—that provided technical as well as cultural explanations about the building of pyramids and mechanical toys in ancient Greece; we established early many of the issues which would recur throughout the course.

The historian basically developed the last half of the course, which looked to the development of the current engineering profession in the context of American scientific and social history. Her tendency was to rely more on discussion and to assign literary and historical texts that revealed and analyzed the deep, but never unambiguous, basis for technology in our culture. Together we tackled issues of ethics in modern industrial engineering and the embeddedness of technology in the political (especially military) and economic aspects of contemporary society.

Our relationship grew as we jointly planned and implemented the course. Developing the goals and content, establishing a list of

Stephen Zaima, *The Brooklyn Bridge,* 1986. Photograph.

readings, discussing how classes were to be conducted—these provided a useful basis for the exchange of viewpoints and an introduction to the other faculty member's discipline, eventually shaping
the joint course. Inevitably, perhaps, the more comprehensive and
open the discussions, the closer the collaboration and the more effective the teaching. Student evaluations indicate that the class sessions in which debate or disagreement between the professors (and
among students) occurred were those most thought-provoking and
remembered.

An essential ingredient of collaboration is the joint participation of the faculty in all the class sessions. The attendance of both
faculty members creates an atmosphere of respect for one another's ideas, and this attitude is conveyed to the students. Given a
spirit of collaboration and clear goals, the individual professors can
speak up about their ideas and, on occasion, challenge assumptions
being acted upon by the other. Having students submit multiple
copies of all assignments, grading them independently, and then
exchanging comments was also helpful in letting each of us see
more clearly the expectations of the other for the course and for
individual students.

Perhaps the most discomforting aspect of teaching in a team is
that the individual members are required to give up some of the
autonomy usually enjoyed in the classroom. How much and what
reading will be assigned? How will presentations and discussion be
balanced? What will be the basis for evaluation and who will make
it? All such questions are negotiable, and the answers often require
compromise. There are ongoing adjustments as well. Students
and faculty must adapt to varying methods of presentation and
changing expectations regarding their participation. The engineer
felt the limitations of time in a course which went from ancient
"techne" to NASA, and worked to "get through all the important
material on a topic." The historian encouraged more discussion on
particular topics, but found it difficult to make those discussions
probing and imaginative with students used to taking notes from
an expert.

In its best moments, the team teaching proved refreshing and
exhilarating, with the edge of "the unexpected," typically encountered the first time through a new course, heightened by having
another "authority" present. Over a longer term, the collaborators
would have to update their portion of the course regularly and find
ways to preserve the excitement of new discoveries with the other
faculty member. We could also do much more to integrate what too
often remained separate halves of the course. Student comments
revealed how much they learned from the occasional difference
in point of view, good-humored challenges, and distinctive ap-

proaches to particular readings or problems in the history of engineering. Knowing that the course was only the first step toward genuine integration of history and engineering, we suspect that collaboration may be one of the few ways to foster connectedness as well as debate on issues which link and differentiate disciplinary and professional fields. We would do it again, having found team teaching rewarding in both professional and personal terms.

In a variant of team teaching, some of our courses used writing consultants to introduce students and faculty to the many ways writing can be a mode of discovery or a tool for learning. Their specific contributions are documented in chapter 13, "Everyone Writes,"[2] as well as in chapters about the individual courses.[3] Initially, the writing consultant's role was to be a resource for writing strategies and assignments that would promote learning and engage students more critically with the course material. While not peripheral to the course, neither were the writing consultants thought of, except as a courtesy, as actual team teachers of the course. What we learned rather quickly, however, was that the role of the writing consultant determined the role of the writing. As long as he or she remained, either literally or figuratively, outside the class, the writing seemed secondary, an afterthought, rather than an integral part of the course. Bringing the consultant into the classroom community made the writing a natural and logical way for students to express their ideas.

Faculty members who had a writing consultant have all written about his or her usefulness and how this changed either the courses they teach or the way they think about and plan those courses. Some now design and use their own writing assignments, while others still prefer to have a consultant work with them, but most agree that writing was one of the most effective teaching and learning strategies to emerge from the entire project. As it turned out, this form of collaboration was in no way one-sided. In the following paragraphs, the writing consultants describe what they learned from the experience:

> The most obviously enriching part of being a writing consultant is that it allows you the luxury of being a student again with all advantages that entails and none of the drawbacks (no exams, no dorms, no LSATs). It was liberating to listen to a guest speaker without taking notes, to watch movies or slides on management or engineering and see relationships to our own fields. In effect, we

were getting paid to learn as well as teach. But our role in the project had a subtler effect on us as well. As writing teachers, we are accustomed to small, student-centered classes where, often, students and their texts are the main content of the course. Students read their papers aloud, discuss in groups what they tried to do in their writing and what they would like to do in future work. But we do not have content for lectures and discussion in the way, for example, a biologist does. Writing can only be taught by doing it. Writing teachers often accept as a given that students write best about what they know best—their own experience. But what the new courses reminded us of is the role reading can and must play in expanding and broadening that experience. We are freshly convinced of the need to assign student writers a range of readings that encourage them to reflect on their own experience and see themselves in broader contexts—readings that serve not simply as models for writing, but as a common source for creating a stimulating classroom environment of issues and ideas. We find ourselves expanding and modifying our own courses in light of that knowledge.

The writing consultant in "Gender and the Professions" now requires students in her technical writing courses to do reading about non-discriminatory language and to investigate the problem of what being a professional means in their chosen disciplines. The inductive teaching method employed in "Conceptual Foundations of Management" inspired a writing consultant to try a new approach in a literature survey course, organizing it around a central question to which she had no answer, hoping that this departure from the traditional historical overview would allow the classroom to become a site of genuine intellectual inquiry. All of us sense other presences in our classrooms now—the personalities and professions of those whose classes we shared.

The varieties of team teaching benefitted students and faculty alike by providing them with a broader perspective of learning and an excitement about the possibilities created by their involvement in a dynamic and open-ended learning process. As we have noted, however, it is not for everyone. Team teaching requires a very strong commitment on the part of all the faculty involved and often a willingness to devote extra time to shaping and reshaping the course as the semester goes on. It is also an expensive alternative to traditional classroom instruction, particularly when the team-taught classes have small enrollments.

As we discussed the role of team teaching, it became dramatically clear that another sort of collaboration was occurring within the

faculty seminar. Those not involved in team teaching were also finding themselves changing or modifying their courses as they looked
upon their subject through new eyes—the eyes of a historian or an
engineer or an artist. As we shared viewpoints in the seminar or
argued over interpretations of the reading, we were ourselves engaging in the kind of learning and thinking process we hoped to
provide for students. The seminar was becoming a collaborative
learning experience that was shaping both the courses and the philosophy of the project. It was a forum for intellectual and pedagogical issues, opening new ways of seeing within and between
disciplines.

It was the literary theorist who gave voice to what was happen-
ing to us. Accustomed to teaching alone within his department, he
said it was sometimes difficult to determine why he did what he did.
But the faculty seminar provided him with insights and interpretations from other disciplines, enabling him to see his own material "in
view of" someone else, achieving a team-teaching effect without the
team. While leading an English class in a discussion of a Platonic distinction between the inside and outside of human beings, he now
quite naturally dealt with culturally rooted conceptions of disease,
such as the biomedical model that is critically considered in the
course for pre-medical students.[4] He would often quite spontaneously find himself wondering how an actor or a journalist might respond to something he was teaching, a reflection that shaped and
sometimes transformed his teaching in a very natural way.

The faculty seminar became a collaborative learning resource
that enabled all of us to share our classrooms with our colleagues.
Sometimes we did this literally by inviting them as guest speakers,
but more often we included each other as ghosts, unseen by our students, but almost palpable to us. We began to refer to this broadening of perspective as "Mellonization."[5] As we taught "in view of"
one another, we became ourselves the means of integrating professional and liberal education. Teaching in each other's view is like
travelling to a foreign country—upon our return, the familiar is
subtly changed; we have gained, through absence, a distance from,
or perspective on, our own discipline that enables us to see things
differently. The drama professor summarizes this in the following
paragraph:

> Guided by our colleagues through representative readings in
> each field, we have come to understand the particular nature of

their attention to the world, the specific criteria which inform their vision, and to enter empathetically into that vision. While the experiment is far from complete, we can to a greater degree read history with a historian's eye, view medicine with a biologist's eye, judge business with a managerial eye. This does not suggest that we have abandoned the acuity of perception particular to our own disciplines when that is required; but the evidence of our continuing discussions suggests that an altered perspective has begun to inform the courses to good effect, especially when addressing students from various disciplines.

The collaborative learning experience gave all of us, team teachers and soloists alike, a richer teaching perspective tempered and shaped by the visions of our colleagues. We came to rely on the seminar group as both source and resource, and it propelled us into still further forms of collaboration, including writing.[6] No chapter here is the product of a single author. Each has been written and rewritten "in view of" the seminar, making this book perhaps our most exhaustively collaborative effort.

The social psychologist sums up the effect of these varieties of collaborative experience as follows:

> To any colleague at Syracuse who enquires about what we in the Mellon project have been doing during the past two years, I now routinely reply, "We've been learning how to teach."
>
> Usually, this elicits lowered eyebrows, cocked heads, and pursed lips—all of these nonverbal cues meant, I'm sure, to signify, "You've got to be kidding!" Even though university teaching is one of the few professions for which no training is prescribed (or perhaps because of this), most of us university teachers know that we know how to do it, once we have done it. We may be aware that not all of us do it the same way. We may even acknowledge that, by some criteria, some of us are better at it than others. But those minor variations aside, that we do it regularly must prove we know how—just as is the case, for example, with sex.
>
> In these respects, university teaching is also rather like parenting. Most who did it were never formally instructed. And a need for such instruction was never widely felt. But it isn't hard to make the case that training in parenting (or training in sexual practices, for that matter) and training in teaching would have improved life mightily for much of humankind, including all the ill-parented children, all the unfulfilled lovers, and the waves of undergraduates who leave our universities little different from when they entered them.

And there is, of course, the ultimate irony that those who are most confident that they have no need to acquire skills are often those who need them the most. Would it not be well, then, for university teachers who are rather sure of themselves as teachers to be confronted with some good reason to suspect that there is more to good teaching than their own habitual practices affirm?

This kind of confrontation occurred consistently in the seminar. There we were, some twenty teachers (presumably selected to participate because we had each established a track record as good teachers), meeting regularly over an extended period of time, grappling with a variety of conceptual problems, reading and writing, defining goals, planning courses, struggling to detect and understand certain overarching, rather abstract concepts relating to professionalism, to the liberal arts, and, more generally, to higher education. We never explicitly addressed the question "How do I become a better teacher?" Yet, in retrospect, that is what many of us in the seminar saw it to be mostly about.

Moreover, making us all better teachers than we were two years ago, while clearly not the seminar's stated objective, may well have been its most profound achievement. I know that I could be a much better teacher than I ever have been. I now view my steady stream of positive student evaluations, collected over twenty years, with skepticism. I interpret the applause that sometimes has come from students as dangerously misleading. While it may tell me that I am a good performer, whose audiences enjoy the course (they do say, "I really enjoyed this course!"), it does not tell me that many of my students have learned what I wished them to learn. The stark fact that only a few of my students in any semester have ever displayed evidence that they had learned most of what I wanted them to learn, while the vast majority of them provided distinct evidence to the contrary, now means to me that I have repeatedly, semester after semester, failed. I may well have taught much to the students who needed my help the least (those who would have learned whether I was there or not), but I doubt that I have done much for those who really needed me. I think, for example, of all those students who earned Cs and Ds on the first exam, then again on the second one, and once again on the final. Apparently, I did little—perhaps even nothing—for them.

In the seminar we all had our firmly planted, habitual ways of teaching challenged. None of us now is as sure of ourselves as teachers as when we began. We haven't yet become the teachers we wish to be, but we now know that. That awareness is itself an important achievement, one that is probably rare on any campus. And we know, too, what we need to try to do in order to become better, which is probably even rarer.

How has the seminar made us more concerned with how we teach? Ironically, not by conducting itself as a workshop on teaching. Rather, it enabled twenty "good teachers" from a variety of backgrounds, with a variety of specialties and a mix of expertise, technique, style, and personality, to interact on a long-term continuing basis over matters of genuine intellectual substance. And those matters of substance were then linked to problems of course design, so that inevitably, issues of how to teach were always there—just under the surface or sometimes right on the table. We would each begin with an idea of what we wished to achieve, and we each had a preferred way to try to achieve it. But we all had ideas about what ought to be the goal; we also all had different ideas about methods and means. Each of us thus had ample opportunity to see our goals questioned, affirmed, or reshaped by the seminar, and frequent occasion to retailor our methods.

Invariably we would rediscover that the essence of the teaching enterprise is to engage the student. The message was most clearly contained in the view introduced by the writing faculty—and ultimately accepted by most of us—that writing engages by enabling thinking. We saw it, too, in examples from many of the courses as they underwent shaping by the seminar, including techniques of discussion, novel short-term project assignments, presentations of "ancillary" objects (whether paintings, films, or books) to be encountered and reacted to by students, and the introduction of outsiders who could interpose an unexpected viewpoint and force an unanticipated connection. For many of us (it now seems incredible to admit), such features had not been included in our standard teaching practices.

It is perhaps most telling that, as the project neared its end, many of us announced commitments to seek ways to involve more good teachers in the kind of continuing engagement with each other over matters of educational substance that we have been so fortunate to have experienced.

We have learned, taught, and written together, each activity involving us more deeply in boundary crossing and, sometimes, dissolution. The intellectual excitement we experienced as we shared knowledge and arrived—together and separately—at new insights about the relationships between professional and liberal education has been powerful. Far from wishing to withdraw from the process, we are determined to extend it. As the project moves into its next phase, the faces and some of the professions in the faculty seminar will change, but the collaborative process that provided its momentum will remain at the very center of the enterprise.

Notes

1. See p. 21.

2. See also chapter 2, "The Faculty Seminar," 43, n.3.

3. See particularly chapter 6, "Individual, Social, and Professional Identity," chapter 9, "The Impact of Science on Medicine," chapter 10, "Gender and the Professions," and chapter 15, "The Creating Mind."

4. See chapter 9, "The Impact of Science on Medicine."

5. See chapter 2, "The Faculty Seminar: Discourse Communities and Quotation Marks."

6. See chapter 2, "The Faculty Seminar," and chapter 13, "Everyone Writes."

13

Everyone Writes

MARGARET HIMLEY

A quiet change is taking place on college campuses across the country: we are (re)asserting the essential role of writing in liberal and professional education. In the form of reading logs and micro-themes, formal papers that go through multiple drafts, and collaborative projects, writing is being integrated into courses from biology to engineering. Faculty are learning that they can *use writing* in their courses to foster greater intellectual participation and learning, that language use facilitates the process of knowing. In creating text, we discover what we mean. In explaining an idea for a particular audience, we determine connections with other ideas or gaps in our understanding. The intellectual and imaginative activities that constitute writing help us to identify, understand, and appropriate the ideas and interpretive schemes that comprise the fields we study.

In designing courses for the Mellon project we decided early on that we wanted to use writing to engage students more actively, more reflectively in a critical examination of the intellectual concepts, implications, and questions that inform their professions. The particular model that we developed for the project links writing faculty with a new course the first time that it is taught. In this way the writing faculty are right there to demonstrate in concrete, course-specific ways the benefits as well as the pitfalls of using writing in these ways.

Writing "Re-viewed"

A Miss Dowling may still lurk in the far reaches of many of our memories about English classes: the prim schoolmarm wielding a red pen with merciless precision, slashing her way across the page, bloodying the text and leaving a trail of "awks" and "CSs" in her wake. This reign of error has characterized many approaches to writing instruction in the past. It was assumed that student writers knew what they wanted to say and that learning to write was merely a matter of translating or packaging those thoughts into correct, conventional form. The English teacher's task was to detect the dangling modifiers or misspelled words and work hard to eliminate them. It is no wonder that when I tell people I teach composition, they act as though they expect me to turn into a red pencil at their first grammatical faux pas.

This instructional paradigm emerged from a nineteenth-century rhetorical theory that complemented the aspirations of upward social mobility of the emerging middle class after the Civil War.[1] The number of colleges grew as more and more students enrolled to acquire skills necessary for their entrance into an expanding economy. And this notion of what "college" meant profoundly influenced the teaching of writing; the ability to write effectively then (as now) was considered essential to students' economic success. In the late 1800s Harvard made the composition class the sole course required of all students in a generally elective curriculum. Serving the professional ambitions of the middle class, typically these composition classes were devoted to matters of style and form, usage and grammar, with little or no attention given to matters of invention (the discovery of ideas during the composing process) or audience or context. The classes presented writing as the static process of formatting the already-known into the already-given, with as few errors as possible. Like Miss Dowling, "composition teachers became the caretakers of the English tongue, and more important, the gatekeepers on the road to the good things in life, as defined by the professional class."[2]

Until recently, little changed. Relegated to the lower echelons, taught by teaching assistants or perhaps junior faculty, and embedded in a nineteenth-century rhetorical theory that emphasized the superficial aspects of writing, composition classes remained for years the ugly stepsister of the English department. But over the last fifteen years a transformation has occurred; the generative role of writing in the process of learning has been reasserted, with happy results for faculty and students alike.

The catchall (and increasingly problematical) phrase for this reviewing of writing is *process*. While traditional rhetorical theory emphasized the style and correctness of the written text or product, the process proponents began investigating the cognitive and social processes whereby people of different ages and abilities and in different contexts go about making choices as they create text.

The pedagogical implications of this shift included instructor involvement with students who are in the various stages of writing, the teaching of strategies for invention and discovery, attention to context (audience and purpose), and an evaluation of text/product based not on arbitrarily selected textual features, but on how well a text "works."[3] The question became not how correct is this text, but how well does it fulfill the writer's semantic and communicative intention, how well does it meet the audience's needs and expectations?

While the field of composition research is abuzz with activity and debate, one premise has achieved early and easy prominence: writing is a mode of learning. Writing serves a heuristic as well as communicative function in our intellectual life.

Hardly a new or startling idea. It is a familiar experience, I imagine, to begin an article for publication and to discover, *only in the process of writing*, the full implications of the original idea or serious problems in the analysis. This commonsense understanding of writing as a mode of learning has been probed and prodded a bit by language theorists, as they have endeavored to demonstrate the potentially useful role that writing can play in classrooms. This case for writing does not preclude the great intellectual usefulness of talk, of course, although the cognitive and pedagogical functions of written and spoken language may differ, given the different contexts in which they typically occur. Talk, for example, tends to provide a rapid, shifting give-and-take, while writing tends to support a sustained meditation and an elaborated text.

Why Use Writing?

What specifically might the role of writing be in the process of learning?[4] The permanence of the written text may enhance learning by providing feedback. As our thoughts and images become more immediately accessible to us in permanent, or graphic, form, we can rescan and reformulate them. The strong version of this theory contends that it is the very permanence of written text that led, historically, to new intellectual operations and promoted more abstract conceptualizations, analytical thinking, logic, and categorization systems.[5] More recently, cognitive psychologists have worked to establish more specific (and less grand) claims about the connection between literacy practices and cognitive abilities.[6]

A less arguable claim is that writing involves making connections, taking often compact and highly predicated "thought" and transforming it into fully deployed written text, with full sentences, paragraphs, and so on. And making connections is fundamental to the process of learning; we don't just store up bits and pieces of information—we actively establish patterns and connections.

Not a simple translation process, however; to use language is actually to create meaning. "We don't have ideas that we put into words; we don't think of what we want to say and then write. In composing, we make meanings."[7] In a rapid free-write, a text may call forth a far-reaching range of thoughts, and in the process generate new connections and possibilities. Or a formal, fully elaborated text may make conceptual relationships more explicit, more systematic, and hence more available for further reflection, discussion, and modification. And language is not a neutral, ideologically free medium. As Bakhtin notes, it is populated—even overpopulated—with the expressive and semantic intentions of others, and when we create text, we enter into a dialogue with meanings that have preceded us, with understandings that we can't fully anticipate. In the gaps between what we mean and what we say, new understandings may emerge.[8]

Typically when we write, we distance ourselves psychologically from the demands of the immediate situation to some degree, and this distancing may allow for a slower, more mediated thinking process.[9] Many kinds of writing foster, and depend upon, this "deliberate structuring of the web of meaning," a structuring that takes place in a kind of solitude and that depends on the text itself to some degree (rather than the ebb and flow of conversation, for example) for its development. To write in many contexts is to be able to engage in this deliberate, detailed, and developed line of inquiry.

Lastly, in producing a text, even a short written closure statement at the end of a lecture, writers take a stance and locate themselves in the ongoing dialogue. When they write, they become personally engaged with the material in that they make choices—they select, connect, pattern, invest—that help them to appropriate and own the ideas. If in the middle of an animated class discussion, students are asked to write short, perhaps speculative, texts for a class magazine, they each have to "own" a piece of that discourse in particular ways.

The premise that writing is a mode of learning informs how— *and more importantly why*—we decided to incorporate writing into the new courses we were designing in our project.

Faculty response to this premise at the outset was generally (and vaguely) positive—the nodding agreement that typically occurs when academics lament the ways Johnny and Jane can't write—and all agree that we should "do something." Realistically, too, there were hesitations and questions. They voiced concern about having to become "English teachers," about losing valuable class time, about giving up too much content, about having another faculty member in the class with them, about their own lack of experience in working with students on their writing. At this point, too, the faculty members in our project did not share a working definition of "writing," with some faculty envisioning writing instruction as consisting of self-expressive, free-flowing journals, and with others expecting to focus on literacy as style and usage.

The problem, then, was to find ways to ease the faculty into a more comfortable sense of competence about the possibilities of using writing in their classes, and into a more process-oriented notion of writing instruction.

The Mellon Menu

To familiarize the seminar members with the use of writing in their courses, the writing faculty compiled a list of writing assignments. The list was designed to expand the idea of "writing" beyond the term paper and formal essay, and to illustrate the many varied kinds of writing students might be asked to do. We dubbed this list "The Mellon Menu," laying out a smorgasbord of possible writing tasks, from informal free writing to major term papers (Table 3).

Like a Japanese flower that opens up into a rich display of colors and shapes when placed in water, the idea of writing as learning, when placed in the classroom, opens up and encourages us to reconceptualize and expand the kinds of writing assignments we make, as well as the ways we respond to student texts.

To demonstrate writing as a process of intellectual discovery and not just as a semi-annual skill called into creaky service for term papers, we have suggested that the faculty responsible for the subject matter of a course might ask the writing faculty member to present *invention heuristics*, prewriting activities designed to loosen writers' pens and minds. Through brainstorming or free writing, students record as quickly as possible all the ideas, associations, and connec-

Table 3

The Mellon Menu[10]

I. *Appetizers: Pre-writing and Composing Strategies*
A. Invention Heuristics: Exercises that aid students in discovering and generating ideas.
B. Reading Logs: Journals in which students respond to the material they are reading in class and "talk" with the teacher at the same time.
C. Focused/Unfocused Free Writing: Rapid, nonstop, ungraded writing, often focused on a question or issue or term.
D. Closure Statements: A summary of a class discussion or lecture, an identification of the key point, a final question (jotted down perhaps on three-by-five-inch index cards).
E. Adopt-a-Persona: A short text in which the student role-plays a particular figure (e.g., speaks as B. F. Skinner).
F. Interpretive Paraphrase: A restatement of a key or difficult passage, often completed collaboratively and shared with a class.

II. *Entrees: Short, Informal Writing Tasks*
A. Micro-themes: Essays so short they could be typed on a five-by-eight-inch card, designed to promote specific cognitive skills, such as summarizing or hypothesizing from data.
B. Class Minutes: Summary of the class lecture or discussion, presented by the recorder at the beginning of the next class.
C. Interviews: An account of a discussion with a real or imagined person.
D. Response Papers: Exploratory texts or "think pieces" in which students react to some aspect of an article or book or lecture.
E. Case Studies. Presentations of individual persons or events.
F. Reviews: Critical assessments of books, articles, or guest lectures.
G. Class Dictionaries: Glossary of key terms in a course, with students producing the definitions and examples.
H. Letters to Authors: Personal responses to the reading in the form of a letter.

III. *Side Orders: Classroom Strategies*
A. Peer Response Groups: three to five students who read and comment on one another's texts.
B. Class Magazines: Short, often speculative student texts that are copied and collated for the entire class.
C. Collaborative Learning Projects: Structured, small group, problem-solving exercises.
D. Conferencing: One-to-one discussions with students about their drafts, ideas, intentions.
E. Oral presentations: Student reports.

Table 3 (*continued*)

    F. Revision Strategies: Procedures for "re-viewing" one's own and others' texts.

IV. *Complete Dinner: Process for Writing Formal Papers and Reports*
    A. Identifying the problem.
    B. Using invention heuristic strategies.
    C. Collaborating with peers.
    D. Forming a tentative thesis.
    E. Conducting research.
    F. Drafting for peer response.
    G. Drafting again . . .

tions a phrase may call forth. Once texts are created, faculty can show students how they can use strategies to begin focusing their ideas. These texts need not be graded nor necessarily even read by the faculty.

Or students might be asked to complete *reading logs* for the articles and books required in the course. In these logs students can not only summarize key information (rather than employ the more passive habit of highlighting key passages), but they can also respond to the reading—raise questions, draw parallels, voice objections, confess confusion. And faculty, by joining in the dialogue, have a chance to focus and direct students' attention, point out possible ideas for fuller treatment in formal papers, suggest other reading, answer questions, and challenge assertions.

The suggestions we placed under the "Appetizer" section of the Menu illustrate the role of writing in speculation and reflection, in generating new ideas, and in responding more actively and critically to reading. The resultant texts are short, informal, usually ungraded, safe, and playful—an experience with writing many students have not had, at least in school. Once students see the possibilities of writing that doesn't immediately turn into a finished product, they may develop a new purpose for writing, a more playful experience with "text."

"Entrees," or short and still relatively informal texts, call forth fuller, more elaborated responses from students. Response papers, or two or three page "think pieces," for example, ask students to take an idea that has come up in class, perhaps, and develop it more explicitly. The texts often are exploratory, testing out ideas and possibilities and voices, and faculty need not grade all of them. Students might revise and submit two or three such texts for grading at the end of the term. We have discovered that students enjoy these short texts more when they are assigned (or allowed to choose) a persona to adopt, a situation to respond to, and a particular purpose to fulfill—that is, when the assignments are rhetorically explicit. These texts can be read by other students, worked on collaboratively, or collated in class magazines. The informality, brevity, and rhetorical specificity of these writing assignments allow students a particularly productive chance to express themselves, develop ideas, and participate in the ongoing dialogue in the course.

We presented our seminar members with ideas about classroom strategies—such as peer revision and collaborative learning tasks—and with ideas about working with students during the process of composing a full-scale final term paper or major project. Obviously we did not expect the faculty to use all the ideas we presented; we hoped they would select and modify those assignments that most complemented the goals and teaching strategies they had in mind for their specific courses.

But seeing the ideas wasn't enough; we also wrote in the seminar.

Everyone Writes

In May 1985, during the three-week faculty seminar, we all read books designated by participants as "key" in some way to the intellectual life of their profession or discipline, among them *Seeing is Forgetting the Name of the Thing One Sees*.[11] The seminar discussion was full of conflicting ideas, too provocative to be brought to closure in the designated time limit.

So everyone wrote. Every faculty member was asked to write a short response to become part of our first "class magazine." No topics were assigned, and each faculty member could identify the content, approach, tone, and purpose that they wanted to accomplish. The "assignment" was due for the next seminar meeting, and the leader promptly had copies run off for everyone.

As with a class, this writing assignment accomplished several purposes: (1) it enabled (or forced?) the participants to follow through in greater detail and development with ideas that may have

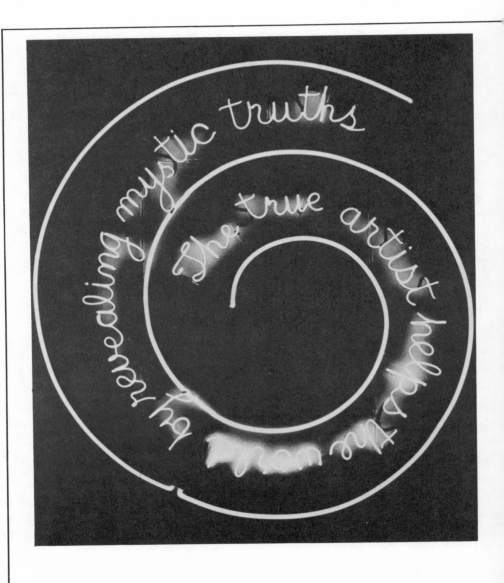

Bruce Nauman, *Window or Wall Sign*, 1967. Blue and peach neon tubing, 59″ x 55″. Photo courtesy of Leo Castelli Gallery, New York.

been strongly felt but were not necessarily fully worked out; (2) it established a sense of community; and (3) it allowed us to read, at our own pace, the ideas, language, voices, and interpretive stances of colleagues from other disciplines and fields.

As with a class, faculty members experienced varying degrees of (dis)comfort with the assignment as they expressed in a questionnaire I asked them to complete the next day. "How did you initially react to the assignment?" The answers varied:

> "With interest and dismay."
> "Liked it. Good opportunity to reflect and restate ideas."
> "Somewhat negatively. As a burden."
> "Negatively, initially, but subsequently very positively."
> "With interest."
> "Oh, no, something else to do! Maybe this will be a way to learn about new writing 'techniques.'"
> "Not well."
> "Positively, I wanted to express my reaction."
> "I thought it was a good idea and would help crystallize the significant points of the discussion for each of us."

Some faculty felt they had expressed themselves fully in the discussion and had no more to say or resented the additional work. Yet others valued the possibility of expressing themselves more fully—and perhaps more forcefully—or of summarizing or bringing to closure what had been a rapid and intense exchange of ideas. They approached the task with different needs and expectations, and then did very different things in their texts, from summarizing to persuading, to raising whole new ideas or connections, to producing a bit of doggerel (from the engineer, no less!).

When asked for their final comments, faculty were generally positive about the intellectual value of the task and about the pedagogical value of actually doing the Menu item themselves:

> "I enjoyed it! I look forward to trying some menu items with students. Obviously this experience is necessary before intelligently using this as a learning tool."
> "The exercise dramatically brought home the value of writing. The exercise really clarified for me the theme(s) of the book."
> "I had said what I had to say during discussion, and had not changed my mind, so the writing did not open up a new space for thought."

"Helpful in sorting out some of my ideas, seeing more clearly where I myself might stand."

"As usual, once I reached the home stretch, I was glad the assignment had been made."

Throughout the seminar, faculty experimented a bit with assignments from the Menu, the terms of this new writing discourse made their way "naturally" into our discussions, and anxiety lessened.

Faculty Collaboration on Writing

When writing faculty are linked to a course the first time it is taught, we have developed four basic roles for them to play:

1. Introduce the other faculty generally to the kinds of writing (the Menu) that can be used in courses to foster greater student engagement and learning.

2. Meet with other faculty in the early stages of course planning (before the semester actually begins) to work out course-specific writing assignments.

3. Do brief in-class presentations on invention heuristics and revision strategies, set up peer editing/response groups, and meet with students early in the semester on a one-to-one basis.

4. Work with other faculty on procedures and criteria for evaluating graded written assignments.

I will describe these four roles in greater detail in this section, with particular attention to the specific benefits and pitfalls we encountered.

Introducing the Menu

Beyond the general introduction of writing as learning in the full faculty seminar, writing faculty began their work with specific courses by reading the proposed syllabus or set of guidelines and making suggestions about the kinds and purposes of writing they might consider.

In "Images of Healing," a course that invites a different guest lecturer to many of its three-hour class sessions, for example, the writing faculty suggested that students write memos or responses to the lecturer during the mid-class break. This system allows the lecturer to respond afterward and answer questions or develop points further—to engage in a fuller dialogue. And it asks students to be more actively involved in the lecture, to draw their own conclusions, to take their own stands, to raise their own points—also to engage in fuller dialogue.

To counter a potential sense of disjointedness that could result from having several different lecturers, students were asked to keep a journal. Faculty and students could then meet and identify themes, concerns, or points of tension threading their way through the various entries; these threads might later be woven into the integrative, critical paper required at the end of the course as the culminating project.

Because this course draws students from all over the University and from all four years, the diversity of interest and ability posed potential problems. We decided that one way writing might address that problem—and indeed take advantage of the diversity—would be to ask students to contribute response papers, or short "think pieces," regularly to a class magazine. When edited and responded to in peer groups selected to reflect this diversity, the class magazine gave each writer the chance not only to express her own perspective, but also to benefit from the reactions of others before submitting the text for class publication and final grading. In forming a community of readers and writers in the classroom, the students can better understand, and enjoy, the diversity among themselves.

As new faculty enter into the Mellon project, we hope that this general introduction to the Menu will be conducted not only by writing faculty, but also by experienced content faculty. We anticipate the possibility of small groups of faculty describing their experiences to each other, or the possibility of a new faculty member sitting in on a discussion between the writing and content faculty about a course, to see in action the nature of the collaboration. We also hope to hold follow-up sessions once a writing faculty member is no longer linked to a course.

Working with Faculty

During our first semester, we discovered altogether too quickly that writing faculty must meet with content faculty during the early stages of course planning in order for writing (and the writing faculty) to be truly integrated. Problems occurred often when the faculty met infrequently, or tried to "catch up with each other" for ten minutes after class. During a lecture, the content faculty might abruptly turn to the writing person with an off-hand request like, "Maybe we need a free-write topic right now?" or a writing assignment hurriedly discussed before class isn't worked out carefully enough and both faculty members get discouraged.

More importantly, early collaboration grants the time and structure for more genuine interdisciplinary give-and-take. Very real discipline boundaries, reflected and revealed in the different ways the faculty members talk about the course, separate the writing and content faculty. To cross those boundaries is, for a time, to apprentice yourself to the other and thereby to lose some power. Under the pressure of actually teaching the course, that mutual apprenticing becomes an unaffordable luxury if it has not been established beforehand. Ironically, this collaboration may have worked in part because a gap in status between the writing and content faculty exists at SU, where most writing faculty are part-timers. The gap may have eased the tensions.

We have found that collaboration succeeds best when both faculty sit down together during the summer—before a syllabus has been pulled together—to talk about the course goals, reading material, and requirements. This is when both faculty members together generate course-specific, sequenced suggestions for writing assignments.

In "Gender and the Professions," for example, the faculty decided to assign (1) summary-response reading logs for key articles and books in the course, (2) a series of micro-themes (essays short enough to be typed on five-by-eight inch cards), (3) a personal journal, (4) class minutes, and (5) a major final project. Due dates for the micro-themes were included in the syllabus, but topics were left open and were worked out specifically as the course proceeded.

Students enjoyed the micro-themes most when they were rhetorically structured—that is, when audience and purpose were defined as part of the assignment, such as: "You are a writer for a major advertising firm. You have been asked to design two written advertisements for a vacation in England, one of which will attract men (*Esquire*) and the other to appeal to women (*Ms.*). You think, however, that two ads are unnecessary. Write a memo to your boss to explain why." Students, it turned out, wrote more cogent, forceful arguments when they were placed in these role-playing situations. Although both faculty read and commented upon all the micro-themes during the term, students revised and submitted only two as part of the final grading process. The micro-theme assignments proved to be beneficial and fun for the students, often providing topics or questions that shaped the final project.

The reading logs turned out to be very time-consuming, and resulted in a small adjustment in the amount of reading that students were assigned. Students found keeping the logs awkward at first. But as the semester progressed, they came to rely upon them more and more during class discussions. Collected and read several times during the semester, the logs also provided faculty with a chance to "talk" to students, to identify themes and questions. Comments written by one student about readings on the topic of male-dominated professions prompted her to look for similarities and differences in her chosen profession, sports broadcasting. Indeed, many of the ideas for the final paper emerged, however nascently, in the log. The logs became resources for the students, records of their own intellectual journey through the course.

There are, obviously, trade-offs. In incorporating the writing assignments, the content faculty found herself with less time to lecture during class. Keeping class minutes meant devoting five minutes at the beginning of each class to them—and then to questions and discussions that resulted. Yet she felt that the trade-off was worthwhile; these writing activities forced students to take more responsibility for their own learning and deepened the role of discussion in the class.

Working with Students

During the first year of our collaboration, we learned that the students saw the writing faculty in the classroom initially as an "aide," someone to help weak writers with their spelling and organizational problems, and they (as "honors" students) didn't seek the writing faculty member out at all. Like most students who have been in traditional composition classes, they perceived writing teachers as final editors or punitive judges, not coaches or collaborators.

To establish a clearer, broader picture of what the writing faculty member actually offers students, we now require a one-on-one conference for each student at the beginning of the course. This meeting allows the faculty member to establish rapport with the students and to talk with them individually about their attitudes and approaches to writing. It is important early in the course to make explicit that a writing conference can be a chance to talk through ideas, to brainstorm on a topic, to have pre-writing activities assigned, to have an early draft read through and commented upon, to share anxiety or alleviate writer's block.

Besides conferencing, the writing faculty is also available to do in-class presentations on: (1) strategies for getting started when writing seems stuck; (2) various formats for organizing information and presenting it to different readers; (3) criteria for an effective oral report; and (4) strategies for rereading and "re-viewing" one's own text in order to improve it in various ways, just to name a few.

Writing faculty are asked also to work with students in setting up peer response groups—groups of students who read and respond to each other's texts without faculty intervention.

Dividing students into pairs or groups of three to five and asking them to read each other's drafts establishes a sense of community in the class; it introduces students (some for the first time) to the effects of an audience on their choices as writers, and results, typically, in more cogent, developed final drafts. Once students learn to trust their peers' responses as authentic and useful, they benefit greatly from this sharing and refining of ideas.

Yet this process of peer response doesn't happen by itself. Faculty need to model it or provide guidelines and questions that call forth text-specific responses and avoid the general "Oh, that's good" comment. Faculty may, for example, discuss the content of a paper with evident respect for the student writer's authority over that paper.

Inevitably, the specific ways the writing faculty could most usefully work with students emerged *during the course*, depending on the abilities of the students, the degree of involvement in writing taken over by the content faculty, and the assertiveness of the writing faculty. Insisting on class time for writing presentations was often the trickiest part of the collaborative process for the writing faculty member, who hesitated at times to intrude or demand time. Here the problems of trade-offs were often most marked, and most touchy.

Developing Evaluative Procedures

All grading in these courses is the responsibility of the content faculty, but they often ask the writing faculty for assistance. In the classes we have worked with, none of which ever had more than fifteen students, we devised two means for collaborating on evaluation.

Dual Reading: In this method, both faculty members read and comment on all written work, with students turning in two copies of each assignment. The faculty then meet and discuss their individual evaluations, although the content faculty is, of course, the final authority and the grader of record.

This procedure has allowed us to overcome, to an extent, the tendency for writing faculty to grade only on expression and the content faculty only on ideas. That split is unproductive and, in fact, quite false. Our experience suggests that when faculty grade the writing as they normally would, both value clear and forceful argument, original responses, and an organization that reflects logical thinking above matters of style, grammar, and editing.

Students benefit from this dual perspective on their writing, and over the semester, in the process of reading each other's evaluative commentary, each faculty member expands his or her own range of responses.

Ranking: An alternative is for students again to submit two copies of each assignment, but this time the faculty not only write comments but also rank order the texts—not so much to tell each of the students where they are placed among their peers as to sensitize the faculty to each other's canons of assessment. The faculty then meet and talk about the reasons for their ordering and for any differences that might have occurred.

Our experience with this method so far has been that over the semester the two readers come to a shared (and enlarged) set of criteria. And discussions about the rankings have been informative in that each faculty member comes to appreciate the disciplined distinctions in their readings.

In both procedures, talking about evaluation has served to strengthen the content faculty member's confidence in his ability to respond in useful ways to student writing without having to become an English teacher—especially of the Miss Dowling variety. As with peer response, a range of faculty response is inevitable and useful to student writers. There is no uniform or "correct" way to respond to student writing that somehow all English teachers (magically) know.

Faculty can help students immeasurably by reading their texts as informed, reactive, challenging, supportive readers.

Results

In the faculty seminar itself, I sense overall a greater ease and familiarity with the language and ideas of writing as process and mode of learning. Most seminar members have acknowledged the potentially useful role of writing in the design and implementation of courses, and have accepted the responsibility of using writing without having to become "writing teachers." And their anxiety about writing has lessened, although I hear echoes of it when, for example, after a particularly energetic discussion, someone jokes, "Oh, I hope we don't have to write a micro-theme now." Journals, microthemes, reading logs, and multiple drafting have proved particularly useful and particularly easy to incorporate into course syllabi. In general, when faculty integrated writing (and writing consultants) into their courses, they reported that it "forced us to pause and reflect, frame our thoughts, and . . . grasp material." One faculty member even attested, "This experience has indeed transformed my way of looking at writing, and it will affect my own work, my relationship with graduate students, and the assignments in my undergraduate classes."

We have been fortunate in our project to have had the chance (the time and the money) to explore in richly collaborative ways what the possibilities are when writing and subject faculty truly work together.

Notes

1. James A. Berlin, *Writing Instruction in Nineteenth-Century American Colleges* (Carbondale: Southern Illinois University Press, 1984).

2. James A. Berlin, *Writing Instruction*, Berlin, 72.

3. See Maxine Hairston, "The Winds of Change: Thomas Kuhn and the Revolution in the Teaching of Writing," *College Composition and Communication* 33 (1982): 76–88 for a fuller account of the process paradigm.

4. See Janet Emig, "Writing as a Mode of Learning," *College Composition and Communication* 28 (May 1977): 122–28.

5. For further elaboration of this, see Jack Goody and Ian Watt, "The Consequences of Literacy," in Jack Goody, ed., *Literacy in Traditional Societies* (New York: Cambridge University Press, 1968); Patricia Greenfield and Jerome Bruner, "Culture and Cognitive Growth," *International Journal of Psychology* 2 (1966): 89–107; David R. Olson, review of *Toward a Literate Society*, John B. Carroll and Jeanne Chall, eds., *Proceedings of the National Academy of Education* 2 (1975): 109–78; and "From Utterance to Text: The Bias of Language in Speech and Writing," *Harvard Educational Review* 47 (1977): 257–81.

6. Sylvia Scribner and Michael Cole, *The Psychology of Literacy* (Cambridge: Harvard University Press, 1981).

7. Ann Berthoff, *The Making of Meaning* (Montclair, N.J.: Boynton/Cook, 1981), 69.

8. Mikhail M. Bakhtin, *The Dialogic Imagination*, Michael Holquist, ed., Caryl Emerson and Michael Holquist, trans. (Suskin: University of Texas Press, 1981).

9. Lev S. Vygotsky, *Thought and Language*, Eugenia Hoffman and Gertrude Vakar, trans. (Cambridge: MIT Press, 1962).

10. For the term "micro-theme" and some of the other strategies here, we are indebted to *Teaching Writing in All Disciplines*, C. Williams Griffin, ed. (San Francisco: Jossey-Bass, 1982), particularly pp. 27–39; and Barbara E. F. Walvoord, *Helping Students Write Well: A Guide for Teachers in All Disciplines* (N.Y.: Modern Language Association, 1982).

11. See chapter 1, "The Syracuse Experiment."

14

The Liberation of the Humanities

GARY M. RADKE

This is the story of how interaction with colleagues from both professional schools and the liberal arts helped a professor in the humanities to come to a better understanding of what might constitute a liberal education.

At the initial meeting of the faculty seminar in January 1985, we gathered around a large table for general introductions. Then we were asked to divide into two groups. Faculty from the liberal arts met with each other in one room, and their colleagues from the professional schools did the same in another. We were asked to consider how we viewed ourselves and our students; we also were told to discuss how we believed that we and the professional schools' faculty viewed each other.

As part of the liberal arts group, I remember quite distinctly how uncomfortable all of us were at making high claims for what we did. But obedient to our charge, we formulated what we thought were some extravagant—and not quite defensible—generalizations of what a liberal arts education was about. We were convinced that our professional colleagues would find many of the claims risible.

When we reconvened, however, the professional faculty seemed very comfortable in assuming that the liberal arts taught students how to think, and that the arts and sciences courses which the professional schools required for their students would generally "liberalize" them. The arts and sciences faculty members were much more reluctant to make such claims. Not only did we have a sense that many of the probing and questioning attitudes of the liberal arts were present in the best professional courses as well, but it is now my hunch that we may already have sensed how professionalized and specialized the liberal arts disciplines had become.

This became more obvious when the seminar undertook three weeks of intensive readings and discussions in May. Burton Bledstein's book, *The Culture of Professionalism*—with its clarification of the origins of professionalism in America and its analysis of how professions defined themselves through, among other things, a common specialized language, systems of credentialing, journals, and generally exclusionary, centripetal activities—aroused in me and my liberal arts colleagues the full realization that we, too, were indeed professionals. We were, after all, professional educators, and we were professionals in our own scholarly fields.

At first I rejoiced. Here was a way to address the concerns of students from the professional schools in my humanities course— insist on the professional status of the practitioners of the liberal arts. We were not the soft, arcane, pie-in-the-sky professors they thought we were. No, we were professionals, just as they hoped to be. High status in America was accorded to professionals, and we were not to be left out. If students wanted more relevance to their courses in the liberal arts, perhaps all that needed to be done was to show them how specialized and rigorous studies in the humanities could be. My own advanced training in the history of Italian medieval and Renaissance art could supply me with plenty of grist for such a mill.

But as I sat down to formulate a syllabus for the general humanities course, the title that I had inherited, "Humanities and Human Understanding," continued to nag at me. There were pretensions to something grander than the professional nature of the humanities in those words. "Human Understanding"—now there was a big topic. And for me at least, it triggered a probe of what the humanities were and what a humanities course might offer. Clearly the title was promising a lot, much of which I thought I might not be able to deliver.

At this point, I suppose that I could have dispensed with the inherited title. It had been invented, after all, when the course was first offered by a member of the religion department, not by a fellow art historian. And yet I was uneasy to let it get away from me. While a course that demonstrated the professional nature of art history might meet some of the goals of our proposed integration of liberal and professional education, it did not really address the liberal component my colleagues in the professional schools assumed that I was offering their students.

Thus, I was forced to confront just what it was that constituted not only my own professional discipline of art history, but the humanities in general. The working definition that I had carried around with me since my undergraduate days seemed of little use here. "The humanities approach," as it was called, was identified with a methodology, and it was basically rooted in the idea of comparative studies of the arts and a search for common threads among the leading arts and ideas of the times. Implicit here was the assumption that the humanities dealt only with high culture and that the masterpieces of the past, and particularly of the West, had intrinsic, enduring value, even outside their original circumstances of creation.

This assumption was a big—and questionable—leap that seminar members from the English department helped me to scrutinize. And it was their interrogation, their insistence on defining questions, not finding bits of information that would neatly coalesce into a presumably accurate portrait of a certain time and place, that triggered my own move to a more critical and theoretical approach for this course.

Liberated for the moment from names, dates, places, and famous works of art and literature (which I still consider important in other ways), I realized that I might be able to use examples from both history and our own time to have students question fundamental issues of human values—something which my colleagues in the professional schools may have assumed I was doing all along, but which was sorely lacking in our usual introductory surveys of the major monuments of art history. There we usually tried to show what people of other times and places thought or believed, and how these beliefs were intimately tied to what kind of art they produced or appreciated; but little or no time was spent asking students to do the same for themselves and their own culture, let alone humanity in general. If connections were to be made, we assumed that students would be bright enough to do this themselves, just as did most of our colleagues in history, literature, philosophy, and religion, whose introductory courses were frequently as "great works" and fact-oriented as our own.

But learning *about* the humanities and experiencing the liberating power of their lessons were two very different things. With that crucial distinction in mind, I began to try to develop a course that would address the latter concern.

"Humanities and Human Understanding," then, was to be redesigned to introduce freshmen and sophomores to some of the major questions and issues rather than the facts of the humanities. It was not an easy task, and I do not presume to have created the definitive course on the subject. But relying on my own expertise as well as striking out into areas that I myself had not explored previously, I felt that the faculty seminar, especially its discussions and pointed questioning of my initial, much less adventurous syllabus, had fortified me for the challenge. My colleagues in the seminar could not tell me how to teach this course or what material to include in it, but they did keep insisting that a humanities course had somehow to get students to think on their own and to get deeply and personally involved with considering the meaning and value of human experience. Here is what resulted.

In general terms, the course is designed to explore how human beings in a variety of places and at various times in history (including our own) have sought to understand human experience and have found or created meaning and values. To this end, the course explores how both the individual and society may be responsible for the creation and maintenance of personal beliefs. So that students can recognize the cultural basis of their own values, the course highlights the extent to which prior experience and societal expectations have always colored the way people view the world. The overall goal of the course is to make students look at their own world more critically and to enlarge that world by becoming more receptive to alternative interpretations of human experience.

"Humanities and Human Understanding" could be taught by a faculty member from the departments of English, foreign and comparative literature, history, Afro-American studies, religion, philosophy, or—as is currently the case—fine arts (art history and musicology). But in order for the course to continue to be successful, the instructor must be committed to considering multiple points of view and exploring general questions, not dispensing facts about any single discipline. The professor in charge must be willing to accept both contemporary and historical expression, be able and willing to lead extensive class discussions (which may account for more than 50 percent of class time), and be skilled at maintaining a sense of purpose and coherence while the specific examples and subject matter are constantly changing.

Some coherence and substance can be created by grounding the course in examples from the instructor's specific specialty within the humanities. In that case, however, it is necessary to remind students repeatedly that this is not specifically an "art course" or a "literature course," but a wider course in the humanities. To make the wider aspects of the course apparent and to emphasize interdisciplinarity, instructors need to stretch their own fields of expertise, and should consider including the participation of guest lecturers from other humanities departments and from professional schools. Material from outside the Western tradition can serve as a useful facilitator for getting students to explore well beyond their usual thoughts and beliefs.

In its present manifestation, the course uses examples from both Western and non-Western art, and from the literature of art history and art criticism to explore the above issues. In no way, however, is it a course in art history or appreciation; neither is it a course in art historical methodology. It is not organized chronologically, and it pays little attention to individual accomplishments in the arts. Rather, it is a course which explores the viewer's perspective on the visual world, and from this point of view it uses art to help students frame questions about meanings and values.

The entire course is based on the contention that the visual arts and the various other disciplines that are usually described as the humanities do not reside outside of, and distinct from, "everyday" experience, but are as tangled in it as are we ourselves. Thus, topics embrace such issues as how and why controversy arose over the erection of the Vietnam Veteran's Memorial in Washington, or the notion of seeing and being seen in traditional Hindu culture, or how economic factors influenced the character of paintings in fifteenth-century Florence, or to what extent the questions we often apply to works of art might need to be revised in light of the work of nine-teenth-century women photographers. A fair number of topics make particular use of unique materials available in the university's archives, art collections, and Belfer Audio Archive.

This course requires students to think about what they see around them and to examine the value systems that condition their responses. For example, they are challenged by radical works of modern art to consider the processes by which people often define art as something removed from, rather than intimately linked to, other realms of experience. They also explore the role and position of the professional artist in society. In addition, students are pur-posefully exposed to works of non-Western art that disturb and up-set their conventional ways of thinking about representations of the human figure so that they can examine the conditioned relation-ships that exist between what they believe and what they believe they see.

Unlike a traditional course in art history, "Humanities and Hu-man Understanding" does not remain aloof from the works that are studied. Rather, students are encouraged to develop and expand their own ideas and opinions about what they see, and to explore wider ranges of personal and professional experience. As far as I am concerned, bridging the gap between liberal and professional education requires demonstrating that the ideas and information generated in a humanities course are applicable and significant for one's future career in the professions.

As I have already noted, too often we have assumed that this is what we were teaching in our humanities courses, when in fact we were teaching facts and technical skills, not critical or evaluative attitudes. Putting the cultivation and exploration of qualities of mind up front in this humanities course marks it as distinctive and ties it most solidly to the Mellon enterprise at Syracuse. Students keep personal journals as well as write more general theme papers, some on general questions of humanistic interest and others that specifically ask the student to consider how the questions they have discussed in class may have relevance for their future careers. They also grapple with the notion of art in professional fields such as filmmaking and advertising. And they encounter—many of them for the first time—essential questions of value and meaning.

Students learn from each other as well as from readings and lectures. They give group presentations in which their divergences of opinion and their different "ways of seeing" are as much the subject as any common perceptions or understandings they may have. For example, students are shown portrait paintings for the covers of *Time* magazine. The students record their initial reactions to the portraits and compare their reactions with each other. They then go on to find the actual magazine on which the painting was published, read the cover story and other news articles in the issue, and record how their perceptions change as they hear each other's reactions and gather more information, that is, as they see the painting in its new context. In their reports, the students attempt to analyze why they may initially have seen the paintings the way they did and what kinds of changes they witnessed taking place in their own perceptions as well as those of their fellow students. One of the major goals of the course, then, is to help students to see their own biases and to begin to understand how they might change their attitudes and incorporate new ideas and beliefs into their lives.

In more traditional courses it is usually assumed that students need "the facts" before they can begin to think seriously about the humanities. Most introductory courses in the humanities offer sweeping surveys of past artistic or literary accomplishments in the hope that students will recognize their reputedly high or enduring value. And even then, students are encouraged to learn only by imitating and doing, not by questioning or disputing. This course, instead, assumes that students need to learn to question themselves and the world before taking on vast numbers of facts. In this way, they will not get overwhelmed by the particulars and neglect to consider bigger questions.

In recent years this sort of interrogative stance has increasingly been emphasized in critical thinking about the humanities, but it has almost never been brought into an introductory undergraduate course, usually thought of more in terms of indoctrination into the vocabulary and thoughts of the great minds who have preceded us. To be sure, we have much to learn from the past. But the standard approach and its implicit separation of everyday life (read "professions" and "pop culture") from great thought (read "the liberal arts" and "high culture"—the "*fine* arts") has insured that professional and liberal concerns have not been fully integrated. What this fails to recognize is just how "professional" the various humanities disciplines have become, and how introductory surveys in the humanities have too often become quite comparable to skills courses in the professional schools instead of being truly liberal in their attitudes and ways of thinking. What this course does, then, is to return a liberal stance to an introductory course in the humanities, even while calling attention to the common ground shared by the humanities and the other professions.

As part of the project at Syracuse, this course addresses the main issues that we have identified as common concerns. Foremost is the issue of embeddedness.[1] Indeed, the entire course stresses how our perceptions of art and its production are deeply embedded in social norms and practices. Similarly, questions of objectivity[2] and subjectivity are addressed every time students try to interpret and understand a work of art. There are objective facts associated with the objects under consideration, but students learn to what extent subjective analysis may help them to make sense of those facts and to what extent some of these "facts" may be more subjective than they thought. As regards "profession,"[3] students are openly exposed to both the professions of art and art history. Readings and discussions on the nature of art history highlight how a field defines itself, controls its membership, and encourages a particular kind of professionalism from its practitioners. In terms of skill or craft,[4] the course spends most of the time openly considering what skills are necessary to begin interpreting and understanding human values. By a choice of certain topics that specifically address the question of women in the arts and by including non-Western examples, the course also incorporates our concerns about gender[5] and Western ethnocentricity.

The implications for any introductory course are great. The neat and orderly world that we present in our introductory courses is not only misleading, but runs counter to what the entire scholarly process is about: not just acquisition of new data and information but, more importantly, developing modes of thought and inquiry that will move us beyond received wisdom to asking new questions and creating new thought.

Notes

1. See chapter 8, "The Concepts of Embeddedness and Enculturation."
2. See chapter 5, "The Concept of Objectivity."
3. See chapter 3, "The Phenomena of Professions."
4. See page 23.
5. See chapter 10, "Gender and the Professions."

15

The Creating Mind

GERARDINE CLARK

There is a paradoxical functional phenomenon in the educational system as presently structured. Contemporary methods of teaching and evaluation train students to lease ideas and information without encouraging or requiring them to own that knowledge. At the mid-term or the final the ideas are returned and the lease allowed to expire. This is not a cynical activity. Students assume that they have somehow been magically and mysteriously changed; but they know how little they actually retain months or even weeks later if the relevance of the information to their immediate disciplinary interests is not continually emphasized. They fail to realize that this is not so much a function of mental capacity as their failure to engage deeply with the content of the course. Knowledge must be earned to be owned.

The development of our course, "The Creating Mind," was intended from the outset as an inquiry having two concerns, the first content-oriented, the second pedagogical. It was to be devoted, first of all, to the investigation of that nebulous activity most usually described as "the creative process." Secondly, it was a search for a teaching strategy that would encourage students to earn, and therefore own, as much of the knowledge generated by the course as possible. An account of this course necessarily must emphasize the process by which it was created. Moreover, the following report will require frequent reference to the faculty seminar, as it provided not only the original impetus for the course, but eventually served as its model.

When I was invited to join the Mellon project, my first challenge was to determine the kind of course I might develop which would integrate the educational concerns of the College of Visual and Performing Arts with those of the liberal arts. The course would have to differ from those developed under the auspices of the other professional schools in the project; it would not have as its subject of inquiry a single profession such as nursing, nor even several substantially related professions such as those embraced under the rubric of public communications. Each of the four schools represented by the College of Visual and Performing Arts—Music, Art, Drama, and Speech Communication—represents a different and quite separate subject matter. Within each school students are trained in very different skills and for widely divergent careers.

The first question was: Is there a subject matter common to the four schools which gives them coherence as a college and, if so, does that subject matter offer the possibility of a meaningful integration with the concerns of the liberal arts? The sole domain which the visual and performing arts hold in common is that of "creativity." Creativity is not, certainly, a quality exclusive to the arts. Creativity is easier to identify than to quantify. Few would hesitate to describe the activities which led to the creation of the Sistine ceiling, the discovery of the Copernican system of planetary motion, the construction of the Brooklyn Bridge, or the synthesis of the Salk vaccine as creative. It would be impossible, however, to determine their relative quanta of creativity. As our seminar readings have repeatedly reminded us, intuition, invention, innovation, originality, and elegance of expression reside in, and are requisite to, significant accomplishment in all disciplines and professions.

In the arts, however, it is most generally evident that creativity is at the heart of the matter, for it is in the arts that creativity is not only means, but end. The Greek terms *poesis* and *poetes* do not translate as "poetry" and "poet," but "making" and "maker." An artist is one who creates spatial or temporal objects, images, or constructions—"made things"—which are in the nature of original statements about herself, the world, and herself in the world; the purpose of these is to invite an empathetic response from reader, viewer, or listener. The principal effect aimed at is not practical or theoretical, but aesthetic—to cause the audience to feel into and become one with the object of contemplation. One is invited to make sense not only of the art object but of oneself through the art object. Because art is an act of creativity which invites contemplation for its completion, a course whose subject of inquiry is the creative process might naturally be located within the curriculum of the College of Visual and Performing Arts.

Creativity, then, was the unifying concern of the four schools in my professional college, and its bearing on the liberal arts could not be denied. I had long wanted to develop a course whose sole function was to enable students to identify and analyze some of the sources of the creative imagination in order to make them more conscious of the creative process in themselves. This is the course I proposed as my contribution to the Mellon project.

While the subject matter was demonstrably appropriate under the terms of the grant, it was necessary to consider whether such a course served a purpose not already being met in our curriculum. Little research was needed to indicate that it did. That creativity is a fundamental to the artistic enterprise is implicit in the curriculum of the visual and performing arts as a whole, and it is addressed in more than a passing way in courses in aesthetics, theory, history, and studio *practica* of various kinds. In the first three, however, it is discussed most often as a quality inhering and accomplished in great models. In the last, the "skills" courses, the discussion tends to be problem specific: "How do I generate an original solution to my immediate problem?" Nowhere in the curriculum of any of the departments was there a course that dealt exclusively with the fundamental questions of creativity:

> Is there an inherently human "will to create?"
> What is imagination?
> What are some of the strategies for engaging the creative imagination?
> What are some of the elements inherent in the process of creation?
> Is there a necessary order of events in the creative process?
> If there is such an order, what is it?
> If there is not, what are some of the strategies that invite completion?

These are the questions the course would raise at the beginning and readdress throughout the semester in order to achieve developmental answers.

During the first summer of the seminar in 1985 when initial course outlines were being developed and tested, there was considerable discussion about the relationship that they should foster between the liberal curriculum and professional training. Shortly afterwards I read *Sabbatical*, a novel by John Barth, about a couple who, while sailing home from a nine-month regenerative ship-board tour, planned the form and content of a semi-autobiographical novel. (The novel is itself, therefore, an exploration and record of the process of creativity.) In it I discovered what seemed to be a felicitous metaphor for the kind of course I wanted to create. Barth, as the fictional protagonist Fenwick Scott Key Turner, reads from the notes for his novel: "Is a Y a fork or a confluence? Does the Chesapeake diverge into York River Entrance Channel and York Spit Channel, or do they converge into the Chesapeake Channel? The one inbound, the other outbound; or, in tidewater, the one on floods, the other on ebbs. Analysis versus synthesis."[1]

Clearly my course should be a "confluence"—one set in a tidewater. Its purpose would be to facilitate the conjunction of the students' liberal and professional streams into the single channel of the creative self (synthesis); it should permit, however, a way back into the individual streams for purposes of analysis.

At the same time, it was necessary to consider that it was not intended that the course remain my permanent domain. During the term of the grant I would be followed in the third year by the visual artist in the seminar, and afterwards we would be followed, presumably, by others assigned according to the shifting curricular demands of the college. What was required, then, was not a detailed outline, but a structure in which I would be free to experiment for two years and which could be adopted without constraint by subsequent instructors. I might also be able to incorporate to some extent what I learned from this course into my own theoretical and skills courses in drama. All could benefit, I was beginning to believe, from the "confluence" construction. The following is a description of the principal elements of the structure of the course as it came to be formulated through the summer of 1985 and a semester of teaching.

It is offered to students across the curricula. While it may be taught by a professor from any discipline or profession who places a high value on the operation of creativity, it would most appropriately continue to be taught by one of the faculty of the College of Visual and Performing Arts.

It became apparent early on that the lecture method as a style of teaching is inimical to the goals of a course whose function is to stress personal engagement and responsiveness to the sources of creativity in the self. While the specific content of the course may vary considerably according to the disciplinary and artistic background, specific skills, and aesthetic viewpoint of the instructor, if it is truly to fulfill its function it should combine coefficients of both theory and practice. The students initially should be made aware, through a broad spectrum of readings, of what has been thought and written about the creative process. These readings should serve as a springboard to class discussions aimed at focusing and eliciting the students' privately held assumptions on the nature of the creative process. My list of readings included excerpts from Rollo May's *The Courage to Create*, Arthur Koestler's *Act of Creation*, Stephen Sondheim's *Sunday in the Park with George*, Virginia Woolf's *A Room of One's Own*, Betty Edwards's *Drawing on the Artist Within*, Albert Rothenberg's *The Emerging Goddess*, Roger von Oech's *Whack in the Head*, and Diane Arbus's introduction to a portfolio of her magazine photographs.

An example of a typical reading is the first chapter from *Drawing on the Artist Within*,[2] in which Betty Edwards charts the classical model of the act of creativity. This model was first described in abbreviated form by German physiologist and physicist Herman Helmholtz, further developed by French mathematician Henri Poincaré, and completed by American psychologist Jacob Getzels, in this way:

Original insight → Saturation → Gestation → Ah-Ha! → Verification

With the exception of the "Ah-Ha!" effect, which is usually a sudden insight, the relative length of time assigned to each stage varies from encounter to encounter.

Students are asked to respond to such readings, either confirming or challenging their assertions. Toward this end they are required to maintain a reading log in which they summarize major points of interest and their personal responses to the text. The log gives the students an investment in the readings and later helps to heighten and focus discussion.

The second necessary element in the structure of the course is the in-class consideration of *exempla*: creative ideas, works, and gestures, especially those representing a stimulating innovation. The best models would be those which vividly portray the process involved in artistic, scientific, or practical creation. For instance, a chronological viewing of the many studies which preceded the completion of Georges Seurat's *Sunday Afternoon on the Island of La Grande Jatte* is a far more persuasive commentary on the artist's tireless methods of working out the problems of color, light, and composition than any critical exegesis of a single painting could provide. The discussion of these *exempla* should include the consideration of cultural forces at work in them—those which are reflected by the work, those that made possible the innovation represented by the work, and those which may have weighed against that innovation.

These discussions should extend to the related question of gender.[3] This issue is especially potent in the arts since, even in this age of women's liberation, there are scientists and critics who continue to assert that women are constitutionally incapable of significant contribution to the arts, especially in the areas of painting and musical composition. The adaptations to cultural forces (of which gender consideration was the most compelling) represented by the work of such women as Sappho, Aphra Behn, George Sand, and Mary Cassatt provided a potentially challenging focus for discussion.

The third, and most important, constituent of the course is the opportunity for *practica* in a variety of creative problems. While the ways of treating and utilizing this element are manifold and will vary according to the philosophy, artistic orientation, and special interests of the instructor, it may be illuminating to describe the problems encountered and the particular strategies employed to address them the first time the course was offered.

In the design and implementation of this element of the course it is necessary to consider two fundamental problems, the first artistic, the second organizational. The first of these is a difficulty inherent in all artistic endeavors. It is often described in literature on creativity as the problem of "idea generation." An artistic "idea" need not be fully developed or capable of verbal or immediate articulation. Sometimes it may be no more than an interesting association of two or more images, a psychological or emotional problem that invites artistic expression, or perhaps an intriguing physical question of color or composition that engages the attention. The search for the idea is the first—and sometimes the most difficult—task of the artist. There is also the concomitant problem of idea discrimination, determining which of the many ephemeral ideas the mind generates is worthy of artistic investigation or sufficiently engaging to invite the artist's deepest attention and experimentation.

Idea generation requires heightened attention and a certain saturation of information if the ideas are to pass the test of discrimination. While it might be left to the student to discover his own most fruitful area of investigation, assigning a common theme or subject provides a common ground for discussion and permits the students to build on each other's insights. Directing each of the *practica* toward a common theme would also have the effect of connecting the exercises through time and allow for a cumulative effect. Originally I planned to use death as the subject, as the question of mortality figures so intimately in many theories concerning the source of the artistic impulse[4] and because it is so frequently the subject of works of art. I soon found that bisociation of the ideas of creativity and death fruitful. Having already planned for ample reading in creativity, I added readings, listening tapes, and slides of art objects, artifacts and architecture relating to death to provide the basis for discussion and the ensuing *practica*. Students completed a "death quiz" which helped to identify the particular aspects of death that they found personally fascinating. These quizzes were shared in a class newspaper which, combined with the readings, the reading logs, and discussions, provided an abundance of information, opinion, and emotional material to generate ideas for the individual *practica*.

While the theme of death proved very fertile, I thought it a valuable exercise to vary the theme the second time the course was offered. Numerous themes suggested themselves, but the ideal topic needed to provide the students with some intrinsic element of risk or peril. Experience runs deepest, emotions highest, and perceptions are most acute in the presence of danger. All great creative endeavors require a considerable risk of the self. I therefore felt that change, like death, was a topic that invited both attention and risk. College is a period of significant changes which, however long awaited, are also often frightening. One is no longer defined by the family, but is expected to become morally, emotionally, and financially autonomous within the span of a few years.

At this writing, the students have been engaged for half of a semester with the themes of creativity and change. Thus far, change as a subject of investigation has not provoked as deep a quality of encounter as did death. However, it has allowed the students to make a wider spectrum of associations with work in other classes, and has provoked a wider variety of responses.

The artistic problem having been provided for, it was necessary to consider the organizational problem—the nature of the *pactica* to be performed. This course is not, and should not, emphasize the development of skills, since the diverse background and talents of the students who take it precludes rigorous instruction in any one of the arts. Skill building per se is amply addressed in other courses. Indeed, it seemed essential that students be forced to operate for much of the semester outside the comfortable parameters of their own major subject if they were to learn anything fresh about the creative process. Training in the arts or other professions often produces tunnel vision. Neophytes have a tendency to inherit the theoretical stance and methods of their teacher-models without question because they lack knowledge of alternatives. Creativity often comes to seem nothing more than the application of learned methods to specific problems. What this most often produces, of course, is conventionality rather than originality. The result of specialized training is that the attention becomes wholly directed to the result rather than the generative process, which has become to a great extent automatic. If the student is not to be instructed in skills and is to be prevented from working for a considerable portion of the semester in his area of concentration, then of what are the *practica* to consist?

In designing this course I wanted to work through a theory—based on experience, observation, and study—that avocational work in a field in which one is not expert often provides greater insight into the creative process than one's principal work which may have, in some degree, become automatic. I believe, moreover, that insights gained in this way can be fed back into one's own discipline, refreshing it. The operation of the class has provided considerable empirical corroboration for this theory.

Students possess many partially trained skills such as logic, writing, drawing, and music. *Practica* in problems involving those skills in which the student considers himself somewhat knowledgeable, but not expert, would help to draw attention more to the process of creation than to the product. If the exercise is to achieve maximum benefit, however, the students should be made to understand from the outset that it is not the final product that will be judged for purposes of this course, but the originality of ideas and the rigor[5] exercised in addressing the problem.

The students first produced ten small projects from a variety of possibilities such as *haiku*, collage, musical composition, script writing, improvisational acting, magazine and television advertising, cartooning, fables, etc. These were presented in class and discussed in terms of motivating idea, materials, execution, and final effect. The expectation was that engagement with a variety of forms followed by constructive criticism would help students discover resonances with unaccustomed materials and methods which they could still pursue with considerable competence. These mini-projects were followed by a major project in a medium for which they felt a particular avocation. The development and presentation of these projects occupied one-third of the semester. They were accompanied by a process paper in which the students described the search for the originating idea, the selection of medium and materials, the process of execution, the intended effect, and the degree of correspondence they

I saw a photograph of Nicola Tesla who invented the Tesla Coil. He also invented a pair of shoes with soles four inches thick to ground him while he worked in the laboratory. In the picture, Tesla was sitting in his lab, wearing the shoes, and reading by the light of the long streamer-like sparks shooting out of his transformers.

Portrait of Nicola Tesla. Photograph courtesy of Burndy Library, Norfolk, Conn. Quotation from Laurie Anderson, *Words in Reverse,* Top Stories #2 (Buffalo, N.Y.: Hallwalls, 1979).

found between the intended effect and the accomplished form. They were to note especially any discoveries they had made along the way about the process of creativity. The projects were discussed at length and criticized under all those heads.

A final *practicum* required a return to the student's principal discipline, accompanied by increased attention to the process of creation and a determination to carry those insights gained in the previous project into the work. These were similarly reported and discussed in class with particular attention to the changes students had experienced in methods of work. Some of the changes reported included greater consciousness of the process, greater willingness to experiment and to build an element of risk into the encounter, and entry into the process at a different point than was customary. Students who had been accustomed to beginning with an "idea" for which they would then choose the appropriate materials and techniques now began by experimenting with materials or investigating a particular technique, trusting that eventually a suitable idea would come.

The course should include another element, not discrete from the other three, but a concomitant of each: extensive writing. As educators, we know writing to be the best means of focusing thought, recording impressions, playing with ideas, and retaining hard-won insights for further contemplation and exploration. While students may agree with us in theory, they don't necessarily act in conformity to that belief. Indeed, the writing practices which they most commonly employ may actually suggest to them that writing and learning are not congruent activities.

Inspired by the "Mellon Menu"[6] provided by the professor of composition in the seminar, and aided throughout the course by the advice and expert assistance of one of her co-workers, I encouraged the use of writing as a way of thinking. I was helped particularly by the method and exercises described in Gabrielle Rico's *Writing the Natural Way*, which many of my students found liberating. Some of the writing strategies have already been described. Others included frequent opportunities for free-writing, inspirational journals, position papers, and formal and informal critical writing employed both in class and as homework assignments. These were directed toward idea generation, primary and secondary research, responsive writing, and reflective writing to preserve insights. Perhaps the most successful of these was the inspirational journal. Students were required to write a minimum of ten minutes each day, recording striking images, occasions of emotion, ideas for future projects, insights about works in progress, and reflections on the creative process generated by the activities and experiences of the day.[7] Most students carried their journals with them to make entries as they occurred.

Not only did students return to their journals and other writing exercises again and again to find ideas for minor and major *practica*, but in a surprising number of cases they chose *practica* whose means of expression was some form of writing. An industrial design major wrote a twenty-page short story; a theatre major wrote a forty-page screen play; a musical theatre major wrote a sonnet sequence (his first attempt at poetry). Had I imposed such arduous assignments, I would have met with disbelief—if not downright opposition. Because the projects were self-selected and their rigor self-imposed, they were undertaken happily, often with amazing results.

Evaluation is a difficult task in any course in which the measures and judgments are largely subjective. The term "evaluation" may itself suggest two entirely different activities: "grading" and ongoing critical judgment. I believe that, on the whole, our students have become accustomed to focus far too heavily on the former and receive far too little of the latter for their own best interests. I advised the students at the first class meeting that I would (as is common practice in studio classes in drama) return grades on none of the individual assignments, but that they would receive feedback in the form of written criticism or in-class discussion on each of their projects. Moreover, they were to save each of their assignments, which they would present again at individual conferences at the end of term. There they would assess what they had learned and accomplished during the semester. I, in turn, would provide my critique of their work as a whole, including class participation. No student complained about this evaluative method. Many said they found it liberating, and all concurred that they had received ample criticism from myself and other students. In my opinion, this method of evaluation was crucial to the success of the course. Grades on individual projects most often invite either complaisance or complaint, but would contribute little to such a class.

When I first undertook this project I feared that such a course —addressing the "soft" notion of creativity through investigation of a wide range of historical, aesthetic, and cultural concerns across the curricula—would provide breadth at the expense of depth. I felt this as a special danger since the course was not attached to a specific disciplinary or skill-building function. As I hoped, the course required of teacher and students a very high degree of rigor, but of an unusual kind. Each participant soon discovered that, in greater degree than usual, the benefits to be derived from this course were limited only by the individual's capacity to be self-aware and self-directing. A certain spirit of friendly competition soon developed among the students in testing their capacity to challenge their own and each other's hard-won and deeply held assumptions. To that extent, the best model for this course is the Mellon faculty seminar itself. In many ways, what happened in the classroom was very nearly a mirror image of what has been the experience at our conference table: self-discovery achieved at the expense of holding up for contemplation and criticism our best insights and most cherished assumptions. For the students and ourselves it has often proved a surprisingly painful game, but one worth the candle, as we have struggled to earn—and thus own—new knowledge and ideas.

Notes

1. John Barth, *Sabbatical* (New York: G. P. Putnam's Sons, 1982), 137.

2. Betty Edwards, *Drawing on the Artist Within* (New York: Simon & Schuster, 1986), 4.

3. See chapter 10, "Gender and the Professions."

4. "Creativity is a yearning for immortality. We human beings know that we must die. We have, strangely enough, a word for death. We know that each of us must develop the courage to confront death. Yet we also must rebel and struggle against it. Creativity comes from this struggle—out of the rebellion the creative act was born." Rollo May, *The Courage to Create* (New York: Norton, 1975), 27.

5. I refer more than once to the rigor necessary for the act of creativity. By this I mean the extent of engagement with an idea, the commitment to the encounter. As Rollo May suggests: "Creativity occurs in an act of encounter and is to be understood with this encounter as its center. Cezanne sees a tree. He sees it in a way no one else has ever seen it. He experiences, as he no doubt would have said, 'being grasped by the tree.' . . . The painting that issues out of this encounter between a human being, Cezanne, and an objective reality, the tree, is literally new, unique and original. . . . In his book *Poetry and Experience* Archibald MacLeish quotes a Chinese poet: 'We poets struggle with Non-being to force it to yield Being. '" *The Courage to Create*, 87–89.

6. See chapter 13, "Everyone Writes."

7. Care should be taken to provide a mechanism which allows students to protect the privacy of certain observations when journals are turned in to the instructor for evaluation and comment. An artist's journal frequently contains quite intimate feel-

ings, memories, and observations which will later form the basis of artistic work. Their secrecy should be guarded until that transformation takes place if the act of encounter is not to be drained of intensity. A simple solution is to require that journals be kept in loose-leaf notebooks. When turned in for reading, those pages which contain private material can easily be removed by the student and later replaced.

V

Challenges

Preface

PETER T. MARSH

In this final section of our report we appeal for widely extended collaboration among the professional and liberal arts colleges within American universities, for much remains to be done if the boundaries that divide them are to be effectively contested.

It was the questions of undergraduates about the bearing of their required liberal arts and professional courses on each other that initially prompted the Syracuse experiment. Seeking answers for those questions, the faculty seminar at the center of the experiment found itself asking them in ever more searching form. Along the way, we have discovered effective ways of involving small groups of students in the quest to understand the interrelationship of liberal and professional education. But a dozen courses with enrollments of a dozen apiece do not amount to transformation of the undergraduate curriculum, even within the confines of an honors program. Adding to the agenda still to be addressed, the ferment and lines of intellectual advance in the seminar have thrown the harmful consequences of universities' compartmentalized administrative structure into sharp relief.

From first to last, the most searching aspect of the challenge posed by the juxtaposition of liberal and professional education is intellectual. In two years of enquiry we have glimpsed—but barely begun to map—the new configuration of islands and connecting seas that the world of learning is assuming. That is the subject of the first two chapters in this section. We have, we believe, acquired a better compass for our voyage of discovery than our original concept of integration between liberal and professional education provided. In the opening chapter of this section Stephen Melville, who as a literary theorist has persistently induced us to reexamine our conceptual bearings, describes the deficiencies of our first compass and the way we redesigned it. Drawing upon Suzanne Gearhart's analysis of the boundary between history and fiction, he proceeds to chart the direction that we intend and urge others to pursue in ex-

215

ploring the ever interpenetrating boundaries among other fields and forms of learning.

In the following chapter, written from a quite different vantage point—the new field of neuroscience—Erich Harth reinforces the belief that the areas of convergence that are emerging in the world of learning will prove to be more fruitful than the spheres of separate development. His estimate of the extent to which computer technology can help in the search for points of convergence does not command universal agreement, but the new patterns of growing knowledge that he discerns in natural science will encourage those who have despaired at its seemingly ever more remote specialization.

To convince others to join in the pedagogical and intellectual quest on which we have launched, we need to provide more than the essentially descriptive account of the experiment that this book has offered. From the outset we arranged for student evaluations of the courses we were introducing and for evaluation of the students' performance in them. We soon discovered that the customary instruments for these purposes do not fit either the new courses or what students gain from them. Unlike the bulk of the undergraduate curriculum, the courses are not intended to convey bodies of information, but rather look for connections and common themes between subjects on which the students are acquiring information elsewhere. Accordingly, what we wish to foster among the students is not mastery of information, but quickened appreciation of conceptual relationships. The effectiveness of the courses and the performance of the students in them cannot, therefore, be gauged by "objective" measurement of the information transmitted.

The subtitle of chapter 18 on the evaluation of the experiment, "Micrometers and Elephants," is meant to draw attention to the inappropriateness of most existing evaluative instruments for our purposes. Written by three participants in the project with differing kinds of pertinent expertise—Marshall Segall from psychology, John Philip Jones from advertising, and Dennis Gillen from management—the chapter briefly elaborates this problem and indicates how we are attempting to meet it. Evaluation of the courses is being extended beyond the semester in which they are taken, and must be extended still further, beyond graduation. Our pedagogical enterprise will have little worth if it does not influence the students' approach to the rest of their curriculum and to their professions once they have embarked upon them.

Even if these efforts at evaluation demonstrate the value of the courses conclusively, they will have only peripheral impact on the undergraduate curriculum at this university—let alone beyond it—so long as they remain confined to small groups of students through the honors program. We can move beyond some of these confines without difficulty, and have already begun to do so; but escape from others will prove more difficult. The experiment has been conducted within the honors program mainly because of its manageable number of students for purposes of a pilot project, and also because of their representative distribution among the university's liberal arts and professional colleges. Nothing about the new courses need restrict their clientele in future to honors or dean's list students. Lifting the numerical limit of fifteen that we have imposed on enrollment in each course will, however, prove more difficult. The biologist in the project, who was used to large lecture classes to dispense information, soon realized that he must familiarize himself with the format of small seminars conducted through discussion in order to involve students in an exploration of the impact of science on medicine.

But if such a format is indispensable for our purposes, how can courses of the sort that we have created irradiate the whole undergraduate curriculum, as they must do if relating liberal and professional education is to become more than a curricular frill? The concluding chapter of our book, written by the project leader with contributions from several participants in the project, addresses this question and its administrative corollary.

We do not envision a total reconstruction of the undergraduate curriculum. The pedagogical objectives of our enterprise would be adequately served if provision were made to ensure that every undergraduate would take a few courses designed expressly to stimulate enquiry into the relationship between separate subjects, including liberal as well as professional concerns in his or her program of study.

Implementating even such a modest policy may, however, be impossible if we do not at the same time rise to the other challenge to which the concluding chapter draws attention—the challenge to reform the administrative procedures and structures of this and other American universities that now constitute arguably the most effective barrier to movement across the boundaries that separate the disciplines and professions. As currently organized, universities serve the interests of the disciplines and accrediting professions much more than they serve the aspirations of the students who come to learn. The allocation of power and money in universities should be redesigned to offset the natural impulse of departments and colleges to advance their separate interests. The criteria for awarding tenure, promotion, and salary increments among the faculty must be revised, not just to give teaching higher priority, but also explicitly to encourage scholarly enquiry between fields. Cross-campus seminars should become an expected, standard feature of faculty development. A network of bridges and bridge builders, of ships and seafarers, even of submarines and sappers, needs to be established and endowed with resources to foster learning and teaching across departmental and collegiate lines. Only if changes like these are made can the interpenetration of liberal and professional education work its way into the fabric of American undergraduate education.

16

Education in a Transformed Field

STEPHEN MELVILLE

I would like to suggest, after two years and the creation of a number of courses of varying quality and ambition, that we are only now in a position to begin facing the deep challenge hidden in the project of "integrating liberal and professional education," and that this challenge is accentuated by understanding how deeply uninterested we are in *that* formulation of the task.

Early on some members of the seminar, most notably the philosopher, argued that there need be no integration of liberal and professional education beyond what is already in place in (or as) that division itself. He held that there is liberal education and there is professional education, and the only question would be one of fine tuning the relation between them (frequently this position came out as a call for a more professional approach to liberal education). On such a view the Mellon seminar could have no special mission beyond echoing the widely heard call for a clearer articulation of the relevance of the one region to the other. However, the ongoing sense of the seminar has been that there is indeed some special job that needs doing, and that this job is something more or other than creating smoother gateways between particular professional schools and particular disciplines within the liberal arts. In a sense, then, we rejected the most straightforward reading of our initial charge and have instead groped after more complex and contestatory models for our activity, using the notion of reflective or interrogative pauses as encouragement to criticism within and between the disciplines and professions.

We have, I think, been guided in this by some general notions about the instability or uncertainty of boundaries, very much along the lines of Suzanne Gearhart's recent remarks on the distinction between history and fiction as it emerged in eighteenth-century France:

Boundaries are established to separate and distinguish entities one from the other, but by the very same process, they link the delimited entities to one another. As a boundary is traced, it defines the integrity of each entity in terms of and in opposition to the others; it establishes where each begins and ends. A boundary therefore should be clearly marked or posted with visible signs in order to function as a boundary. When one crosses it, one should know immediately that one is in a different place where a different language is spoken, and different laws, rules, and procedures are followed. Because boundaries mark areas and limits, they assure us that we are where we think we are, and that wherever we are, we are on safe, familiar ground—for each area has been charted and defined, made recognizable and mastered before our arrival there. To be at home when we cross over boundaries, all that is necessary is to conform to the practices established on the other side by those inhabiting the area, by those who respect its boundary and remain within it.

The problem with the boundary separating history and fiction is that it does not function this way. It is more open than closed, more often displaced than fixed, as much within each field as at the limits of each. It is in play throughout history, whenever and wherever the question of history or fiction is raised, but nowhere does it function in an unproblematic, unequivocal manner. It is not just open, then, in the sense that it permits passage over it—all boundaries do this. It is open in a more radical sense, for the very domains it is supposed to separate and delimit continually cross over it also.[1]

It seems to me that this way of thinking about boundaries is generalizable well beyond the particular relationship of history and literature. The generalization does not, however, take the form of an appeal to any overarching liberal or loosely humanistic unity. It is a thought that is simultaneously about the permanence of boundaries and about their inadequacy; it does not so much free us from boundaries as ask us to have them as a problem.

I have tried to approach these issues through the image of a "seam" understood to be at once within and without a given discipline, a fissure or overlap that disturbs and complicates any simple notion of disciplinary identity and any simple distinction of inside and outside. This description has been developed in conjunction with a generalized analysis of the disciplinary constitution of any object as always embedded within a complex matrix of disciplines and material conditions. I understand these notions to press toward the acknowledgment of the "outside" of any region as a simultaneously necessary and transgressive condition of its "inside." While this picture is far from receiving any official endorsement from the Mellon project as a whole, it has played its part in allowing us to get on with the work of course creation.[2] Now, with a range of courses more or less acquired, it is perhaps time to look back and try to reformulate the possible drift of our work.

There are, I think, two issues that we were particularly slow to pick up on directly: one is whether there is any historical motive to our coming together; the other is the professionalism of the liberal arts themselves.[3] Full awareness of the latter makes hash out of our explicit project, depriving us of anything to "integrate," and should force us back on the matter of our historical circumstances.

The division of liberal arts and professional studies emerged within a very particular context—one in which class notions, particularly the distinction between gentlemen and those in trade, counted crucially, and one in which the notion of a "profession" was tightly circumscribed, limited to a very few clearly recognized occupations—law, medicine—capable of making some claim to escape the condition of trade and approach that of the gentleman. As recognized professions and institutions for the formation of professionals of increasingly varied stripe have multiplied, our educational institutions have tended, I think, to treat the distinction between liberal arts colleges and professional schools as a distinction between sites for education and sites for training, with education clearly the valorized term, to which every professional school must pay at least lip service at the peril of showing itself finally to be nothing more than a training institute, a trade school.

Our coming together, I would suggest, happened at a time when this picture was simply no longer tenable—too much education was going on in the professional schools and too much training in the liberal arts. To put it another way, professionalism is now so deep a fact of our culture that we are compelled to recognize and reflect upon a profound transformation in the field of our practices at large.[4] I would argue that we are compelled to move toward an attempt at reinventing education as a fundamental reflection upon our practices[5] in such a transformed field. Syracuse University, with its many undergraduate professional schools, seems to offer a particularly apt site for such an attempt, and it seems almost inevitable that our work should tend this way. In the seminar we have taken at least the first steps toward a series of interlinked courses that do some of the work of the liberal arts clusters,[6] but without excluding such salient facts as technology and the inevitable professionalism of students regardless of school or major. Some members of the seminar have suggested that we are moving toward the creation of a cluster that might be called "Background to Professional Studies."[7] I would rather say that we are more broadly in the business of reconceiving general education.

To say that we are moving in a certain direction is not to say that we have arrived somewhere—just that we seem to be working toward a new sense for "the integration of liberal and professional education." If the above account is an accurate description of the current state of the project, then it seems in order for us to go on by trying to gain some greater explicitness about this idea of education in a transformed field of practices. The themes we developed over the course of our meetings should serve as springboards toward a more powerful reflection. The concern with professionalism[8] and the competences demanded by it suggests, for example, that we understand the situation to be one in which no one can claim to have the world whole and apart from the particular perspectives within it that are his or her particular practices. That is, we no longer place much credence in the traditional humanist claims of the liberal arts. This recognition underlies our general lack of interest in trying to establish or rediscover some deep common, liberal, and humane language that would serve as the shared ground of any particular disciplinary or professional specialization. For us, discursive communities, their constraints and conventions, play an essential and unsurpassable role in any educative process.[9]

At the same time we have become sharply aware of the extent to which professionalism itself has developed as an attempt to hold the world at bay, to do and justify the doing of one particular thing within an essentially self-contained structure that erects its own standards and foundations. The risk here is the practical fragmentation of the world into mutually self-enclosed, noncommunicating, and self-justifying practices. We might call this risk that of losing the world (this would be the cost of imagining that our foundations and standards stand in no particular ground). The current arrangement of things at our university (and at many others) works powerfully to ensure such sealing off from one another of the activities the university as such means to unite. The seminar members have never lost their wonder that it took this special grant to introduce us to one another, and we remain acutely aware of how easy it still would be to fade back into our particular buildings, departments, and practices. Indeed, I would suggest that a great deal of the excitement in the seminar has simply been that of rediscovering that there is a world, complex and peopled, and that we have no objects except within it.

It is this sense of objectivity—that of the worldly and discursive conditions under which we can claim to have an object—that should interest us above all. It is within this frame that we can place the particular questions of what counts and is argued over as "objectivity" for any particular pursuit.[10] This frame does not offer solutions to particular disciplinary or professional questions about objectivity so much as it gives them a new urgency by explicitly linking the epistemological issues arising in a particular field to the conditions of possibility of that field itself. Just as we are no longer willing to imagine some common language purer than ordinary language and its appropriation to, and transformation in, diverse practices, so we decline to imagine any general space of knowledge organized by standards of objectivity that stand somewhere above the fray.

The image of embeddedness[11] can then be understood to point toward the complexity that follows from such an interest in objectivity—to point, that is, toward the way in which the principled claim to have an object turns against itself at its limits and places a practice in perilous, critical communication with others (other practices, other persons, other concerns), opening it to discussions that can no longer be constrained by the terms in which that practice understands itself. At the limits of a practice, foundation and context and material effects become entangled in one another. These limits interest us because they are the places where our pursuits are obliged to acknowledge something or someone other; they are the places where the worldliness of objects is marked and enforced. Such acknowledgment is not a passing nod toward the bare facts of context or effect, but a detailed, critical exploration of the "open boundary" that at once unites and distinguishes two fields, at once founding and dismantling their specific objects.

We may then want to turn away from the apparent substantial structure of particular disciplines and professions with which we have been largely occupied and move toward more pointed considerations of our world and the place of our knowledges and practices in it. We need to think more deeply about the relationships between human beings and their practices, or about the relationships between the desire to insure our practices against the contingencies of the world and the world such assurances make, lose, or deny. We need still to find our way to a basic examination of the interlocking of questions of technology, the guarantees of knowledge, and the goals of education—no doubt the most difficult questions we have faced and for which we have yet to produce a satisfactory approach.[12]

For some of us at least, it seems increasingly clear that in the long run—and our project is still very much in the short run—we are moving toward a vision of practices, disciplines, and professions as essentially relational, organized by and responsive to no standards above or apart from the web of relations in which they are knotted and tangled together. In this sense, we are asking of ourselves and the various practices we address how far these activities can be conceived, not in terms of guaranteeing and defending some essential internal stuff, but in terms of relations to an outside. The first curricular question would then be not, What is the knowledge that defines our particular and protected terrain? but, Where are we? The underlying impulse would be to reduce the particular and protected terrain to "what we are stuck with having to teach" rather than to the core of our pedagogy. To the extent that the Mellon project pursues this track, it seems committed to finding ways to suspend or deflect the credentialing pressures that control so much of the curricula and so much of our image of education, whether overtly professional or not. (The foolishness of pretending that a liberal arts curriculum is not structured by quite explicit market pressures is something we can no longer afford.)

But the questions we begin to open in this fashion are dangerous. Whatever we may want to make of ourselves as educators and whatever our ambitions for our students, we are deeply embedded within a demand for certified products. To suspend this function is to deprive ourselves of social ground. We can hold this ground just so long as we can continue to assume the validity of a picture of education that begins from the liberal voice and heritage of our common humanity, and refines it down to one or another professional point without loss of continuity, sponsored every step of the way by overarching standards. This is not the path the Mellon seminar has followed. Instead, we have tried to follow out the consequences of the assertion, implicit in the very project of undergraduate professional education, that particular practices seriously pursued—pursued to their limits and with a view to their highest standards—can and should open beyond themselves.

Turning the very idea of a department or school inside out is not easy. For many programs, whether liberal or professional, this kind of change may well seem inconceivable. And where credentialing pressures are most acute, such change, even if conceivable, may well be impossible. But it does seem to me that the Mellon project calls at the least for the intellectual effort of imagining such radical change, because it is only in such imagining that there is any real promise of sorting out the complex and highly problematic interlocking of skills, technology, and teaching. Our discussions of these matters have veered wildly between bland agreement about the necessity of teaching certain core skills and an inarticulate, sometimes fierce, mutual incomprehension. Perhaps our closest approach to this interlocking has lain in the recognition that within the new courses our teaching has changed, and that one aspect of this change has been that we teach less and less in view of the central knowledges claimed by particular disciplines and professions, and more and more in view of one another.[13]

It is clear that, throughout the seminar, questions of ethics and adequate knowledge have been deeply interlocked, although this interlocking has rarely been addressed with any explicitness. Some remarks by Martha Nussbaum may point in the direction I am urging:

> If it is reason, and reason's art, philosophy, that are supposed to save or transform our lives, then, as beings with an interest in living well, we must ask what this part of ourselves is, how it works to order a life, how it is related to feeling, emotion, perception. The Greeks characteristically, and appropriately, link these ethical questions very closely to questions about the procedures, capabilities, and limits of reason. For it is their instinct that some projects for self-sufficient living are questionable because they go beyond the cognitive limits of the human being; and, on the other hand, that many attempts to venture, in metaphysical or scientific reasoning, beyond our human limits are inspired by questionable ethical motives, motives having to do with closedness, safety, and power. Human cognitive limits circumscribe and limit ethical knowledge and discourse; and an important topic *within* ethical discourse must be the determination of an appropriate human attitude towards those limits.[14]

These are a philosopher's questions, raised simultaneously at the heart and margins of her profession; answering them carries her beyond the limits of that profession.

Our interest lies in finding other angles that open such ques-

Mark Tansey, *Triumph Over Mastery,* 1986. Oil on canvas, 60″ x 144″. Collection, the Museum of Contemporary Art, Los Angeles. Gift of Steven and Patsy Tisch. Photograph courtesy of Curt Marcus Gallery.

tions, in finding where in our various disciplines and professions such issues become central and inevitable. The goal is to get us out from under the phrase "integration of liberal and professional education" and the protective shadow it casts over our imagination of the limits of particular practices so that we can push ourselves toward an active exploration of a new and uncertain terrain where boundaries shift inside one another. Here the only word from our initial charter that will continue to matter to us may well be nothing more than "education."

> In place of the story of salvation through new arts, in place of the stratagems of the hunter and the solitary joy of the godlike philosopher, we are left with a new (but also very old) picture of deliberation and writing. We see a group of sailors, voyaging unsafely. They consult with one another, and take their bearings from that rock, which casts (under the liquid sky) its shadow on the sea.[15]

Notes

1. Suzanne Gearhart, *The Open Boundary of History and Fiction* (Princeton: Princeton University Press, 1984), 4–5. Gearhart is here giving particularly clear voice to a position implicit in much recent work at the margins of literary study.

2. See, in particular, the various discussions in Section III of this book on "Embeddedness and Enculturation."

3. Some of the readings in literary theory might have raised the question for us, except they were themselves deeply internal to the ongoing professional retrenchment of literary study that has accompanied the emergence of theory; the question finally emerged clearly from art history, a field deeply aware of its own professional crisis.

4. See, in this respect, chapter 4, "The Liberation of the Humanities."

5. I use the general term "practices" here with the simple intent of not reimposing the distinction presupposed by such phrases as "disciplines and professions."

6. Liberal arts clusters of four courses selected from a menu of departmental courses constitute the core requirements for the lower division at Syracuse University.

7. See chapter 18, "Evaluation: Micrometers and Elephants."

8. See chapter 3, "The Phenomena of Professions."

9. For a fuller discussion of these points, see chapter 2, "The Faculty Seminar: Discourse Communities and Quotation Marks."

10. See chapter 5, "The Concept of Objectivity."

11. See chapter 8, "The Concepts of Embeddedness and Enculturation."

12. See chapter 1, "The Syracuse Experiment."

13. See chapter 12, "The Varieties of Collaborative Experience."

14. Martha Nussbaum, *The Fragility of Goodness: Luck and Ethics in Greek Tragedy and Philosophy* (Cambridge: Cambridge University Press, 1986), 8.

15. Nussbaum, *The Fragility of Goodness*, 421.

17

From Specialization toward Integration
A Scientist's Perspective

ERICH HARTH

The seminar in which we engaged has made us all reexamine our particular functions within the educational process. On pondering education itself, I was led to conclude that it is an absurd venture that should not be contemplated by a sane person. What it comes down to is the attempt to take an untutored individual, a Stone Age brain, if you will, and load into its memory banks the fruits of millennia of cultural advances. The process is to be accomplished in a few years' time, and is expected to give the recipient an appreciation of the thoughts of the great thinkers, the art of the great artists, in short, the accomplishments of all the great accomplishers of the past. On top of this it is to introduce the student to a specialty. If majoring in physics, he or she is to learn what has happened in physics from Galileo to the present and will, on becoming a young professional, be considered mediocre (unable to get tenure at any reputable institution of higher learning) if he or she hasn't by the age of thirty provided answers to several problems that have vexed the best minds of the past.

Viewed this way, education seems indeed to be a foolish and doomed undertaking—except that we are doing it and that at times we are even reasonably successful. We may wonder whether this miracle could still be worked a hundred years hence, given the present rate of accretion of knowledge. To contemplate this situation is an intellectual exercise that may serve to alert us to some of the limitations and anachronisms in current educational practices.

When I spoke of Stone Age brains I meant this quite literally, and not as an aspersion on our students. The birth of civilization can now be traced back to the appearance of *Homo sapiens* some hundred thousand years ago, which was marked by the addition of a few hundred grams of gray matter to the brain of his predecessor *Homo erectus*. It is believed by many anthropologists that few, if any, significant changes in our brain structure have occurred since then.

This belief is reinforced by the observation that individuals from contemporary "Stone Age" cultures can readily adapt to the ways and challenges of a technological society.

This leaves us with a profound conundrum. Is it possible that humans possessed the latent ability to deal with the complex issues of a modern technological culture many millennia before civilization arrived at this stage? Did the evolutionary process, perhaps as a last gift, confer upon humans what has been called the *Promethean gene*, a kind of all-purpose ability to deal inventively and imaginatively with novel problems?

It appears that as a result of this remote genetic change the human environment itself has become more and more the product of our culture. The inherently slow processes of genetic adaptation have given way to a rapid, mind-driven cultural evolution.

The fruits of the Promethean gift are manifold and appeared early in civilization. They include toolmaking skills, knowledge and hypotheses about nature, the ability and drive to create objects of art, and the need for ritualistic expression and mythological fancy. Looking back, we are likely to call these the roots of technology, science, art, and religion respectively, but it is safe to say that originally such divisions were not recognized, and that the practitioners of one art were frequently also the masters of another.

I wish to emphasize also that the abilities of *Homo sapiens* to fashion tools, make images, search for truths, and create myths are closely related. The appreciation of this relatedness has been, throughout our seminar, a profound experience. From the point of view of the neuroscientist, the related abilities all seem to have occurred almost precipitately following the last addition to the human brain, which somehow gave us the ability to envision situations we have never encountered, to sample and manipulate mental images, to construct hypothetical situations, and to confabulate. "Creativity" is a term that covers a good many—but not all—of these, and much discussion during the seminar was devoted to comparisons between artistic and scientific creativity. The aim on the part of the scientists present was not so much to convince others that they too were creative, but to point to a unifying feature of the human mind.[1]

The diverse human talents, though rooted in the same brain, have through the ages served different human needs and often been in sharp conflict with one another. The rift between science and the humanities that C. P. Snow was later to characterize as two cultures appears already in antiquity. Xenophon tells us of Socrates' profound disdain of natural philosophy:

He did not even discuss that topic so favored by other talkers, "the Nature of the Universe" and avoided speculation on the so-called "Cosmos" of the Professors, how it works, and the laws that govern the phenomena of the heavens. Indeed he would argue that to trouble one's mind with such problems is sheer folly. In the first place, he would inquire, did these thinkers suppose that their knowledge of human affairs was so complete that they must seek these new fields for the exercise of their brains? . . . His own conversation was ever of *human things*. The problems he discussed were What is godly, what is ungodly; what is beautiful, what is ugly; what is just, what is unjust; what is prudence, what is madness; what is courage, what is cowardice; what is a state, what is a statesman; what is government, what is a governor . . . ?[2]

No better definition of the humanities nor a more passionate indictment of the sciences has been given since. Religion and the sciences, similarly, have had an uneasy and often turbulent coexistence, although throughout long periods they were cultivated by the same individuals. But we are more aware of instances of conflict such as the inquisition of Galileo, the Scopes trial, or—in our own time once again—the controversies over evolution versus "creation science". The materialistic and deterministic trend of the natural sciences during the eighteenth and nineteenth centuries made the cleavage between science and religion not just one of fundamental beliefs, but, more profoundly, one of temperament. The progressively hard-nosed attitude of nineteenth-century physicists also added distance between them and scholars in the humanities, many of whom would have subscribed to Socrates' sentiments quoted above.

The sciences themselves did not remain unified. Physics, given the tools of Newtonian mechanics and later of Maxwell's theory of electromagnetism, began to outdistance all other disciplines. It presented, by the end of the nineteenth century, a system of knowledge that was powerful and unassailable. The physicist Eddington was quoted as remarking that physics was really the only science. "Everything else is stamp collecting."

This apparent lag of the other sciences precipitated in the twentieth century a scramble to reduce their problems to recognized physical principles. This reductionism led to some spectacular successes in the life sciences, as well as to some dead ends.

The progressive mathematization of the sciences, especially physics, further contributed to the estrangement between sciences and humanities. It also caused a permanent division between experimentalists and theoretical physicists (those who understood the intricate mathematical structures used to account for what the experimentalists observed). In rapid order, specialties and subspecialties evolved in all the sciences, each with its own rapidly growing body of knowledge, special techniques, and—alas—its own scientific jargon.

The outstanding trend in the sciences for the past century or so has been an intensification of research in all directions with enormously improved tools and techniques, an explosive growth of the body of knowledge, and a seemingly endless fragmentation of the fields. These aspects appeared inevitable and irreversible. The illusion of the Renaissance scholar was shattered, and there seemed to be no hope of putting Humpty Dumpty together again.

But more recently the trend has begun to point in almost the opposite direction. Instead of existing fields subdividing, new areas have appeared at the boundaries of established fields, often straddling the older disciplines and blurring formerly sharp divisions. Among the many new hybrids are geophysics, biophysics, molecular biology, biochemistry, and even physical biochemistry.

In physics, which during the last century or so has undergone more fragmentation than most other disciplines, the magic word now is "unification" or even "grand unification." To accomplish this lofty goal—the construction of a theory of everything—theoreticians have been forced to learn types of mathematics they never used before, and extend their expertise over areas that had been distinct specialties. Steven Weinberg of the University of Texas at Austin and a Nobel laureate in physics put it bluntly: "Deep and narrow is a grave."

Sometimes a new field swallows up a whole cluster of established disciplines. This happened when new attempts to understand brain function made it necessary for researchers to pool knowledge from neurophysiology, neuroanatomy, and neurochemistry, combined with such mathematical tools as the dynamics of nonlinear systems, theory of chaos, and extensive use of computer technology. All these and more are now incorporated in a vast new enterprise called neuroscience. Training programs in neuroscience leading to advanced degrees now exist on many university campuses along with the traditional departments of liberal arts. At Syracuse University, a graduate program in neuroscience was started in 1985, bringing together faculty from the Institute for Sensory Research and the departments of physics, chemistry, and biology. The Society for Neuroscience, with more than 10,000 members, is now one of the most active professional societies in America.

The emergence of interdisciplinary areas was first viewed with considerable suspicion by those in the more traditional fields. The biochemist, during one of our discussions, related that when biochemistry first appeared, a German chemist disparagingly remarked that "Tierchemie ist Schmierchemie"—Animal chemistry is messy chemistry. Such criticism was partly based on the feeling that a single field offered enough difficulty, and that combining fields could only lead to shallow dilettantism.

This stigma remained attached to interdisciplinary research for some time and has not yet been completely erased. Meanwhile, more and more hybrid fields are formed, often making unlikely combinations. A few years ago one of the leading physicists in the country, whose specialty was the physics of elementary particles, conceived of the idea of using cosmic ray telescopes to search for hidden chambers in one of the large Egyptian pyramids. The idea is similar to the novel way x-rays are now used to generate two-dimensional slices through body tissues (CAT scans). Another addition to the pantheon of science is the still controversial—but lively—field of sociobiology.

One of the puzzles in paleontology has been the apparent mass extinction of fauna at the border between the two geologic periods known as the Tertiary and the Cretaceous. Some evidence points to the repetition of global catastrophes roughly every 65 million years. Several theories of mass extinctions have now been proposed, invoking bombardment of the earth by debris from comets, triggered perhaps by an unseen companion star of our sun (appropriately called Nemesis), or periodic passage of the solar system through the plane of the galaxy. This field of investigation spans paleontology, geology, and astrophysics.

The new trend is more than just the application of research results from one field to another, as in the use of x-rays in medicine, but the bringing together of expertise from different fields in order to deal with a new—or at least newly conceived—field of research. Such novel integrations involving not only the natural sciences, but often combining with humanities or social sciences, give new meaning to the concept of liberal arts, not as a collection of disparate fields of endeavor, but of one large territory of scholarly activity with fluid boundaries and the potential for lively interchanges between any of its parts. It is clear that the same trend also tends to draw together the professional schools and the liberal arts.

The problems of preparing the future scholar or professional are, therefore, even more severe than stated at the outset. The sheer

mass of potentially useful information is overwhelming, and any selection of material appears arbitrary and inadequate. For a while our
seminar was engaged in a controversy regarding the function of liberal arts courses in the training of the pre-professional. One of the
participants suggested a careful tailoring of courses to be "gateways"
to the particular profession for which the student was preparing. In
connection with an honors course in the natural sciences given to
non-science students, I responded as follows:

> It is one thing to be sensitive to the needs of students from dif-
> ferent schools and colleges. It is quite another thing to crystalgaze,
> and to pretend being able to foresee all such needs, and design a
> course around such notions. Let me give an example: A close rela-
> tionship has always existed between engineering and the sciences.
> Every engineering student must, during his first two years, take
> a two-semester course in basic physics. Over the years there have
> been many discussions concerning the desired course material.
> Should it be especially selected to fit the engineering needs? Should
> it perhaps be taught by engineers?
>
> In the current arrangement all engineering students take a
> calculus-based course that they share with science majors, premed
> students, and anyone else interested in physics. The philosophy is
> that this is not just good mental discipline (like Latin), but that we
> try to teach the best physics course that can be taught at that level,
> realizing the impossibility of anticipating just where and how a par-
> ticular piece of information may become meaningful in the future.
> Such liberal allowance for serendipity, and for the rapidly changing
> circumstances in all professions, is the best the liberal arts can give
> to the pre-professional, and in the long run far more beneficial
> than a seemingly pragmatic *gateway* approach. Selection of material
> is, of course, always a difficult process, and a certain amount of ar-
> bitrariness is inevitable. But I believe it would be a disservice to the
> students to omit the mention of black holes (to pick an example)
> just because future physicians or engineers are not soon likely to
> run into one.

We must accept as necessary the trend toward more interdisciplinary studies. But how can we expect to subject the student to
such an inflated program of courses when each discipline is continuously growing? Will the future professional have to sacrifice depth
for the breadth that now seems to be called for? This is where both
liberal arts and the professional schools face their greatest challenge.

It would be folly if, in our zeal to integrate, we were to injure existing training programs that have proven effective in turning out competent professionals in established fields. But innovation must come because needs are changing rapidly. We must look, in particular, for changes in educational practices that promise to increase the amount of useful knowledge that can be transmitted, and its rate of acquisition. I offer a few suggestions.

We have been in the habit of formalizing and packaging virtually all knowledge, and presenting it as a menu of courses. Much of this effort, I believe, is wasted. Not everything that should be learned needs to be taught. Schools should do more to provide ambience and encouragement for students to be intellectually engaged in ways not connected with course work, but as part of their leisure activities. A modicum of guidance might direct them toward wider use of our libraries. Students' attention should also be directed to the cultural offerings of the community (films, lectures, exhibits, concerts) and to such sources of information in the news media as science news, book and art reviews, and coverage of current affairs in general. For the student who wishes to know about important advances in the sciences, there are now several popular magazines that present clear and engaging accounts for the general reader.

But by far the most revolutionary and most promising development with regard to educational practice has been the arrival of the computer on the American campus. It has brought unprecedented computational power to some who have never computed anything before. Linguists, psychologists, and economists are tapping into the same mainframe computer as the natural scientists or are using personal computers. Almost everyone now uses word processors.

Even more significant than the computational power is the use of the computer as a device for storage of, and ready access to, information. Instead of using card catalogues, students have become accustomed to consulting a computer terminal in the library. It has the added advantage that they can search for sources using key words. More sophisticated computer searches are also available.

But the computer revolution has barely begun. In the future we may expect to be able to shift a considerable amount of educational baggage onto conveniently accessible external storage. Such peripheral memory could relieve our brains of much tedious memorization, leaving them free to carry out the more creative, imaginative tasks.

There will be some reluctance to enter this transition, in part due to extravagant claims of computer intelligence and to myths of computers that are ready to develop a will of their own. The computer is, in fact, the ideal servant. It does exactly what it is told, and does it with unparalleled efficiency. I am confident that we will soon overcome residual feelings of alienation and view computers as useful extensions of ourselves. They will become as inseparable from human culture as the printing press that was once considered an impersonal monster, depriving us of the beauty of handwritten texts. I believe that future generations will chuckle at our portrayal of the computer as the ogre that was just waiting to take control over our lives.

Computers, it must be said once and for all, are not brains. They don't have ideas or ambitions. They create only under our direction. A faulty instruction, and they will produce reams of utter nonsense until we turn them off. They are like the brooms in *The Sorcerer's Apprentice*.

This situation is likely to remain true even for the so-called "fifth generation" computers, which to date are but a gleam in the eyes of Japanese and American computer scientists. These silicon marvels will not only be bigger (in memory capacity) and faster, they should overcome the chief bottleneck that still exists between the thinking human and the perfect machine—the slow and cumbersome way in which information is communicated across the interface between the two. One of the aims of fifth generation computers will be the understanding of speech or printed text. No coding or decoding should be required, nor any rigid input format. Questions asked in conversational language should be answered rapidly and succinctly by the computer if it knows the answer.

The terms "knowing" and "understanding" raise the question of the true nature of artificial intelligence, or AI. In one interpretation—sometimes called "hard AI"—represented by A. Newell and H. A. Simon at Carnegie-Mellon, there is no fundamental difference between human intelligence and that of a machine.[3] John Searle rejects this notion, pointing out that a machine that successfully translates Chinese into English understands neither language, but merely responds in prescribed fashion to strings of symbols that are fed into it.[4] An advocate of hard AI would argue that humans do precisely that and no more.

I believe Searle is right. There is an open-endedness to the human mind and an unpredictability to its powers of reasoning. As long as we fail to understand the brain mechanisms responsible for inventiveness, adaptability, creativity, and drive, we have no right to expect these faculties to emerge spontaneously from any machine or program, however cleverly designed. Until the time when we grasp the nature of the Promethean gene, we will remain the sorcerers, and computers the brooms.

I want to come back once more to the Stone Age brains that we are trying to imbue not only with knowledge (to bring them into the twentieth century), but also with wisdom (to make them survive into the twenty-first). Education is likely to be the watershed in the struggle to overcome the great threats of our time—environmental degradation, population explosion, and nuclear doom.

We look with justification to the natural sciences to provide us with answers and means. But most of these will be temporary solutions, many will create new problems, and some, such as the Strategic Defense Initiative (Star Wars), are downright silly. We also look to science to teach us an analytic mode of thinking that rejects sentimentality and makes us reexamine all premises. We hope this will prevent our national, ethnic, and religious loyalties from slipping into the kind of pre-Darwinian typological thinking and ethical blindness[5] that has mankind divided into the good and the bad, and always argues for one more crusade to save the world.

Notes

1. See chapter 15, "The Creating Mind."

2. Xenophon, *Memorabilia*, I, trans. E. C. Marchant (Cambridge, Mass: Harvard University Press, Loeb Classical Library, 1923), 9–11.

3. A. Newell and H. A. Simon, "Computer Simulation of Human Thinking," *Science 134* (December 1961), 2011–17.

4. J. Searle, "Minds, Brains, and Programs," *The Behavioral and Brain Sciences* 3 (September 1980), 417–8.

5. The expression "ethical blindness" was coined by Daniel Coleman in *Vital Lies, Simple Truths: The Psychology of Self-deception* (New York: Simon & Schuster, 1985).

18

Evaluating the Experiment
Micrometers and Elephants

JOHN PHILIP JONES, DENNIS GILLEN,
and MARSHALL H. SEGALL

We believe that we have developed, through two years of collaborative learning, some atypical and unusually effective ways to teach professionally oriented undergraduates. In the present chapter we ask how this belief is to be confirmed. We are not yet sure how to evaluate the courses we have developed or the growth of the students who have taken them; but we are sure that, whatever and whenever we wish to measure something, the measuring instrument must be appropriate to that something. Hence, much of this chapter is devoted to a consideration of evaluation techniques and instruments.

Two intersecting objects of evaluation concern us: courses and students. Since we attempted to design and implement new courses, we obviously need to evaluate the courses themselves. Various approaches to course evaluation must be considered and tried as an essential part of the Syracuse experiment. Like any experiment, it must yield data that permit us to draw conclusions regarding its outcome. We need to know how well the experimental procedures work and what effects they have. Have the course contents and formats resulted in the kinds of learning that were expected? To answer these sorts of questions, whereby the courses themselves are the target of evaluative scrutiny, evaluation functions simply as a tool.

On the other hand, when we consider the evaluation of students, we must examine evaluation itself. No longer just a tool to be employed, the assessment of student performance becomes for us an object of evaluation itself. The manner in which we evaluate the growth of the students in the new courses is one of the substantive issues of the educational reform effort that constitutes the Syracuse experiment. Therefore, when we turn in this chapter to a discussion of student evaluation, we must evaluate evaluation.

Evaluating the Syracuse Experiment

The most concrete product to have emerged from our enterprise thus far is a set of twelve new courses, each implemented as "Honors courses." Their overarching goal—to induce professionally oriented undergraduate students to take interrogative pauses, to challenge the precepts, ethos, and culture of the profession or career to which they aspire—should provide the ultimate standard to be employed in the evaluation of the courses. In baldest form, the object of the evaluation of the experiment is to discern how far these courses have brought their students toward this interrogative state, this essentially critical frame of mind. If it can be shown that the students are, at some point after completion of one of the new courses, less ethnocentrically pursuing the skills and techniques of their particular career and less blindly imbibing the values that are part of the cultural baggage of their chosen profession, and instead seeking ways to transcend the skills and consciously examining the values, then surely the course may be branded a success. But how to show all this?

Most of the courses introduced to date have administered a fairly simple evaluation form to the students at the end. Results have revealed widespread enthusiasm, epitomized by the frequent assertion that "this course really made me think." However, the data collected with such instruments throw very little light on whether the project goals are being met by the courses.[1]

There is also the difficulty that these courses were not intended primarily to impart a corpus of knowledge, but rather to affect students' apparatus of mind. The former could easily be measured, but some would doubt that it is possible to measure how far a course might have brought students to an interrogative state, to a critical frame of mind.

We could, of course, construct attitudinal measures that provide students an opportunity to reveal how enthusiastically they endorse or express doubts about their chosen profession, and these measures could be applied more than once in order to assess change in attitudes. For example, a questionnaire could be administered early and late in the course. But such a strategy involves problems, not the least significant of which is the reactive effect of the first measurement. By alerting the student to our interest in attitudes, the course might be made to appear more successful in changing attitudes than it really is. As in a study done many years ago in Cincinnati of the effectiveness of a political advertising campaign, which showed it to be effective *only* for persons whose attitudes were measured before the campaign began (and then, of course, later as well), the pre-test/post-test design that seems to recommend itself for our present purposes could artificially enhance the apparent effectiveness of our courses.

There is also the Hawthorne effect—an improvement in performance of whatever kind by persons due simply to their knowing that they are involved in an experiment and that someone is paying attention to them.[2] Since undergraduates generally feel—rightly or not—that faculty care little about them, those undergraduates who are in the Mellon courses, knowing that they are special and that the faculty is doing some unusual things with them, may be motivated to respond positively to whatever is being done, quite independent of its content. In the present case, this so-called Hawthorne effect would be most apt to show up in student-supplied evaluations, but it could also be manifest in other more objective measures as well. Thus, if students work harder simply because they know they are the object of concern, their actual performance on some course-related task might be enhanced. While this would be all for the good, since an enhancement of student performance is what we hope for, we would be fooling ourselves if we attributed that enhancement to something specific that we did rather than to the fact that we simply paid a little more attention to the students than they are accustomed to.

Perhaps the most serious of all methodological problems we face in trying to evaluate our experiment is that as a design for research it is not an experiment at all. It lacks both of the two defining characteristics of a bona fide social science experiment: control groups and random assignment.[3] With what other courses do we compare ours? If our students are self-selected, as they are in the main, how do we attribute any apparent effects we have on them to what we have done with them rather than to what they were already well on the way to doing for themselves? And even if we could, by some miracle, show that an "X" that we did in the course had an effect "Y" on the students, could we with any degree of confidence generalize to a population of students in the abstract and claim that "X" produces "Y" for any other than this specific self-selected group of students?

These caveats regarding the threats to validity that necessarily plague any effort to evaluate our enterprise definitively do not discourage us from trying to do an evaluation, but rather make us realistic about the tentative nature of any conclusions that might be drawn from it. Aware of these methodological hurdles, we must concede that our evaluation of the overall project will be limited at best to a quasi-experiment, and we must seek ways to get as much information as possible that is at least suggestive. We know in advance that we cannot demonstrate with quantitative data that the program has succeeded. But we know that we can gather data—some of it qualitative and subjective—that can guide us in continuing our experimental effort. For while we lack an experimental design for evaluative research purposes, we do have an experiment in the sense of a continuing exploration of ways to teach professionally oriented students to examine critically what they are being taught by their professional tutors. It is that experiment that will be propelled onward by the "evaluative" data we collect.

Course Evaluation

There are three means for securing essentially qualitative[4] data pertaining to evaluation of each course in our project: soliciting student opinion, querying faculty who teach the courses, and consulting professionals.

Student Opinion

Student data can be collected in relatively routine fashion, employing the somewhat standardized techniques designed by the Syracuse University Center for Instructional Development. Their standard course evaluation forms can be applied as is, or supplemented by additional closed-ended or open-ended questions. For all of the courses in the project that have already been put into practice, such questionnaires have been administered. Their findings in the main reveal a highly enthusiastic response. On the other hand, as is always the case with student evaluations, student reaction ranged from complaints about unrealistically demanding assignments through to complaints that the course (sometimes the same course) was too easy.

What have we learned from these course evaluations by students? Probably not much. The data suggest that the courses satisfy most of the students, but we have few leads as to why. Moreover, these kinds of data don't really tell us about the success of the courses in achieving the project goal; they merely inform us—not very clearly—about the degree of student satisfaction. Still, even if we don't know for sure why the students were satisfied with particular courses, we know the degree to which they were and we know why they *think* they were satisfied.

The routine procedure of collecting opinions from students at the end of the course should probably be continued, and we should endeavor to analyze the opinions longitudinally, tracking over several semesters any changes in student opinions.

We need also to note that these student-provided course evaluations are all, thus far, of a short-term nature. We have begun to extend this particular data collection technique to a longer-term version by asking students months after completing a particular course the ways in which the course impacted on them, left a residue, and affected their subsequent work in courses outside our project.

As faculty members responsible for the course on "The Conceptual Foundations of Management" realized from the outset, only a delayed study of student opinions could reveal whether their participation a year earlier in this course had subsequently shaped their academic programs, or caused them to reconceptualize their field or to revise their career goals. Through the delayed questionnaire, the faculty hope to come to grips with the way in which the students' thinking patterns have been shaped by the course. As of this writing, the delayed questionnaire has not been administered, but plans are in place for distributing it to "graduates" of the course and to a comparable group of students in management who were not involved.

Faculty Opinion

While it might appear naive or ingenuous to suggest that evaluation of the courses in the project include assessment by the courses' own faculty, in fact not to do so would be to lose an opportunity. We know what we are trying to accomplish. We know what we've done in meetings with students. We know when we've had a sense of achievement and when we've felt disappointed or foiled. So, to the degree that we can overcome the biasing effects of wanting to succeed, and to the extent we can overcome our own need to appear successful, we teachers of the project courses are a potentially rich source of information about what seems to work and what does not.

Interpreted with caution, the reports by teachers themselves of what they think happened in their experimental courses can be very informative. Also relevant are self-appraisals of the effect that the seminar had on each of us as teachers. Have we gained insights from interactions with each other, as well as with students in the preliminary go-rounds with the new courses—insights which have helped us become better teachers? After two years of rigorous self-examination and challenge from colleagues in the faculty seminar, it may not be too much to expect that "Mellonized"[5] faculty can provide information that contributes validly to the overall effort to evaluate our courses.

While we do, therefore, include the course faculty's own subjective impressions in the evaluation arsenal, we propose that input also be sought from faculty not directly engaged in teaching a Mellon course. When we carry out the kind of longer-term evaluations mentioned earlier in this chapter, we can include in them interviews with teachers whose current students were students in courses developed in the project. We can try then to ascertain whether these students strike their current teachers as somehow different from their "un-Mellonized" classmates, and if so, how. (Of course, it would be highly desirable if the current teacher did not know which students had been "Mellonized" and which not.) Once again, however, we must caution that a positive outcome in such a study (former project students more likely to be described as thoughtful, mature, well informed, or the like) could not be attributed confidently to their experience in the project, since they might well have appeared so without it. Remember, they are self-selected. Nevertheless, this proposed portion of an overall evaluation effort has two notable virtues—it involves outsiders' views (which could be more objective) and it could show long-term effects which comprise a more stringent "test" of the course.

Talking to Professionals

It has been suggested that a thoughtful and rigorous evaluation by certain selected professionals might be a rich source of insight into our courses. We have not pursued enquiries in this direction very extensively so far, but the procedure has been pilot-tested on "The Impact of Science on Medicine."[6] Responses have been received by four physicians of distinction, and can be found in the appendix to this chapter. Their responses, limited to descriptions they received of the course content, are not casual nor anodyne, but specific, constructive, and actionable. We look forward to seeking outside, professional opinions for other courses as well.

Evaluating Student Growth

Higher education as we know it today, which we refer to as "traditional education," employs, not surprisingly, traditional means of student evaluation. If we are to move beyond traditional education, an essential part of this movement includes escaping from the traditions of student evaluation.

Although exceptions abound, student evaluation, or "grading" as normally practiced in American colleges and universities today, is an attempt objectively to assess relative levels of knowledge possessed by a coterie of students at the end of a course. Students are graded "A" if they display more knowledge than other students who are graded "B," and so on down the line. They are compared with each other rather than with themselves at some earlier stage. The possibility that some "A" students at the end of the course could have earned the "A" by taking the final exam before the course began is usually overlooked. Our assessment procedures tend not at all to measure individual growth, but simply relative standing across students. Furthermore, we tend to assess "knowledge," which usually consists of factual information included in the course content, rather than acquired ability to process information, analyze it, put it into new contexts, employ it creatively, and the like. And, finally, traditional assessment procedures tend to employ modes of examination that engender rather passive responses by students, as in recognizing the "right answer" in multiple-choice items, as opposed to the more active process of writing essays.

These traditional features are all, to a considerable extent, anathema in our project. We clearly would prefer to focus on individual students and assess the degree to which each one of them has grown in response to our mentoring. We would like to be able to detect, from early on in a course and continuing throughout the semester, the changes in a student's ability to grasp and employ facts, ideas, concepts, conceptual schemes, and, yes, even values. We want to do this primarily in order to provide continuing feedback to the student and guidance to ourselves as we shift and adjust emphases in content and conduct of the courses.

What we don't want to do is merely give a grade to put on a transcript that signifies the attractiveness (or lack thereof) of a person to a prospective employer or postgraduate school admissions officer. Of course, we know that whatever we do by way of assessment, the grades we ultimately record will be interpreted in this light—that is, they will serve, for better or for worse, as criteria for subsequent selection—but we insist that that is not the best purpose served by student evaluation. Rather, it is the worst one.

For us in the Mellon project to succeed as teachers, we must also succeed as evaluators; we must make evaluation a tool of our teaching. And just as we are still learning how to be teachers, we are surely still learning how to be evaluators. With respect to evaluation, we are probably at an early and steep stage of the learning curve.

We have collectively been given a big boost in our effort to ascend this curve by insights provided by the writing expert, Margaret Himley. Her teaching the project faculty how to employ various types of writing assignments as means of producing in the students the kind of growth that is the objective of our courses[7] has given us also some valuable tools for more appropriate student assessment, and some new emphases in communicating with students, such as giving them marginal comments on papers but not "grading" them in the sense of marking a sign of relative goodness in a record book. Since "learning how to think" is what faculty and students in this project have come already to identify as a central objective of the enterprise, and since writing is the preeminent procedure for doing this, it seems obvious to us that students' growth must be evaluated through their writing. They must write often; we must read and react often and with great care and attention.

Looking at the problem of student assessment at a more macro level, we must pay closer attention to the "tyranny of grades" and the implications of American higher education's complicity in the process of "credentialing." By "tyranny of grades" we refer to the demonstrably anti-educational impact of students' concern for grades as opposed to concern for learning for its own sake. This debilitating concern shows up, for example, in students' worries about entry into competitive graduate programs (such as medical school) or transfer into undergraduate professional schools which currently have high admission standards based on grade point averages (such as the S. I. Newhouse School of Public Communications).

By "credentialing" we refer to the circular process whereby people get ahead in life (or not) on the basis of access to successive levels of credential-granting institutions, with that access heavily depen-

Still from the 1964 movie *My Fair Lady* with Audrey Hepburn and Rex
Harrison. Courtesy of the Museum of Modern Art/Film Stills Archive.

dent on their acquiring grade records, certificates, and diplomas earlier on. We in higher education are accomplices in this system which maintains and reinforces the social status quo, and a persuasive case can be made that, by so doing, we keep higher education from those who need it the most and make it available to those who need it the least. The testing industry, handmaiden to education, speaks with a loud voice and has oversold us on the virtues of traditional student assessment. But we, too, have participated willingly in the circular process because it is one that has filled our classrooms with persons who are relatively easy to teach. Hiding behind pious declarations of our commitment to the maintenance of something called "standards," we have, generation after generation, endorsed the employment of selection procedures, based on allegedly objective measures of ability, to keep out those who are harder to teach but have possibly the greatest potential to grow.

So, there is a difficult job to be done. We cannot become better teachers without simultaneously becoming better evaluators. We need to find ways to make evaluation of our students' performance a feature of courses that contributes to student growth. This is a job that we have only begun to conceptualize; we hope to pursue it vigorously because it comprises the most obvious of our unfinished tasks.

Appendix

Responses to the Course "The Impact of Science on Medicine"
1. "I'm sorry to be late in answering your letter of May 1, but my telephone call really covered most of the ground. Your plan is excellent and I would encourage it strongly. Next year will perhaps be crucial. Keep the discussion *relevant* (horrible word, but essential) to the students' interest. You have enough material to satisfy a wide range of interests.

"I had originally thought of suggesting some more readings. But apart from my own collections of essays . . . I would recommend only one more reading, a remarkable study in the scientific method. It is Oliver Wendell Holmes' *The Contagiousness of Puerperal Fever*. And is found in Holmes' Collected Works or in the special volume *Medical Essays*. It can be excerpted."

Lester S. King, M.D., physician and
medical historian

2. "I was delighted to have your letter and excited by the course you have put together, a daring and challenging venture. You have my congratulations and admiration.

"I have gone through the course description and the list of readings and am impressed with how well you have covered the major themes and issues."

George L. Engel, M.D., Professor
Emeritus of Psychiatry and
Medicine, University of
Rochester Medical Center

3. "I enjoyed the opportunity to learn about the course that you have developed. I have also looked at the list of readings and am glad to offer a few comments based on my own interests in the subject and experience in teaching the humanities in medical schools where there is less time for reflection than in premedical education.

"I very much applaud your idea of a critical pause and an attempt to see the connections between the humanities, the social sciences and medicine. I am certain that your course will indeed sensitize pre-medical students to problems that may arise when they become physicians. I suspect that sensitization will, in some of the students, remain despite their immersion in medical education itself which notoriously can obliterate even some of our better grounded sensitivities.

"The course cannot expect—and you certainly do not suggest that it can—to substitute for a liberal education. Neither can those of us who try to teach the humanities in medical school hope to substitute for the inadequacies of a previous liberal education. Like you, we hope to provide a period of critical reflection and often it turns out to be a much shorter period than the one you have available before they come to medical school.

"It is also in part due to the general failure of liberal arts colleges to provide a true liberal arts education, that is to say, one that is directed at the developing of those attitudes of mind that classically have been associated with liberal studies. This means serious study in depth of some of the classical humanistic disciplines—philosophy, literature and history.

"However, it does not follow that taking a course in the humanities is equivalent to advancing one's liberal education. Too many of today's "humanities" courses are taught as specialties or as propadeutics to a career in a specialized field of humanistic research. The humanities are indeed the most valuable instruments for teaching the liberal arts but this requires that they be taught with that end in mind, and also that they be taught liberally as well.

"Scientists often assert that the sciences can be taught as liberal arts. This is possible of course but not likely, given the education of most scientists (or physicians for that matter).

"In any case, I think that a course like yours can only be beneficial. It can help students appreciate that medicine is not solely science, not solely art, not solely practice but a combination of all three.

"Thank you very much for the opportunity to look at your prospectus. To spell out a little further one of the points I have made in this letter, I am sending you a reprint that I wrote some time ago . . ."

Edmund D. Pellegrino, M.D., John
Carroll Professor of Medicine
and Medical Humanities,
Director of the Joseph and
Rose Kennedy Institute of
Ethics, Georgetown University

Notes

1. On first offering, the courses had small enrollments, which further reduces the usefulness of data collected by standard course evaluation forms. The fact that student numbers in most of the courses on second offering were considerably larger is itself better evidence of favorable student opinion, provided we can assume that the increase in enrollment reflected word-of-mouth advertising.

2. In the early days of industrial psychology, a study in a Hawthorne, Illinois factory uncovered this potential source of invalidity in social science research.

3. We could, of course, evaluate these courses in a much more definitive way by designing pairs of courses, one member of each pair possessing Mellon attributes, the other not, assign the same teacher to both courses in the pair, assign students randomly to them, collect data in a post-test-only design for some students and in a pre- and post-design for others, transform all data to numbers, and subject any numerical differences which obtain to statistical tests of significance. However, to do so would epitomize micrometers and elephants.

4. Opinions, whether expressed as responses to open-ended questions or as check marks on a rating scale, can, of course, be "transformed" into quantitative data by coding or otherwise assigning numbers to the responses, adding them up, dividing by the number of responses to produce a mean, calculating standard deviations, and otherwise imbuing the "data" with the magical power of statistics. But what begins as qualitative remains qualitative, however it is clothed.

5. See chapter 2, "The Faculty Seminar."

6. See chapter 9, "The Impact of Science on Medicine."

7. See chapter 13, "Everyone Writes."

19

Of Bridges, Ships, and Sea Dogs

PETER T. MARSH

The preceding pages have described an attempt by twenty faculty at one university, through collaborative enquiry and course creation, to engage undergraduates in exploring the bearing of their liberal arts and professional fields of study upon each other. That exploration has carried the participants considerably farther and has proved much more rewarding than we originally envisioned. The dividends have been as much conceptual as pedagogical. Led on by the identification of themes of concern—professionalism,[1] objectivity,[2] skills,[3] and embeddedness[4]—that run through all fields of learning, we moved beyond the original objective of integrating liberal and professional education toward a more incisive, conceptually more valid, and pedagogically more fruitful sense of the relationship between the two.[5] "Liberal" and "professional" are indeed dimensions present in every field of learning; and that simple statement, which needs to be much more widely appreciated, scarcely begins to suggest the benefits for learning and teaching that follow from it.

Meanwhile, we have created a dozen courses, each with an element of originality. Four are in the arts and sciences, including one for each of the major divisions—humanities,[6] social sciences,[7] and natural sciences—plus one on "Reading and Interpretation." Five are in the professional colleges that participated in our project: engineering, management, nursing, public communications, and visual and performing arts.[8] A further three were developed once our project started, each looking beyond a single college: courses on "The Impact of Science on Medicine,"[9] on "Gender and the Professions,"[10] and on the intersection between postmodernism in art and poststructuralism in literature.[11] Though arrangements were made from the outset to incorporate into these courses substantial amounts of writing, we underestimated the importance that this component of the enterprise would acquire. The team of writing consultants in the project not only introduced the students to a liberating repertoire of approaches to writing,[12] but pumped fresh ped-

Mark Tansey, *The Myth of Depth*, 1984. Oil on canvas, 39″ x 89″. Collection Rose and Morton Lansdowne, N.Y. (Clement Greenberg points toward Jackson Pollock while Helen Frankenthaler, Arshile Gorky, Robert Motherwell, Kenneth Noland, and Mark Rothko look on.) Photo courtesy of Curt Marcus Gallery.

agogical air throughout the enterprise. In this as in so many other ways, collaboration proved to be the key to the project's effectiveness;[13] and the crucial vehicle for this collaboration was the prolonged seminar that brought faculty from the liberal arts and professional colleges together to learn from each other.[14]

These dividends and discoveries have moved us effectively beyond the false conventional dichotomy between liberal and professional education. But obviously we have conducted nothing more than a pilot project. The courses we created have not yet significantly affected the general undergraduate curriculum at Syracuse. Nor have the processes that we found indispensable for cross-college collaboration worked their way into the structure of the university. Until headway is made on both fronts, our enterprise will have no more than peripheral importance to the undergraduate education provided by this university, let alone by others.

Because the intellectual seas that we proposed to explore were uncertain and the pedagogical demand pressing, scholar-teachers, rather than the chairs of curriculum committees or divisional and central administrators, were recruited to conduct the Syracuse experiment. From the outset, that limitation bred some anxiety, which deepened as the benefits to be derived from the project expanded beyond first hopes. In the absence of administrators, what we learned and accomplished was largely conceptual and pedagogical. We alluded to, but rarely explored, the administrative implications of what we were learning.

We nevertheless present this account of the project as much to appeal to administrators as to faculty. Though the division between faculty and administrators in American universities sometimes runs deep, the future character of American undergraduate education is the responsibility of both. Indeed, the prospects for interpenetration of liberal and professional education, the objective of our enterprise, depend heavily on central administrators. They alone have a permanent mandate that explicitly transcends the dichotomy between the liberal arts and professional colleges. We therefore draw our account toward a close with some suggestions to reinforce that mandate and make it effective throughout the undergraduate curriculum.

Curricular Reform

The demand for effective interpenetration between the liberal and professional components of universities' curricula has deep historical roots. Educators in early modern Europe devoted much of their curriculum to the ancient world of Athens and Rome, partly in order to show their students the bearing of different fields of study—literature, philosophy, and history—upon each other. The rise of science and the proliferation of specialized professions shattered confidence in that antique curriculum. The abandonment of its substance may not cause much regret now, but its underlying pedagogical principle has also fallen into neglect. That loss contributes to the frustration of undergraduates in search of intelligible coherence amid the atomized world of higher education that sends them out too often unable to meet the complex demands of work and life in the professions for which they were supposed to be educated.

Yet to cut the curriculum back to study of great periods of civilization or great books is to avoid rather than to solve the problem. It is the specialized diversity as much as the connectedness of the world of learning, life, and work to which our students need preparatory introduction. Here again, old roots of study generate fresh responses. However strange their new language, literary studies have made a prominent contribution to the project at Syracuse quite naturally, "not only because [to quote from a recent review[15]] literature reminds us of the diversity of mankind . . . but also because it enables us to look at ourselves from outside, as it were, and to assess our own existing ways of behaving and thinking." Whatever intellectual tools may serve our purpose, we need to rediscover [as the same reviewer puts it] "the virtues of an education that encourages a free interplay between special knowledge and general understanding, both profiting from the reciprocity which is at once the hallmark and the justification of pluralism and the open-textured society." The curricular reform to which we aspire must bring about free interplay among the specialized fields of learning in the professions, the arts, and the sciences, among which there is at present notoriously little general understanding.

Interplay among specialized fields of learning is what the courses we created are all about. The intent is reformist, not revolutionary. As the biologist in the project has put it:

> Our aim is not to *supplant* the usual kind of courses with Mellon courses, but to *supplement* the curriculum with an array of Mellon courses so that, eventually, all students will have some understanding of the embeddedness of their field, or profession, in the rest of the world. This should not be viewed as a threat in any way to the conventional curriculum; without the conventional curriculum, Mellon courses could not exist. My course, for example,[16] does not in any way lead to the conclusion that physicians should be exposed to less science, but rather that they should reflect on the impact science has on their profession.

This is essentially the same point that one of the engineers makes in chapter 4 with regard to the curriculum in his college.

The curricular measures necessary to extend the effect of the project throughout the undergraduate curriculum are threefold: (1) the creation of courses for fields and intersecting concerns that we have not yet addressed; (2) the addition of these courses to standard degree requirements; and(3) the development of ways, if possible, to increase enrollment in such courses without damaging their essential quality.

We hoped from the outset to extend enrollment beyond the Honors Program. The professor of advertising put the case this way: "No matter how intellectually stimulating it may be for faculty to work with the best students, it is the *less* gifted students who are actually in greater need of our attention."[17] No one disagreed. But when he went on to plead for a much higher limit on class size, at least doubled to admit thirty or forty students to each, the unanimity ended. "Large classes in 'thinking' subjects (i.e. those involving reciprocal exchanges between faculty and students) are hardly uncommon either in Syracuse or in other universities," he argued. "In the Harvard Business School, classes of 100 students are the norm, and they are all vigorously participative." But most other faculty in the project—including those who handle large lecture classes for other purposes effectively—have continued to insist that, given the kind of inquiry we hope to stimulate in the new interpenetrating courses, they should be given to groups of no more than fifteen.

Insistence on small class size increases the need for more such courses. We have yet to create them here for computer science, education, human development, information studies, and social work, and for many lines of pre-professional interest within the College of Arts and Sciences including public administration and law. There should be more courses like "Gender and the Professions"[18] to deal with concepts, themes, and forces that run through all fields of learning. The possibilities for courses on the points of convergence that are emerging with increasing frequency among the disciplines and professions are almost boundless.

As soon as the supply of these courses permits, they should be woven into the curricular requirements of every undergraduate degree program. The courses could be placed in any number of configurations. Our professor of advertising suggests the creation of a cluster of courses entitled "Background to Professional Studies," which he sketches as follows:

> It might comprise twelve credits (four courses) of specialized electives from a "menu" of thirty-six credits (twelve courses). The majority of students singly enrolled in one college could accept such a cluster, at the price of a reduction in their choice of free electives.
>
> The courses should probably be at the upper level and should be adapted versions of those developed in the Mellon program. They must be taught both by faculty in the relevant professional schools and in Arts and Sciences, and should be of equal importance to professional schools and Arts and Sciences students.
>
> For students in the professional schools, this cluster would have great value in its contribution to depth in their professional studies. It should also help students understand the points of similarity and difference between different professions and types of business.
>
> For students in the College of Arts and Sciences, the value of the cluster is that it would provide a baptism into the business/professional activities to which these students may eventually devote their lives.

Such a cluster, like the general education or liberal arts core requirements common at many universities,[19] would run the risk of reaffirming the demarcation between liberal and professional education. That risk might be overcome by an alternative arrangement, clustering together courses like "Humanities and Human Understanding"[20] and "The Creating Mind"[21] that transcend those boundaries, assigning them to the lower division curriculum, and thence directing students toward upper division courses that examine individual professions within an interpenetrating frame of reference. In yet another arrangement, confluence or capstone courses could be developed for any of the four undergraduate years. The impact of this configuration would naturally be enhanced by sustaining it in a succession of forms from year to year. However it is done, courses that explore the bearing of liberal and professional education upon each other should, we believe, become a standard, prominent feature in all undergraduate curricula.

Administrative Reform

The structure of the curriculum is closely bound up with the administrative structure of the university. Potentially far-reaching change in the one is not likely to occur—and certainly will not endure—without some modification of the other. Preoccupied with courses and concepts, the seminar usually suppressed its anxiety about the long-term administrative outlook for the enterprise, and has little to offer under this heading but statements of principle. Still, the central principles—whether for the enquiry in which we engaged, the courses we created, the curricular reform we envision, or its administrative implications—are the same. The paramount needs are twofold: recognition of the embeddedness and interconnection of every field of learning, and hence collaboration among them.

Currently the situation, as analyzed by the professor of organization management in our project, is quite different. Alert to the structural affinity between administration and curriculum and to the disembeddedness of the various fields of learning at present, he observes that:

> Universities have been structured in a functional manner that allows for specialization in order to foster technical competence. They have also been primarily concerned with scholarly pursuits that demonstrate causal relationships among variables by isolating limited numbers of phenomena, treating all other influencing forces as contamination. This approach has produced valuable outcomes for business, medicine, and other areas of study. It has, however, been carried to a point where the phenomena being studied are relegated to the background in the learning process. You might say that we are experiencing our experiments more than we are experiencing life. As a result, students are exposed to a linear series of ever more specialized forms of knowledge.

Drawing upon his experience of business as well as his academic field, he goes on to suggest adapting for university purposes the internal task forces that American businesses have used to restructure their efforts in face of stiffened competition:

> The curriculum and, as a necessary concomitant, the organization of the university need to be restructured to apply both integrative and specialized approaches to learning and teaching. Many industrial firms have adopted new structures to protect and legitimize innovative processes to cope with rapid change. Universities would be in a much better position to prepare their graduates for the complex organizational environment they will be entering if they institutionalized and empowered the Mellon project's kind of configuration for learning and teaching.
>
> Such structural change, in fostering the development of more Mellon-type courses, would help to establish two major foundations for students that are rare among today's graduates. These foundations are a conceptual base that integrates the many complex forces in our society such as religion, economics, politics, technology, science, and the arts, and an experiential base in which the actual class process emulates task-force functioning so prevalent today in our major institutions. Employers and graduates themselves have complained about the absence of this development in higher education. Our professional schools continue to churn out experientially and conceptually naive graduates who are hence unable to make sense of the increasingly complex organizations whose employ they seek to enter.

Devising the adaptations in university administration needed to bring liberal and professional education to bear upon each other will require as much creativity as any advance of learning in the arts, sciences, or professions. However it is accomplished, one thing is clear. Collaborative forms of learning and teaching such as we have described must be regularized, reliably funded, and empowered to forward their objectives and protect their participants in the face of the entrenched interests of the separate liberal and professional departments and colleges. Ideally, collaborative and unidisciplinary forms of learning would be recognized as complementary. Ultimately that may prove to be the case. But at present universities are constituted for all practical purposes as feudal federations of liberal and professional fiefdoms among which central administrators hold the ring and annually distribute financial resources. Such an arrangement provides little protection—let alone encouragement—for those who venture beyond the bounds of the fiefdom to which they originally pledged allegiance.

These martial metaphors are harsh, and undoubtedly distort the situation. The administration of universities is a civilian, essentially political art reliant on forms of persuasion rather than coercion. Furthermore, the dividends that the separate departments and colleges have contributed to the world of learning are massive and continue to mount. The interests that they seek to protect are fully legitimate. The annual struggle to meet even existing demands in colleges and departments where faculty resources are scarce and enrollments are high does not encourage newfangled experimentation.

The fact remains that the enterprise described in the foregoing pages does not coincide with the vested interests, standard curricular demands, and research expectations of the departments and colleges to which its participants in the final analysis belong. Contesting the boundaries of liberal and professional education is of marginal interest, where it is not a threat, to the administrative units into which universities are currently divided. Deans and department chairs may recognize collaborative learning and teaching as of general interest. Still, the general interest is proverbially weak unless it is reinforced by particular material interests and strong central command.

At present, interest in the relationship between liberal and professional education is widespread in the United States among undergraduates, educators, and employers. But that interest has to date been vaguely articulated, poorly organized, and ineffective. Overcoming this weakness requires yet another form of collaboration, in this case particularly between the central administration of universities and interested faculty. Collaboratively, they could transform inter-college faculty seminars into flexible task forces regularly renewed and empowered to intersect the existing administrative composition of universities by discipline and profession. Only through such collaboration can the needed network of communicative transport be established among the separated fields of learning, a network of bridges and bridge builders, of ships and seafarers. Like Elizabeth I of England with her "sea dogs," adventurous mariners such as Sir Francis Drake, the challenge to those who govern our universities is to encourage exploration past the known coastlines of liberal and professional learning into the uncharted seas beyond.

Notes

1. See chapter 2, "The Phenomena of Professions."
2. See chapter 5, "The Concept of Objectivity."
3. See chapter 1, "The Syracuse Experiment," page 23.
4. See chapter 8, "The Concepts of Embeddedness and Enculturation."
5. See particularly chapter 16, "Education in a Transformed Field."
6. See chapter 14, "The Liberation of the Humanities."
7. See chapter 6, "Individual, Social, and Professional Identity."
8. See chapter 15, "The Creating Mind."
9. See chapter 9, "The Impact of Science on Medicine."
10. See chapter 10, "Gender and the Professions."
11. See chapter 11, "On Seeing and Reading."
12. See chapter 13, "Everyone Writes."
13. See chapter 12, "The Varieties of Collaborative Experience."
14. See chapter 2, "The Faculty Seminar: Discourse Communities and Quotation Marks."
15. Philip Drew, review of *The Crisis of the Democratic Intellect: The Problem of Generalism and Specialisation in Twentieth-century Scotland*, by George Elder Davie, the *Times Literary Supplement*, 24 October 1986, 1201.
16. See Chapter 9, "The Impact of Science on Medicine."
17. Cf. chapter 9, "The Varieties of Collaborative Experience."
18. See chapter 10, "Gender and the Professions."
19. See chapter 1, "The Syracuse Experiment."
20. See chapter 14, "The Liberation of the Humanities."
21. See chapter 15, "The Creating Mind."

Background Reading

Barnes, Michael, ed. *The Three Faces of Advertising*. London: Advertising Association, 1975.

Baxandall, Michael. *Painting and Experience in Fifteenth Century Italy: A Primer in the Social History of Pictorial Style*. Oxford: Oxford University Press, 1972.

Bennis, Warren. "The Artform of Leadership." *The Executive Mind*, edited by Srivastva & Associates. San Francisco: Jossey-Bass, 1985.

Bledstein, Burton J. *The Culture of Professionalism: The Middle Class and the Development of Higher Education in America*. New York: Norton, 1976.

Brook, Peter. *The Empty Space*. New York: Atheneum, 1978, chap. 1.

Brumberg, Joan Jacobs, and Nancy Tomes. "Women in the Professions: A Research Agenda for American Historians." *Reviews in American History* X (1982).

Callow, Simon. *Being an Actor*. New York: Methuen, 1984, chaps. 1 and 2.

Campbell, Donald T. "Ethnocentrism of Disciplines and the Fishscale Model of Omniscience." In *Interdisciplinary Relationships in the Social Sciences*, edited by Muzafer Sherif and Carolyn W. Sherif. Chicago: Aldine, 1969.

Cavell, Stanley. *Must We Mean What We Say?* Cambridge: 1976, foreword.

Donahue, M. Patricia. *Nursing, the Finest Art*. St. Louis, Mo.: Mosby, 1985.

Drucker, Peter F. *Managing in Turbulent Times*. New York: Harper & Row, 1980.

Eagleton, Terry. *Literary Theory: An Introduction*. Minneapolis: University of Minnesota Press, 1983.

Elbow, Peter. "Teaching Writing by Not Paying Attention to Writing." In *Forum: Essays on Theory and Practice in the Teaching of Writing*, edited by Patricia L. Stock. Upper Montclair, N.J.: Boynton/Look, 1983.

Engel, George L. "The Biopsychosocial Model and the Education of Health Professionals." *Annals of the New York Academy of Science* 310 (1978): 169–81

Engel, George L. "The Clinical Application of the Biopsychosocial Model." *American Journal of Psychiatry* 137 (May 1980): 535–44.

———. "The Need for a New Medical Model: A Challenge for Biomedicine." *Science* 196 (1977): 129–36.

Eyal, Chaim, Jim Winter, and Maxwell McCombs. "The Agenda-Setting Role of Mass Communication." In *Readings in Mass Communication: Con-*

cepts and Issues in Mass Media, edited by Michael Every and Ted Curtis Smythe. Dubuque, Iowa: Brown, 1983.

Fagin, Claire M. "Nursing's Pivotal Role in American Health Care." In *Nursing in the 1980s,* edited by L. Aiken. Philadelphia: Lippincott, 1982.

Florman, Samuel C. *Engineering and the Liberal Arts: A Technologist's Guide to History, Literature, Philosophy, Arts, and Music.* New York: McGraw-Hill, 1968, chapters 1, 2, and 3.

Foster, Kurt W. "Critical History of Art, or Transfiguration of Values?" *New Literary History* 3 (1971/72):

Fulwiler, Toby, and Art Young, eds. *Language Connections.* Urbana: National Council of Teachers of English, 1982.

Gould, Stephen Jay. *The Mismeasure of Man.* New York: Norton, 1981, introduction and epilogue.

Griffin, C. W., ed. *New Directions for Teaching and Learning: Teaching Writing in All Disciplines,* no.12. San Francisco, December 1982.

Harth, Erich. *Windows on the Mind: Reflections of the Physical Basis of Consciousness.* New York: Morrow, 1982.

Haskell, Thomas L., ed. *The Authority of Experts: Studies in Theory and Practice.* Bloomington: Indiana University Press, 1984, introduction.

Hegel, G. W. F. *Phenomenology of Spirit.* Translated by A. V. Miller. Oxford: Clarendon Press, 1977, introduction.

Hopcroft, John E. "Turing Machines." *Scientific American* 250, no. 5 (May 1984).

Hull, S. Loraine. *Strasberg's Method.* Woodbridge, Conn.: Oxbow Press, 1985, chaps. 1 and 2.

Johnson Graduate School of Management (Cornell University). *Survey of CEOs Regarding Attitudes toward MBA Education: Summary report* (January 1986).

Jones, John Philip. *What's in a Name?: Advertising and the Concept of Brands.* Lexington, Mass.: Lexington Books, 1986), chap. 10.

Kasson, John F. "The Aesthetics of Machinery." In John F. Kasson, *Civilizing the Machine: Technology and Republican Values in America, 1776–1900.* New York: Grossman, 1976.

Keller, Evelyn Fox. *Reflections on Gender and Science.* New Haven: Yale University Press, 1985. chaps. 4 and 9.

Kirkhorn, Michael J. "The Virtuous Journalist: An Exploratory Essay." *The Quill* (February 1982).

Koen, Billy Vaughn. "Toward a Definition of the Engineering Method." *Engineering Education,* 75, no. 3 (December 1984): 150–55.

Kuhn, Thomas S. *The Structure of Scientific Revolutions.* 2d ed. Chicago: University of Chicago Press, 1970.

Kurzweil, Raymond. "What is Artificial Intelligence Anyway?" *American Scientist* 73 (May–June 1985): 258–64.

Lambert, J. W. "Politics and the Theatre." *Theater Quarterly* 13, no. 30 (Summer 1978).

Lehninger, Albert L. *Biochemistry*. 2d ed. New York: Worth Publishers, introduction.

Levitt, Theodore. *The Marketing Imagination*. New York: The Free Press, 1983, chap. 1.

Lumsden, C. J., and E. O. Wilson. "Toward a New Human Science." In C. J. Lumsden and E. O. Wilson, *Promethean Fire*. Cambridge, Mass.: Harvard University Press, 1983.

McWhinney, Ian R. "Medical Knowledge and the Rise of Technology." *Journal of Medicine and Philosophy* 3 (1978): 293–304.

Mayer, Martin. *Madison Avenue U.S.A.* New York: Harper & Brothers, 1958, chap. 19.

Molotch, Harvey, and Marilyn Lester. "News as Purposive Behavior: On the Strategic Use of Routine Events, Accidents, and Scandals." *American Sociological Review* 39 (February 1974): 101–12.

Munson, R. "Why Medicine Cannot Be a Science," *Journal of Medical Philosophy* 6 (1981): 183–207.

Nash, Thomas. "Derrida's 'Play' and Prewriting for the Laboratory." In *Writing Centers: Theory and Administration*, edited by Gary A. Olson. Urbana: National Council of Teachers of English, 1984.

Ogilvy, David. *Confessions of an Advertising Man*. New York: Atheneum Press, 1963, chap. 5

Pellegrino, Edmund D. *Humanism and the Physician*. Knoxville: University of Tennessee Press, 1979, chap. 12.

Phillips, E. Barbara. "Approaches to Objectivity: Journalistic vs. Social Science Perspectives." In *Strategies for Communication Research*, edited by Paul M. Hirsh, Peter V. Miller and F. Gerald Kline. (Beverly Hills, CA: Sage Publications, 1977): 63–78.

Prown, Jules David. "Editor's Statement: Art History vs. the History of Art." *Art Journal* (Winter 1984).

Quinn, James Brian. "Managing Strategic Change." In James Brian Quinn, *Strategies for Change: Logical Incrementation*. Homewood, Ill.: R. D. Irwin, 1980.

Reither, James A. "Writing and Knowing: Toward Redefining the Writing Process." *College English* XLVII, 6 (October 1985): 620–28.

Rhodes, Frank H. T. "Reforming Higher Education Will Take More Than Just Tinkering With Curricula." *The Chronicle of Higher Education*, 22 May 1985.

Rose, Frank. "The Mass Production of Engineers." *Esquire*, May 1983.

Schneider, Alan. "Things to Come: Crystal-Gazing at the Near and Distant Future of a Durable Art." *American Theatre*, April 1984.

Scholes, Robert. *Textual Power: Literary Theory and the Teaching of English*. New Haven: Yale University Press, 1985, chap. 1.

Schwartz, Michael Alan, and Osborne Wiggins. "Science, Humanism, and the Nature of Medical Practice: A Phenomenological View." *Perspectives in Biology and Medicine* 28 (Spring 1985): 331–61.

Singer, Aubrey. "Television: Window on Culture or Reflection in the Glass?" *American Scholar,* 35 (Spring 1966): 303–9.

Steinberg, Leo. "Objectivity and the Shrinking Self." *Daedalus* 98 (1969): 824–36.

Tarkov, John. "A Disaster in the Making." *American Heritage of Invention and Technology* 1, no. 3 (Spring 1986).

Thomas, Lewis. *The Youngest Science: Notes of a Medicine-Watcher.* New York: Viking Press, 1983.

Vild, Kathleen A. "The Civil Engineering Degree: Education or Training?" *Journal of Professional Issues in Engineering* 90, no. 1 (January 1984): 25–30.

Weschler, Lawrence. *Seeing is Forgetting the Name of the Thing One Sees: A Life of Contemporary Artist Robert Irwin.* Berkeley: University of California Press, 1982.

Young, James Webb. *How to Become an Advertising Man.* Chicago: Advertising Publications, 1963, chap. 16.

Index

265

CONTESTING THE BOUNDARIES OF LIBERAL AND PROFESSIONAL EDUCATION

was composed in 10 on 12 Baskerville on a Linotron 202
by Eastern Graphics;
printed by sheet-fed offset on 50-pound, acid-free Glatfelter Natural Hi-Bulk,
Smyth sewn and bound over binder's boards in Holliston Roxite C,
and notch bound with paper covers printed in two colors
by Braun-Brumfield, Inc.;
designed by Will Underwood;
and published by

SYRACUSE UNIVERSITY PRESS
SYRACUSE, NEW YORK 13244-5160